THE POLITICAL WRITINGS

OF JOHN ADAMS

The American Heritage Series

THE POLITICAL WRITINGS OF JOHN ADAMS

Representative Selections

Edited, with an introduction, by
GEORGE A. PEEK, JR.

BOBBS-MERRILL EDUCATIONAL PUBLISHING
Indianapolis

John Adams: 1735-1826

The Bobbs-Merrill Company, Inc.
4300 West 62nd Street
Indianapolis, Indiana 46268

First Edition
Twelfth Printing—1980

Library of Congress Catalog Card Number: 54-4998
ISBN: 0-672-60010-2

PREFACE

This volume is one of a series designed to present in reasonably short compass some of the best of American literary and political writings. John Adams is chosen because, along with John C. Calhoun, he best represents the American republican conservative statesman who despite a full and active political life attempted to formulate a consistent political theory. Though it is not difficult to formulate some sort of political philosophy from the public speeches and private correspondence of many political figures, it is a rare thing to find that one of these has devoted himself to the more laborious and reflective task of attempting to erect a more or less complete political system, proceeding logically from stated assumptions to political conclusions. This very thing John Adams attempted to do in his *Defence of the Constitutions of Government of the United States of America* and *Discourses on Davila*. This is his political system in essence. At the same time he was an active leader of the struggle for independence and made a significant contribution to a constitutional analysis of the nature of the relation between the American colonies and Great Britain. And again in old age he reflected on the constitutional system Americans had constructed. To cover the various phases of his thought and to present a picture of that thought rather fully as it developed, it was decided to proceed chronologically.

The first piece included, written by a young and vigorous Adams, reveals his insistence on self-government for the colonies and a devotion to the rule of law, or, as some would put it, constitutionalism. The other pieces of his pre-revolutionary writings indicate a changing position until the formulation of the mature constitutional view on the nature of the British Empire found in the Novanglus letters.

The post-revolutionary writings establish his hastily written, though not hastily conceived, plan of government, the working out of this plan in the constitution of Massachusetts of 1780, and the climax of his thought in his *Defence* and *Davila*. The final selections are reflections on the Constitution of the United States and, at a later date, a spirited defense of the *Defence*. Taken together these pieces form a consistent whole and, it is believed, give a fairly good view of Adams' political thought.

The selections are chosen not only for their content but also to illustrate Adams' methodology as a political theorist. Like Aristotle long before him Adams studied many constitutions and many political systems in order to get the raw material out of which to construct his own. Surely he was selective in his choice of raw material and tended to ignore that which did not buttress his view, but keep in mind that he usually wrote with a purpose —namely, to defend constitutional, balanced government. If he was less an objective writer than he was an advocate, the answer probably lies in his devotion to a cause—the cause of independence and the rule of law.

On the whole I have chosen his public pieces in preference to his private correspondence for the reasons, first, that the former, usually of some length, are a fuller statement of the case than the latter and, secondly, that the private letters on the whole appear to add little to these more comprehensive statements. Furthermore, it is my belief that one gets a better view from a few pieces quoted at length than from many pieces with frequent elisions. For a detailed account of the editorial arrangement of the text, the reader is referred to the Note on the Text, page viii.

I am indebted to the General Editor, Mr. Oskar Piest, for his encouragement and wise counsel in the preparation of this volume. Finally I should like to thank my wife, Marion, and my good neighbor, Mrs. Henry Malcolm, for their valuable assistance in reading proof.

G. A. P.

CONTENTS

. . . .

THE POLITICAL WRITINGS
OF JOHN ADAMS

NOTE ON THE TEXT

With the exception of the Massachusettensis letters, the material included in this volume is taken from *The Works of John Adams,* edited by Adams' grandson, Charles Francis Adams, and published by Little, Brown and Company, Boston, 1850–56. The *Works* were published in ten volumes. In the editor's notes and footnotes, *Works* followed by a Roman numeral or simply a Roman numeral always refers to this edition and indicates the volume in which the selection appeared. The Massachusettensis letters are taken from *Novanglus and Massachusettensis,* by John Adams and Jonathan Sewall (sic!),[1] printed by Hews and Goss at Boston in 1819.

The text follows the original except for minor editorial changes in spelling, capitalization and punctuation. Relevant footnotes of *The Works of John Adams,* which are either those of John Adams himself, added at a later time, or of his grandson, have been retained. The editor's footnotes have been bracketed.

The editor has provided a set of notes divided into Headnotes, Appendix Notes, and a Biographical Index. The latter two are designed to help the reader identify Adams' frequent and sometimes obscure references to events and persons respectively. Appendix Notes are marked by a superior letter in the text. The Biographical Index is organized in alphabetical order.

[1] Cf. editor's note on page 26.

INTRODUCTION

"He is vain, irritable, and a bad calculator of the force and probable effect of the motives which govern men. This is all the ill which can possibly be said of him. He is as disinterested as the being who made him; he is profound in his views; and accurate in his judgment, except where knowledge of the world is necessary to form a judgment. He is so amiable, that I pronounce you will love him, if ever you become acquainted with him. He would be, as he was, a great man in Congress."[1] This perceptive judgment was rendered by Thomas Jefferson on John Adams. It is based on first-hand experience, rooted in thoughtful insight, and tempered by real affection. It reaches the mark. History, on the other hand, has dealt more harshly with Adams. First of all, he occupied the Presidency of the United States between George Washington and Thomas Jefferson and in the public mind suffers grievously from the comparison. In addition no political party has rallied to his support. The demise of the Federalist Party[a] is charged to John Adams, who insisted on being a patriot first and party adherent second. In the election of 1800 he was roundly attacked by the Republican Party,[b] which had the windfall of Alexander Hamilton's ill-advised letter criticizing Adams, and in later years when Adams approved of some Republican actions, that party was still suspicious. He was well aware that he could expect support from neither party. "For my part I always thought and am still determined to support every administration wherever I think them in the right," he wrote to his friend Benjamin Rush.[2] "I care not whether they call me Federalist, Jacobin[c] or Quid."[d] His view that titles were neces-

---

[1] Thomas Jefferson to James Madison, January 30, 1787. *The Writings of Thomas Jefferson,* edited by H. A. Washington (New York, 1859). II, 107.

[2] John Adams to Benjamin Rush, April 18, 1808. *Old Family Letters: Copied from the Originals for Alexander Biddle* (Philadelphia, 1829). I, 181.

ix

sary even in a representative democracy led to charges that he
secretly favored monarchy; his consistent advocacy of balanced
government, that he was anti-republican. It was not enough for
him to deny some of the charges which reached his ears. "I am
a mortal and irreconcilable enemy to monarchy," he protested,
again to Rush. "I am no friend to *hereditary limited* monarchy
in America. . . . Do not, therefore, my friend, misunderstand
me and misrepresent me to posterity." [3] He was too bluntly
honest, almost to the point of rudeness, to curry public favor, and
this very honesty made him sensitive to the fact that "Mauso-
leums, Statues, Monuments will never be erected to me. I wish
them not. Panegyrical Romances will never be written, nor flat-
tering orations spoken to transmit me to Posterity in brilliant
colors." [4] Adams prophesied rather well, though historians have
for some time been cognizant of his accomplishments as a patriot
and statesman and in a measure have wondered why he has
not received more acclaim.

But here we wish to talk about him as a political thinker.
Vernon Louis Parrington, avowedly "liberal and Jeffersonian,"
stated that, "In spite of his dogmatisms and inconsistencies he
remains the most notable political thinker—with the possible
exception of John C. Calhoun—among American statesmen." [5] In
1858 Theodore Parker asserted, "With the exception of Dr.
Franklin, I think of no American politician in the eighteenth
century that was his intellectual superior. For though Hamilton
and Jefferson, nay, Jay and Madison and Marshall surpassed him
in some high qualities, yet no one of them seems to have been
quite his equal on the whole." [6] These evaluations seem just.

John Adams was no closet philosopher. His major sustained
literary efforts on politics—*A Defence of the Constitutions of
Government of the United States* and *Discourses on Davila*—are
discursive, disorderly, and repetitive. They are not so much

---

[3] John Adams to Benjamin Rush, April 18, 1790. *The Works of John
Adams*, edited by Charles Francis Adams (Boston, 1850–56), IX, 566.
[4] John Adams to Benjamin Rush, March 23, 1809. *Op. cit.*, I, 226.
[5] Vernon Louis Parrington, *Main Currents in American Thought* (New
York, 1927), I, 320.
[6] Theodore Parker, *Historic Americans* (Boston, 1878), pp. 200–201.

original treatises on government as they are dialogues between some ancient, medieval and eighteenth-century writers on the one hand and John Adams on the other. In fact Zoltán Haraszti has suggested "that the *Defence* would benefit enormously . . . by placing the borrowed texts and Adams' comments in dialogue form." [7] The bulk of these two pieces consists of quotations, frequently *in extenso*, with Adams' pungent comments interspersed at will. Rather than an author of extended tracts on government, he was a pamphleteer, letter writer, and above all, political thinker. He was too much a man of action, too impatient with continued and laborious writing, despite a voluminous correspondence, to produce any single piece wholly his own of length. But his reactions to the political events of his times, to which he added deep reflection based on wide and intensive reading, result in outstanding discussions on politics—using that word in its original and Aristotelian sense.

Adams' political writings form a remarkably consistent whole, and one can perceive that the *Defence* was a logical development of theories advanced in the *Dissertation* and *Novanglus*. Of course, there was a change in emphasis as current affairs forced Adams to think and write on different problems—he is answering a Tory [e] charge in the *Boston Gazette*, or summing up thoughts on constructing a constitution, or replying to Turgot's attack on separation of powers—but there was no change in fundamental belief. As he wrote about himself, "John Adams remains *semper idem*. . . . " [8] Hence the classification, sometimes used, of his writings into early democratic views and later post-Revolutionary reactionary views is not only without utility but does violence to the facts.

A Dissertation on the Canon and Feudal Law, published in the *Boston Gazette* in 1765, was John Adams' first major contribution on politics. It received attention in both Boston and London. The title is misleading, for it is essentially an attempt to

[7] *John Adams and The Prophets of Progress* (Cambridge, Mass., 1952), p. 155.
[8] John Adams to Benjamin Waterhouse, July 12, 1811. *Statesman and Friend*, edited by Worthington Chauncey Ford (Boston, 1927), p. 64.

analyze the origins of the American tradition, to make this tradition explicit to New England, and lastly to defend it against encroachments from England. America had rejected the despotism of the canon and feudal law, Adams argued. Hers was the heritage of the Reformation, the Magna Charta,[f] and the Bill of Rights,[g] and this heritage had to be protected even against Parliament itself, which was not the grantor of fundamental, natural liberties. In his *Instructions of the Town of Braintree to Their Representative,* written in the same year, Adams simply attempted to spell out within a particular context what he had hinted at in his *Dissertation*—namely, the Stamp Act[h] violated the principles of the English Constitution since it was a tax levied without the consent of those taxed.

By far the most significant of his contributions to the American-British controversy preceding the act of revolution itself was the *Novanglus* letters, a series of essays published in the *Boston Gazette* in 1774–1775, designed to refute the traditional Tory position that Parliament was supreme over the entire empire. In the debate with Great Britain American arguments had taken three forms: dependence on the colonial charters, the principles of the English Constitution, and lastly an unconstitutional appeal to natural law or the right of revolution. Adams in the course of the debate took each of these positions. Initial American protests were based upon the nature of the charters, which were viewed as contracts, but this argument was without much substance. The second appeal based on the nature of the English constitution was really twofold. First, the thesis was advanced that the constitution embodied right reason or natural law; hence any act of Parliament contrary to right reason was *ipso facto* void and should be judged so by the courts. This was the position so dramatically asserted by James Otis in his speech on the Writs of Assistance. The second phase of the constitutional argument, more technical and more subtle, revolved around the nature of the British Empire, and this John Adams developed fully. Simply stated, he held that the American colonies owed allegiance not to Parliament but only to the King, that there was an intermediate position between absolute dependence on Parlia-

ment and complete independence, though he did admit that fo
the sake of convenience Parliament should control strictly imperial matters. Adams' argument was not free of difficulties, both
legally and in principle, but it was penetrating and imaginative.
Randolph G. Adams writes that "he [Adams] has . . . a claim
to a position among the pioneers of a new class of Britannic
thinkers (in the commonwealth of nations concept). . . ." [9] And
Charles H. McIlwain holds that "John Adams' answer (to Massachusettensis, representing the British view) is the most elaborate
exposition extant of the American interpretation of the constitutional problem of the empire. . . ." [10] The idea of a commonwealth of nations bound together through the person of the
King was premature. Constitutional solutions proved unaccept-
able and the colonies proceeded to "appeal to heaven," to declare
"That these united colonies are and of right ought to be free and
independent States." In the battle in Congress [i] for independence
Jefferson in later years recalled that Adams was "the great Colossus of that Congress—the great pillar of support to the Declaration of Independence, and its ablest advocate and champion on
the floor of the House." [11]

In a time of social revolution two types of activity prevail,
demolition of the old and formation of the new. It is not usual
for a person to engage well in both of these, but this John Adams
did. Even before independence was declared, he had in November, 1775, sketched some of his ideas on constructing a framework of government for each of the colonies, a framework later
elaborated in his letter to George Wythe and published in 1776
as *Thoughts on Government*. This piece, the *Defence*, the *Discourses*, and many of his later letters may be viewed as constituting the essence of his speculation on politics.

[9] *Political Ideas of the American Revolution* (Durham, North Carolina,
1922), p. 108.
[10] *The American Revolution: A Constitutional Interpretation* (New York,
1923), p. 139. The Massachusettensis, or British position, is defended by
Robert L. Schuyler in his *Parliament and the British Empire* (New York,
1929).
[11] *The Writings of Thomas Jefferson*, Memorial Edition (Washington,
D. C., 1905), Vol. XIII, p. xxiv.

John Adams built his political system upon so-called self-evident truths. The nature of man determined the nature of society and government. What, then, was the essential nature of man? Adams did not rely solely on his own judgment but marshalled the views of philosophers and historians. He quoted Machiavelli to the effect that "'those who have written on civil government lay it down as a first principle, and all historians demonstrate the same, that whoever would found a state and make proper laws for the government of it must presume that all men are bad by nature: that they will not fail to show that natural depravity of heart whenever they have a fair opportunity.'"[12] The opinion of Montesquieu was that "'constant experience shows us that every man vested with power is apt to abuse it. He pushes on till he comes to something that limits him.'"[13] Swift, Junius, Beccaria, Rochefoucauld and De Lolme were cited to the same end. "Shall we say that all these philosophers were ignorant of human nature?" Adams inquired, "With all my soul, I wish it were in my power to quote any passages in history or philosophy which might demonstrate all these satires on our species to be false. But the phenomena are all in their favor; and the only question to be raised with them is whether the cause is wickedness, weakness, or insanity?"[14] According to Adams the reason is weakness rather than wickedness or insanity. The passions of men are unlimited and nature has purposely left them so, for if the passions could be bounded, they would soon be extinct. Though men do feel benevolent and generous to their fellows, on the whole each prefers his own interest to that of his neighbor. Ambition, pride, avarice, self-interest, and private avidity exist in every society and determine every form of government.

If the philosophers are to be credited, Adams went on to say, the ability to reason is the faculty which distinguishes man from other animals. If men were wholly reasonable and practiced the rule of doing as they would be done by, no external restraint of their passions would be necessary. The moral government of God

[12] *Works, IV,* 408.
[13] *Ibid.*
[14] *Ibid.,* 409.

would be sufficient to make men just and benevolent. But the nature of man is one thing; his reason is another. Passion and appetite are as much a part of man as reason and moral sense. "In the institution of government, it must be remembered that, although reason ought always to govern individuals, it certainly never did since the Fall, and never will, till the Millenium; and human nature must be taken as it is, as it has been and will be." [15] The passions of men must be restrained. This is the function of government.

Given these premises with regard to the nature of man and the necessity for the restraining power of government, John Adams could have employed the social compact,[j] either in the tradition of John Locke or possibly Thomas Hobbes, whose view of the nature of man he tends to follow. But Adams in his political system rejected the contract, despite his reference to it in the Preamble of the Massachusetts Constitution of 1780, a reference probably inserted to reflect the climate of opinion in New England following the break with the King. "Men, in their primitive conditions, however savage, were undoubtedly gregarious; and they continue to be social, not only in every stage of civilization but in every possible situation in which they can be placed." [16] Adams agreed with Aristotle that God intended that men should live in society. But while for Aristotle society, or the state, which commences for the sake of mere life, exists for the sake of the good life; for Adams, society exists for the sake of life or even for the satisfaction of egoism. Man seeks his own kind to herd with, Adams reasoned, for only in the social condition can man satisfy to the full his universal passion, pride—the "passion for distinction."

Having established the nature of man and the consequent necessity for social existence, Adams proceeded to analyze the nature of society. All men have one common nature and from that may be inferred equal rights and duties. "But equal ranks and equal property can never be inferred from it, any more than equal understanding, agility, vigor or beauty. Equal laws are all

[15] *Works,* VI, 115.
[16] *Ibid.,* 232.

that ever can be derived from human equality."[17] In every state God has implanted inequalities which no legislator can erase. No two objects are perfectly alike; no two creatures are perfectly equal. "The people in all nations are naturally divided into two sorts, the gentlemen and the simplemen, a word which is here chosen to signify the common people."[18] The factors which cause this division of society are essentially threefold—inequality of wealth, inequality of birth, and inequality of merit. By virtue of these factors are the few separated from the many, the natural aristocracy from the common people. The basis of a natural aristocracy rests upon the possession of influence. "By aristocracy, I understand all those men who can command, influence or procure more than an average of votes; by an aristocrat, every man who can and will influence one man to vote besides himself."[19]

With the nature of man, his tendency to gregariousness, and the essential ordering of society into classes accepted as fundamental data, Adams asked himself, "What combination of powers in society, or what form of government will compel the formation, impartial execution, and faithful interpretation of good and equal laws, so that the citizens may constantly enjoy the benefit of them and may be sure of their continuance?"[20] Or what system of government will hold in check these natural orders of mankind, orders constantly struggling for power? Simple government whether of the one, few, or many will not satisfy the requirement; simple government is despotism. Only a mixed government properly balanced can insure stability, for it is built on the natural order of society and hence is built on the very nature of man. By balanced government Adams meant a tripartite balance of executive, upper house, and lower house representing essentially the one, few, and many in society. There is some difficulty in this scheme.[21] It is quite easy to see how the

[17] John Adams to Thomas Brand-Hollis, June 11, 1790. *Works*, IX, 570.
[18] *Works*, VI, 185.
[19] John Adams to John Taylor, 1814–1824. *Ibid.*, 451.
[20] *Works*, IV, 406.
[21] *Cf.* Correa M. Walsh, *The Political Science of John Adams* (New York, 1915). Chap. VI.

upper house represents the natural aristocracy; the lower house, the people; but more difficult to determine what order in society is represented by the executive. There is no one or "King's friends" in a republic corresponding to the one in society. The primary function of the one, it might be suggested, is not so much to represent an order in society as it is to preserve the balance between the few and the many.

This system of government was not, of course, original with Adams. One may trace its origins back to Aristotle; it was elaborated fully by Polybius; it was current in 17th and 18th century political thought. In this tradition Adams divided simple governments into monarchy, aristocracy, and democracy. Each of these in turn degenerates of necessity into its evil counterpart, tyranny, oligarchy and anarchy. The way out of this dilemma lies in formulating a government made up only of the good forms, monarchy, aristocracy and democracy. This in Rome would be a government made up of consuls, senate, and tribunes; in England, King, Lords and Commons; in the United States, chief executive, upper house, and lower house. In each system monarchy, aristocracy and democracy or the one, few, and many are properly represented and balance is achieved.

It was in elaborating on the simple forms of government that Adams may have laid himself open to charges that he was anti-republican. On the whole the least evil of the simple governments is monarchy, he argued, because the people have more liberty under it than under the other two. Even under a simple monarchy a modicum of balance exists in the nobility and the courts of judicature. In the struggle for power the aristocrats by their very nature have an advantage, and the result is oftentimes an oligarchy. It is the people, wearied of aristocratic intrigues, bribes, and outrages, who have set up monarchy and fortified it with an army. Monarchy is ". . . the eternal resource of every ignorant people, harassed with democratical distractions or aristocratical encroachments." [22] The people need a champion to defend them against the nobility, and this champion is a king. Monarchy and aristocracy are not natural allies. A man might as well take up abode with Daniel in the Lion's Den, as monarchy

[22] *Works,* IV, 347.

take up abode with aristocracy. "Aristocracy is the natural enemy of monarchy; and monarchy and democracy are the natural allies against it, and they have always felt the necessity of uniting against it, sooner or later." [23] The common people, not the gentlemen, have established simple monarchies over the world. Simple aristocracy, Adams continued, is half way between simple monarchy, which is the least evil of the simple forms, and democracy, which is the most evil. It is probably true that if government must reside in a single assembly, it is more safe and durable in the hands of a few than in the hands of the many. Aristocracy generally prefers merit to wealth and preserves in some degree the morals of the people. But aristocratic government is oppressive government, and there will be intrigues and rivalries among the few. The result of necessity will be violence, war, and catastrophe. Adams reserved his strongest invective for simple democracy. It is the most evil of the simple forms—the most ignoble, unjust and detestable. It is more to be feared than simple monarchy or aristocracy. "We may appeal to every page of history we have hitherto turned over for proofs irrefragable that the people, when they have been unchecked, have been as unjust, tyrannical, brutal, barbarous, and cruel as any king or senate possessed of uncontrollable power. The majority has eternally, and without one exception, usurped over the rights of the minority." [24] In its last stages democracy reaches the most complete despotism. Nowhere does human nature show itself so completely depraved, so nearly approaching brutality and devilism, as in the last stages of democracy. It has only one saving grace. It never lasts long. "It soon wastes, exhausts, and murders itself. There never was a democracy yet that did not commit suicide." [25] Adams should not be misinterpreted on this point. These remarks were made after the French Revolution, and Adams may well have had it in mind. In addition he was employing this invective against simple democracy to bolster his case for *republican* balanced govern-

[23] "Review of the Propositions for Amending the Constitution submitted by Mr. Hillhouse to the Senate of the United States in 1808." *Works*, VI, 533.

[24] *Ibid.*, 10.

[25] *John Adams to John Taylor*, 1814–1824, *ibid.*, 484.

ment. After an examination of the simple forms Adams again concluded: "We have all along contended that a simple government, in a single assembly, whether aristocratical or democratical, must of necessity divide into two parties, each of which will be headed by some one illustrious family and will proceed from debate and controversy to sedition and war. . . . Having no third order to appeal to for decision, no contest could be decided but by the sword." [26] In this fashion did Adams make out his case for balanced government; that is, a government consisting of a strong executive, a selective upper house, and a broadly representative lower house.

Each of the three separate branches in Adams' system had a distinct and peculiar function. In the first place, he asserted, "The great desideratum in a government is a distinct executive power of sufficient strength and weight to compel both these parties (gentlemen and simplemen), in turn, to submit to the laws." [27] The executive is the mediator, the arbitrator between the senate representing the few and the lower house representing the many. Not only is the executive distinct, but he must be a single person with power to protect his office by an absolute veto. His authority, like all governmental authority, is derived from the people in whom sovereignty finally rests, for the executive represents the people as well as the legislature. The upper house, the senate, is derived from and represents the rich, the well-born, the natural aristocracy. This group must not sit in a single body with the representatives of the "simplemen." "The rich, the well-born, and the able acquire an influence among the people that will soon be too much for simple honesty and plain sense in a house of representatives. The most illustrious of them must, therefore, be separated from the mass, and placed by themselves in a senate, this is, to all honest and useful intents, an ostracism." [28] In addition, it is the peculiar function of the senate

---

[26] *Works,* V, 10.

[27] *Ibid.,* 473.

[28] *Works,* IV, 290. By "ostracism" Adams meant that illustrious figures in the House of Commons would be "ostracized" to the House of Lords where their influence on the people and governmental affairs in general would be considerably curtailed.

". . . to be guardians of property against levellers for the purpose of plunder. . . ."[29] It must be remembered, Adams cautioned, that the rich are people as well as the poor, and the rich have as much right to their property, which is great, as others have to theirs, which is smaller. "The moment the idea is admitted into society that property is not as sacred as the laws of God and that there is not a force of law and public justice to protect it, anarchy and tyranny commence."[30] The lower house, the popular branch, Adams always insisted, is the *sine qua non* of freedom. The people, in truth, are the origin of power of all three branches, but the lower house is closest to them. ". . . there can be no constitutional liberty, no free state, no right constitution of a commonwealth, where the people are excluded from the government; where, indeed, the people have not an independent equal share with the two other orders of the state and an absolute control over all laws and grants of money."[31] The function of the popular branch in addition to law-making and voting appropriations is to watch the other two branches and to preserve the balance.

In view of the modern American interpretation of separation of powers as a separation of the executive, the legislative, and judicial branches of government, it is of some interest to notice that in John Adams' scheme the judiciary does not form a part of the major balance which, as we have seen, was between the executive, senate, and house of representatives. The judiciary was a secondary, not a primary check in government. Adams did insist that the judiciary be separate and that judges have their independence and salaries protected by law. In a letter to John Taylor he even suggested that the judiciary would act as "a salutary check" upon the other branches.[32] As a lawyer in the 18th century tradition of the English common law, however, an independent judiciary preserved liberty and government by law, but it was not integrated closely into the essential balance of the one, few, and many.

[29] *Works*, VI, 118.
[30] *Ibid.*, 9.
[31] *Ibid.*, 113.
[32] *Ibid.*, 488.

We may summarize Adams' thoughts on politics by employing two quotations from his letters. To Samuel Adams, a cousin, he wrote: "It is a fixed principle with me that all good government is and must be republican." [33] A quarter of a century later, in his old age, he wrote to Thomas Jefferson: "The fundamental article of my political creed is that despotism, or unlimited sovereignty, or absolute power is the same in a majority of a popular assembly, an aristocratical council, an oligarchical junto, and a single emperor. Equally arbitrary, cruel, bloody, and in every respect diabolical." [34]

What were the sources of John Adams' political theory? [35] He laid no particular claim to originality; his works abound with quotations from Aristotle, Machiavelli, Harrington, Bolingbroke, Swift, De Lolme and others. Because of his extended quotation of other writers it is not difficult to single out those who were apparently most influential on his thinking. On the other hand, to suggest that only these writers determined his politics would be to suggest that he was a theorist in an ivory tower and that his system was merely an eclectic exercise. Such an assumption, of course, would be incorrect. At the outset Adams' writings reflect his temperament; there is something distinctive in the way he constructs his system. Furthermore, he has a particular view of human nature, a view obviously influenced by his early Puritan religious training and, though mellowed in later years, one never wholly abandoned. The peculiar emphasis which Adams placed on pride in human nature, found in his *Discourses on Davila,* is in large part derived from Adam Smith's *The Theory of Moral Sentiments.* At the same time it must be remembered that Adams' theory was an expression of the age in which he lived and it may not be torn out of that context; it is an expression, in part, of the "climate of opinion" of 18th and early 19th century America and Europe. Just as Plato wrote in terms of the

[33] John Adams to Samuel Adams, October 18, 1790. *Ibid.,* 415.
[34] John Adams to Thomas Jefferson, November 13, 1815. *Works,* X, 174.
[35] On the sources of Adams' political ideas, *cf.* Haraszti, *op. cit.,* especially chapters IX and X, Walsh, *op. cit.,* Chapters XV and XVI, and Alfred Iacuzzi, *John Adams, Scholar* (New York, 1952), Chapters IV through VIII.

Greek city-state, and Hobbes wrote in terms of the national state emerging from medievalism, so did Adams write in terms of institutions familiar to him. The very fact that Adams came to political maturity under a colonial government composed of a strong governor, a council, a popular lower house, and an independent judiciary and that the colonists enjoyed individual liberty under such a government certainly influenced his thinking. State governments and the government of the United States itself took the forms they did because of our colonial forms. It will be recalled that two of the colonies simply readopted their old colonial charters as State constitutions. Adams recognized "That it was not an affected imitation of the English government, so much as an attachment to . . . old colonial forms, in every one of which there had been three branches—a governor, a council, and a house of representatives"—which in reality determined the forms of the state governments.[36]

Among the many authors Adams quoted with approval, a few may be singled out as being of critical importance in his political thinking. Polybius, among the ancients, might be cited. The system he erected is significant in political theory as the first elaborated exposition in a formal way of check and balance in constitutional organization. He followed Aristotle's cycle theory of monarchy, aristocracy, and polity degenerating respectively into tyranny, oligarchy and democracy, and found the solution in a mixture of the three good forms. Among 17th and 18th century English political thinkers Adams was particularly influenced by James Harrington, whose *Oceana* he often quoted. Harrington's thesis that "Empire follows dominion" or, to rephrase it, "Power follows property" [37] Adams believed to be ". . . as infallible a maxim in politics as that action and reaction are equal is in mechanics." [38] Like Harrington, Adams was impressed with the way mankind was naturally divided into two classes, with the way in which single assemblies invariably divide themselves, and with the necessity for three orders in government.

---

[36] John Adams to John Taylor, 1814–1824. *Works*, VI, 487.
[37] *Cf., The Commonwealth of Oceana*, Collected, methodized, and reviewed by John Toland (London, 1777).
[38] John Adams to James Sullivan, May 26, 1776. *Works*, IX, 376.

Both men tempered their democratic proclivities with the necessity for the guidance of "gentlemen"; both insisted that balanced government "is a government of laws and not of men."

Since Adams was so widely read in 18th century political writing, we will suggest only a few works of that period that particularly appealed to him. Jonathan Swift's essay, *A Discourse of the Contests and Dissensions between the Nobles and Commons of Athens and Rome; with the consequences they had upon both those states,* reads so much like Adams that Adams had to caution the reader of the *Defence* that it was Swift, not Adams speaking.[39] Their agreement on the nature of man, society, and mixed government is in most respects all but identical. Lord Bolingbroke's *Dissertation Upon Parties* and *The Idea of a Patriot King,* Montesquieu's *The Spirit of the Laws,* Sir William Blackstone's *Commentaries on the Laws of England,* Jean Louis De Lolme's *Constitution of England,* all works current in the 18th century, formed a part of Adams' intellectual background; all were cited by him to support his general views on politics. On the other hand, there were many 18th century writers whom Adams read, but not with agreement; Rousseau, Turgot, Condorcet—to suggest only three. In fine, Adams was an educated eighteenth-century man of affairs, familiar with his age, widely and deeply read in its literature, and obviously influenced by what he saw and read.

In appraising John Adams' political thought one must be careful not to take it out of context. If the notion of perfect balance in government somehow seems contrived to us today, we should recall that Adams wrote in an age still under the influence of Sir Isaac Newton. Newton's law that to every action there is an equal and opposite reaction had its counterpart in political life. If each one of the heavenly bodies is kept in its precise orbit by the nice poise and balance of other bodies, then the branches of government can be balanced one against the other to achieve order and symmetry.[40] Or so the 18th century

[39] Cf. *The Works of Jonathan Swift,* edited by Sir Walter Scott (London, 1883). Vol. III; also *Works,* IV, 382–389.

[40] Cf. Woodrow Wilson, *Constitutional Government in the United States* (New York, 1921), pp. 54–56.

advocates of balanced government reasoned. The following century fell under the shadow of Charles Darwin, whose theories of evolutionary development also affected social and political thought, a fact well documented in Herbert Spencer's *First Principles*. One can only speculate concerning what succeeding centuries will write about our age of relativity under the influence of the scientific thinking of Albert Einstein.[41] The difficulty, of course, with the theory of balanced government is that government is not a contrivance; it is a social institution and cannot be constructed with one part precisely balanced against the other. Government itself is subject to change and growth; it reflects the community it represents, and communities also are not mere balanced mechanisms. The reason for Adams' advocacy of balanced government lies in the fact that he was seeking a scheme to preserve the order of society and to reconcile that order with individual liberty. Adams was tackling one of the fundamental problems of political science. The fact that his solution has weaknesses does not reflect too much to his discredit, for no political philosopher has fully and satisfactorily reconciled social order with individual liberty.

Adams' basic conservatism is apparent from his early writings. He was trained in the English common law, approached each problem in a pragmatic and realistic fashion, and attempted to justify his position in the light of precedent, not wishing too much to break the "cake of Custom." In his *Dissertation* and *Novanglus* we see that he defended individual and colonial rights in terms of the fundamental rights guaranteed by the English Constitution. Thoroughly committed to a system of representative democracy, he nevertheless saw the difficulties of unchecked majority rule and sought to formulate a system that at one and the same time allowed for popular sovereignty and still restrained it. The liberal Thomas Jefferson recognized the same problem when, commenting on the Constitution of Virginia for want of separation of powers, he wrote that, "One hundred and seventy-three despots would surely be as oppressive as one."[42] Taking

---

[41] Cf. Walter Lippman, *Public Opinion* (New York, 1922), p. 106.
[42] *The Writings of Thomas Jefferson*, Washington edition, VIII, 361.

the Christian view that man has a capacity for good but a tendency to evil, Adams was distrustful of the French thinkers in the tradition of Rousseau who founded their systems on the inherent goodness of man. He was cognizant in part of the possibilities of tyranny involved in such assumptions. This very fact would today cause him to perceive one of the major fallacies in the doctrines of Karl Marx, whose followers would reconstruct and perfect the world in the image of the proletariat. Because Adams firmly believed in a "government of laws and not of men," he defended the perpetrators of the "Boston Massacre," [k] despite the fact that he thought such an action would bring him only ruin. Lawful, orderly government, he insisted, should not yield to transient whims of the majority or the selfish pressure of the minority. Not an original thinker, he was nonetheless a bold, penetrating, imaginative, and at times even a profound one. In American political thought one might place him between Alexander Hamilton on the one hand and Thomas Jefferson on the other. His is the tradition of Edmund Burke and John C. Calhoun. In mid-twentieth century his staunch republican conservatism still has relevancy and continues to offer insights into our social and political problems.

GEORGE A. PEEK, JR.

UNIVERSITY OF MICHIGAN
January, 1954

CHRONOLOGY

1689 William and Mary proclaimed King and Queen of England by Parliament, concluding the Glorious Revolution.
King William's War (1689–1697) between French and English colonists.

1690 John Locke publishes *Two Treatises on Government,* justifying the Revolution of 1688.

1691 Massachusetts ceases to be a charter colony and becomes a royal colony.

1702 Accession of Anne to the English throne. Queen Anne's War (1702–1713) between the English colonists and the Indians backed by the French.

1714 George I succeeds Queen Anne on the British throne.

1727 George II succeeds George I on the British throne.

1734 Great awakening (revival in fundamentalist religious thinking) in American colonies begins at Northampton, Massachusetts, in the church of Jonathan Edwards.

1735 John Adams born at Braintree, Massachusetts.

1744 King George's War, 1744–1748, between England and France, American phase of the War of Austrian Succession.

1754 French and Indian War, 1754–1765, American phase of the Seven Years' War.
Albany Plan of Union for union of the American colonies, drafted by Benjamin Franklin, tentatively adopted by Albany Congress, not accepted by colonies or Great Britain.

1755 John Adams graduated from Harvard College.

1758 John Adams admitted to the bar at Boston.

1759 British defeat the French on the Plains of Abraham overlooking Quebec. Quebec surrenders to the British.

1760 All New France passes into hands of Great Britain. George III ascends the British throne.

1761 James Otis delivers fiery address before the Superior Court of Massachusetts against use of Writs of Assistance by British customs officers.

1763 Treaty of Paris ends French and Indian War. France cedes to Great Britain Canada and all her territory east of the Mississippi except Isle d'Orleans.

1764 John Adams marries Abigail, daughter of Rev. William and Elizabeth (Quincy) Smith of Weymouth.

1765 John Adams publishes *Dissertation on the Canon and Feudal Law*.

1765 Stamp Act becomes law, providing stamps on newspapers, legal papers, pamphlets, playing cards, etc. Internal tax to raise revenue within the colonies. Colonies react by meeting in New York on request by Massachusetts. Stamp Act Congress protests to the King and Parliament. The following year the Stamp Act is repealed.

1770 "Boston Massacre" perpetrated by the British soldiers, three persons killed, two mortally wounded, six injured.

John Adams defends Capt. Preston and his men on a charge of murder resulting from the "Boston Massacre."

John Adams elected a representative of Boston to the General Court.

1772 Committees of Correspondence first organized in Massachusetts under Samuel Adams and Joseph Warren, to be followed by similar committees throughout the colonies.

1773 Boston Tea Party. Boston citizens throw tea from ships into harbor.

1774 First Continental Congress assembles in Philadelphia and protests British treatment of American colonies in Declaration of Rights and Grievances.

John Adams chosen a delegate from Massachusetts to the Continental Congress.

1774–75 John Adams contributes the Novanglus letters to the *Boston Gazette* defending the colonies against the Tory view.

1775 Battles of Lexington and Concord commencing American War of Independence. Second Continental Congress meets in Philadelphia.

John Adams chosen a delegate from Massachusetts to the Second Continental Congress.

John Adams nominates George Washington as Commander of the Colonial Army.

John Adams appointed Chief Justice of the Superior Court of Massachusetts. He accepts, but never sits, and resigns in 1777.

1776 Continental Congress adopts the Declaration of Independence, drafted in the main by Thomas Jefferson, declaring that "these United colonies are and of right ought to be free and independent states."

John Adams an active member of the Continental Congress. He is a member of the committee to draft a declaration of independence.

John Adams "the pillar of support" for independence in Congress.

John Adams writes his *Thoughts on Government* which is published anonymously.

1777 Articles of Confederation adopted by Congress and submitted to states for ratification.

France declares war against Great Britain and comes to the aid of the American states.

1778 John Adams embarks from the United States as a duly elected Commissioner to France.

1779 John Adams returns from France, is chosen to represent Braintree at the Massachusetts Constitutional Convention, and is the principal "engineer" of the constitution formulated.

1779 John Adams returns to France as one of the ministers to negotiate peace.

1780 Massachusetts in convention adopts a new constitution and submits it to the voters.

John Adams is the principal author of this constitution.

1781 Articles of Confederation become effective when signed by delegates of last state. United States in Congress assembles. British Lord Cornwallis surrenders to American and French forces at Yorktown, Virginia. End of hostilities.

1782 John Adams, as a minister to Holland, secures a loan for the United States.

Along with Franklin and Jay, Adams represents the United States in peace negotiations.

1783 End of war proclaimed by Congress. Definitive treaty of peace signed by Great Britain and United States at Paris. John Adams one of the signers of the treaty of peace with Great Britain.

1785 John Adams appointed the first Minister to the Court of St. James.

1786–87 John Adams publishes the three-volumed, *A Defence of the Constitutions of Government of the United States.*

1786 Shays's Rebellion in Massachusetts reflecting social and economic discontent.

1787 Federal Constitutional Convention meets in Philadelphia on call from Congress. A new constitution drafted and submitted to the states.

1788 New Federal Constitution accepted by sufficient number of states and Constitution becomes effective.

1789 George Washington elected President of the United States; John Adams elected Vice-President; both officially assume office.

1791 John Adams publishes the *Discourses on Davila.*

1792 Political parties emerge, largely from division over Hamilton's policies: Washington, Adams and Hamilton lead Federalists; Jefferson leads Republicans.

Washington re-elected President; Adams re-elected Vice-President.

1793 Washington issues proclamation of neutrality toward the French and British engaged in war.

1794 Jay's Treaty with British concluded.

1796 John Adams elected President of the United States; Jefferson elected Vice-President.

1798 Quasi-war with France commences.

Alien and Sedition Acts, concerning aliens in time of peace and curtailing criticism of the government, passed by Congress and signed by President Adams. Not vigorously enforced by the President.

1800 Through Adams' persistent efforts, a convention with France signed in Paris, ending naval war. He concludes peace with France, despite Federalist objections. Adams defeated in his bid for re-election to the Presidency.

1801 John Adams appoints John Marshall Chief Justice of the United States.

In the disputed electoral vote, the House of Representatives finally elects Thomas Jefferson President and Aaron Burr Vice-President of the United States.

John Adams retires to his home in Quincy. He participates no more in active politics except to attend the Constitutional Convention of Massachusetts in 1820.

1812 John Adams renews his friendship with Thomas Jefferson and carries on an extended and lively correspondence until his death.

1820 John Adams attends the Constitutional Convention of Massachusetts.

1825 With no electoral majority in the Electoral College the House of Representatives chooses John Adams' son, John Quincy Adams, President of the United States.

1826 John Adams dies, July 4, at Quincy.

SELECTED BIBLIOGRAPHY

The Author's Writings

Familiar Letters of John Adams and His Wife Abigail Adams during the Revolution. Edited by Charles Francis Adams. Boston, 1876.

Correspondence between John Adams and William Cunningham. Boston, 1823.

Correspondence of John Adams and Thomas Jefferson 1812–1826. Selected with comment by Paul Wilstach. Indianapolis, 1925.

Old Family Letters: Copied from the Originals for Alexander Biddle. Philadelphia, 1892. (This publication is in two volumes but only the first contains letters from John Adams to Benjamin Rush.)

"Some Unpublished Correspondence of John Adams and Richard Rush, 1811–1816." *The Pennsylvania Magazine of History and Biography.* Volumes 60, 61.

Warren-Adams Letters, Being Chiefly a Correspondence among John Adams, Samuel Adams, and James Warren. 2 volumes. Boston, 1917, 1925.

Correspondence between John Adams and Mercy Warren in *Collections of the Massachusetts Historical Society,* Fifth Series, IV. Boston, 1878.

Statesman and Friend, Correspondence of John Adams with Benjamin Waterhouse, 1784–1822. Edited by Worthington Chauncey Ford. Boston, 1927.

Correspondence between John Adams and Professor John Winthrop in *Collections of the Massachusetts Historical Society,* Fifth Series, IV. Boston, 1878.

The Works of John Adams. Edited by Charles Francis Adams. 10 volumes. Boston, 1850–56.

Novanglus and Massachusettensis. John Adams and Jonathan Sewall. Boston, 1819.

COLLATERAL READING

Adams, Charles Francis, *The Works of John Adams.* (Volume I of the *Works* is a biography by the editor.) Boston, 1850–56.

Adams, James Truslow, *The Adams Family.* Boston, 1930.

Bowen, Catherine Drinker, *John Adams and The American Revolution.* Boston, 1951.

Chinard, Gilbert, *Honest John Adams.* Boston, 1933.

Ford, Worthington Chauncey, "John Adams". *Dictionary of American Biography,* Volume I. New York, 1937.

Haraszti, Zoltán, *John Adams and the Prophets of Progress.* Cambridge, Massachusetts, 1952.

Iacuzzi, Alfred, *John Adams, Scholar.* New York, 1952.

Merriam, Charles E., *A History of American Political Theories.* New York, 1903.

Morse, John T., *John Adams.* Boston, 1885.

Parker, Theodore, *Historic Americans.* Boston, 1878.

Walsh, Correa Moylan, *The Political Science of John Adams.* New York, 1915.

Warren, Charles, "John Adams and American Constitutions," *Massachusetts Law Quarterly.* Volume XII, No. 5.

Whitney, Janet P., *Abigail Adams.* Boston, 1947.

PRE-REVOLUTIONARY WRITINGS

I. A DISSERTATION ON THE CANON AND FEUDAL LAW [1]

In 1765 John Adams wrote this essay on ecclesiastical and civil despotism while a member of Jeremiah Gridley's "Sodalitas Club," [a] a small group of Boston lawyers. It attracted attention and was reprinted in the *London Chronicle* by Thomas Hollis but was wrongly attributed to Gridley. In a later edition of the essay published with other pieces in 1768, Hollis acknowledged his error by writing in his own copy that the essay was penned by "John Adams, Esq., a young gentleman of the law." [2] A few years later Adams said the piece had been "written at random, weekly, without any preconceived plan, printed in the newspapers without correction, and so little noticed or regarded here, that the author never thought it worth his while to give it either a title or a signature." He regretted that it had been attributed to Gridley because "the mistakes, inaccuracies, and want of arrangement in it are utterly unworthy of Mr. Gridley's great and deserved character for learning." [3] In spite of Adams' rather deprecatory reference to the essay in later year as a "lamentable bagatelle," [4] it is still of considerable interest for it presages much of his later thinking and indicates a genuine feeling for liberty coupled with a warning to the British not to attempt a "subversion of the whole system of our fathers by the introduction of the canon and feudal law in America." Furthermore, he argued that it was a struggle against civil as well as ecclesiastical tyranny that peopled America. "It was not religion alone, as is commonly supposed; but it was a love of universal liberty, and a hatred, a dread, a horror, of the infernal confederacy [of the canon and feudal law] before described, that projected, conducted, and accomplished the settlement of America."

[1] [*The Works of John Adams,* edited by Charles F. Adams (Boston: Little and Brown, 1851), III, 448–464.]
[2] [IV, 447.]
[3] [IX, 332.]
[4] [IX, 589.]

3

"Ignorance and inconsideration are the two great causes of the ruin of mankind." This is an observation of Dr. Tillotson with relation to the interest of his fellow men in a future and immortal state. But it is of equal truth and importance if applied to the happiness of men in society on this side the grave. In the earliest ages of the world, absolute monarchy seems to have been the universal form of government. Kings and a few of their great counsellors and captains exercised a cruel tyranny over the people, who held a rank in the scale of intelligence in those days but little higher than the camels and elephants that carried them and their engines to war.

By what causes it was brought to pass that the people in the middle ages became more intelligent in general would not, perhaps, be possible in these days to discover. But the fact is certain; and wherever a general knowledge and sensibility have prevailed among the people, arbitrary government and every kind of oppression have lessened and disappeared in proportion. Man has certainly an exalted soul; and the same principle in human nature—that aspiring, noble principle founded in benevolence, and cherished by knowledge: I mean the love of power which has been so often the cause of slavery—has, whenever freedom has existed, been the cause of freedom. If it is this principle that has always prompted the princes and nobles of the earth by every species of fraud and violence to shake off all the limitations of their power, it is the same that has always stimulated the common people to aspire at independence and to endeavor at confining the power of the great within the limits of equity and reason.

The poor people, it is true, have been much less successful than the great. They have seldom found either leisure or opportunity to form a union and exert their strength; ignorant as they were of arts and letters, they have seldom been able to frame and support a regular opposition. This, however, has been known by the great to be the temper of mankind; and they have accordingly labored in all ages to wrest from the populace, as they are contemptuously called, the knowledge of their rights and wrongs and the power to assert the former or redress the latter. I say RIGHTS, for such they have, undoubtedly, antecedent to all earthly government—*Rights* that cannot be repealed or restrained by human laws—*Rights* derived from the great Legislator of the universe.

Since the promulgation of Christianity, the two greatest systems of tyranny that have sprung from this original are the canon and the feudal law. The desire of dominion, that great principle by which we have attempted to account for so much good and so much evil, is, when properly restrained, a very useful and noble movement in the human mind. But when such restraints are taken off, it becomes an encroaching, grasping, restless, and ungovernable power. Numberless have been the systems of iniquity contrived by the great for the gratification of this passion in themselves; but in none of them were they ever more successful than in the invention and establishment of the canon and the feudal law.

By the former of these, the most refined, sublime, extensive, and astonishing constitution of policy that ever was conceived by the mind of man was framed by the Romish clergy for the aggrandizement of their own order.[5] All the epithets I have here given to the Romish policy are just and will be allowed to be so when it is considered that they even persuaded mankind to believe, faithfully and undoubtingly, that God Almighty had entrusted them with the keys of heaven, whose gates they might open and close at pleasure; with a power of dispensation over all the rules and obligations of morality; with authority to license all sorts of sins and crimes; with a power of deposing princes and absolving subjects from allegiance; with a power of procuring or withholding the rain of heaven and the beams of the sun; with the management of earthquakes, pestilence, and famine; nay, with the mysterious, awful, incomprehensible power of creating out of bread and wine the flesh and blood of God himself. All these opinions they were enabled to spread and rivet among the people by reducing their minds to a state of sordid ignorance and staring timidity and by infusing into them a religious horror of

[5] Robertson's *History of Charles V*, Ch. V, pp. 54, 141, 315.
This work did not appear until the year after the publication of this dissertation in England. The two references are in the handwriting of Mr. Adams in the margin of his printed copy.—C. F. A.

letters and knowledge. Thus was human nature chained fast for ages in a cruel, shameful, and deplorable servitude to him and his subordinate tyrants, who, it was foretold, would exalt himself above all that was called God, and that was worshipped.

In the latter we find another system, similar in many respects to the former,[6] which, although it was originally formed, perhaps, for the necessary defense of a barbarous people against the inroads and invasions of her neighboring nations, yet for the same purposes of tyranny, cruelty, and lust which had dictated the canon law, it was soon adopted by almost all the princes of Europe and wrought into the constitutions of their government. It was originally a code of laws for a vast army in a perpetual encampment. The general was invested with the sovereign propriety of all the lands within the territory. Of him, as his servants and vassals, the first rank of his great officers held the lands; and in the same manner the other subordinate officers held of them; and all ranks and degrees held their lands by a variety of duties and services, all tending to bind the chains the faster on every order of mankind. In this manner the common people were held together in herds and clans in a state of servile dependence on their lords, bound even by the tenure of their lands to follow them, whenever they commanded, to their wars, and in a state of total ignorance of everything divine and human, excepting the use of arms and the culture of their lands.

But another event still more calamitous to human liberty was a wicked confederacy between the two systems of tyranny above described. It seems to have been even stipulated between them that the temporal grandees should contribute everything in their power to maintain the ascendency of the priesthood, and that the spiritual grandees in their turn should employ their ascendency over the consciences of the people in impressing on their minds a blind, implicit obedience to civil magistracy.

Thus, as long as this confederacy lasted and the people were held in ignorance, liberty and with her knowledge and virtue too seem to have deserted the earth, and one age of darkness succeeded another till God in his benign providence raised up the

[6] *Ibid.*, Ch. V, pp. 178ff.

champions who began and conducted the Reformation. From the time of the Reformation to the first settlement of America, knowledge gradually spread in Europe, but especially in England; and in proportion as that increased and spread among the people, ecclesiastical and civil tyranny, which I use as synonymous expressions for the canon and feudal laws, seem to have lost their strength and weight. The people grew more and more sensible of the wrong that was done them by these systems, more and more impatient under it and determined at all hazards to rid themselves of it; till at last under the execrable race of the Stuarts, the struggle between the people and the confederacy aforesaid of temporal and spiritual tyranny became formidable, violent, and bloody.

It was this great struggle that peopled America. It was not religion alone, as is commonly supposed; but it was a love of universal liberty and a hatred, a dread, a horror, of the infernal confederacy before described, that projected, conducted, and accomplished the settlement of America.

It was a resolution formed by a sensible people—I mean the Puritans [b]—almost in despair. They had become intelligent in general and many of them learned. For this fact I have the testimony of Archbishop King himself, who observed of that people that they were more intelligent and better read than even the members of the church, whom he censures warmly for that reason. This people had been so vexed and tortured by the powers of those days for no other crime than their knowledge and their freedom of inquiry and examination, and they had so much reason to despair of deliverance from those miseries on that side the ocean, that they at last resolved to fly to the wilderness for refuge from the temporal and spiritual principalities and powers and plagues and scourges of their native country.

After their arrival here, they began their settlement and formed their plan, both of ecclesiastical and civil government, in direct opposition to the canon and the feudal systems. The leading men among them, both of the clergy and the laity, were men of sense and learning. To many of them the historians, orators, poets, and philosophers of Greece and Rome were quite familiar; and some of them have left libraries that are still in being, consisting chiefly of volumes in which the wisdom of the most enlightened ages and nations is deposited—written, however, in languages which their great-grandsons, though educated in European universities, can scarcely read.[7]

Thus accomplished were many of the first planters in these colonies. It may be thought polite and fashionable by many modern fine gentlemen, perhaps, to deride the characters of these persons as enthusiastical, superstitious, and republican. But such ridicule is founded in nothing but foppery and affectation and is grossly injurious and false. Religious to some degree of enthusiasm it may be admitted they were; but this can be no peculiar derogation from their character because it was at that time almost the universal character, not only of England, but of Christendom. Had this, however, been otherwise, their enthusiasm, considering the principles on which it was founded and the ends to which it was directed, far from being a reproach to them, was greatly to their honor; for I believe it will be found universally true that no great enterprise for the honor or happiness of mankind was ever achieved without a large mixture of that noble infirmity. Whatever imperfections may be justly ascribed to them, which, however, are as few as any mortals have discovered, their judgment in framing their policy was founded in wise, humane, and benevolent principles. It was founded in revelation and in reason too. It was consistent with the principles of the best and greatest and wisest legislators of antiquity. Tyranny in every form, shape, and appearance was their disdain and abhorrence; no fear of punishment, nor even of death itself in exquisite tortures, had been sufficient to conquer that steady, manly, pertinacious spirit with which they had opposed the tyrants of those days in church and state. They were very far from being enemies to monarchy; and they knew as well as any men the just regard and honor that is due to the character of a dispenser of the mysteries of the gospel

---

[7] "I always consider the settlement of America with reverence and wonder, as the opening of a grand scene and design in Providence for the illumination of the ignorant and the emancipation of the slavish part of mankind all over the earth."

of grace. But they saw clearly that popular powers must be placed as a guard, a control, a balance, to the powers of the monarch and the priest, in every government, or else it would soon become the man of sin, the whore of Babylon, the mystery of iniquity, a great and detestable system of fraud, violence, and usurpation. Their greatest concern seems to have been to establish a government of the church more consistent with the Scriptures and a government of the state more agreeable to the dignity of human nature than any they had seen in Europe, and to transmit such a government down to their posterity with the means of securing and preserving it forever. To render the popular power in their new government as great and wise as their principles of theory, that is, as human nature and the Christian religion require it should be, they endeavored to remove from it as many of the feudal inequalities and dependencies as could be spared, consistently with the preservation of a mild limited monarchy. And in this they discovered the depth of their wisdom and the warmth of their friendship to human nature. But the first place is due to religion. They saw clearly that of all the nonsense and delusion which had ever passed through the mind of man, none had ever been more extravagant than the notions of absolutions, indelible characters, uninterrupted successions, and the rest of those fantastical ideas, derived from the canon law, which had thrown such a glare of mystery, sanctity, reverence, and right reverend eminence and holiness around the idea of a priest, as no mortal could deserve and as always must, from the constitution of human nature, be dangerous in society. For this reason they demolished the whole system of diocesan episcopacy; c and, deriding, as all reasonable and impartial men must do, the ridiculous fancies of sanctified effluvia from episcopal fingers, they established sacerdotal ordination on the foundation of the Bible and common sense. This conduct at once imposed an obligation on the whole body of the clergy to industry, virtue, piety, and learning and rendered that whole body infinitely more independent on the civil powers, in all respects, than they could be where they were formed into a scale of subordination from a pope down to priests and friars and confessors—necessarily and essentially a sordid, stupid, and wretched herd—or than they could be in any other country where an archbishop held the place of a universal bishop, and the vicars and curates that of the ignorant, dependent, miserable rabble aforesaid—and infinitely more sensible and learned than they could be in either. This subject has been seen in the same light by many illustrious patriots who have lived in America since the days of our forefathers and who have adored their memory for the same reason. And methinks there has not appeared in New England a stronger veneration for their memory, a more penetrating insight into the grounds and principles and spirit of their policy, nor a more earnest desire of perpetuating the blessings of it to posterity, than that fine institution of the late Chief Justice Dudley, of a lecture against popery and on the validity of presbyterian ordination.[d] This was certainly intended by that wise and excellent man as an eternal memento of the wisdom and goodness of the very principles that settled America. But I must again return to the feudal law. The adventurers so often mentioned had an utter contempt of all that dark ribaldry of hereditary, indefeasible right—the Lord's anointed— and the divine, miraculous original of government with which the priesthood had enveloped the feudal monarch in clouds and mysteries, and from whence they had deduced the most mischievous of all doctrines, that of passive obedience and non-resistance. They knew that government was a plain, simple, intelligible thing, founded in nature and reason and quite comprehensible by common sense. They detested all the base services and servile dependencies of the feudal system. They knew that no such unworthy dependencies took place in the ancient seats of liberty, the republics of Greece and Rome; and they thought all such slavish subordinations were equally inconsistent with the constitution of human nature and that religious liberty with which Jesus had made them free. This was certainly the opinion they had formed; and they were far from being singular or extravagant in thinking so. Many celebrated modern writers in Europe have espoused the same sentiments. Lord Kames, a Scottish writer of great reputation, whose authority in this case ought to have the more weight as his countrymen have not the most worthy ideas of liberty, speaking of the feudal law, says, "A constitution so contradictory to all the principles which govern mankind can never be brought about, one should imagine, but by foreign conquest or native usurpations." Rousseau, speaking of the same system, calls it, "That most iniquitous and absurd form of government by which human nature was so shamefully degraded." [8] It would be easy to multiply authorities, but it must be needless, because, as the original of this form of government was among savages, as the spirit of it is military and despotic, every writer who would allow the people to have any right to life or property or freedom more than the beasts of the field, and who was not hired or enlisted under arbitrary, lawless power, has been always willing to admit the feudal system to be inconsistent with liberty and the rights of mankind.

To have holden their lands allodially or for every man to have been the sovereign lord and proprietor of the ground he occupied would have constituted a government too nearly like a commonwealth. They were contented, therefore, to hold their lands of their king as their sovereign lord; and to him they were willing to render homage, but to no mesne or subordinate lords; nor were they willing to submit to any of the baser services. In all this they were so strenuous that they have even transmitted to their posterity a very general contempt and detestation of holdings by quitrents, as they have also a hereditary ardor for liberty and thirst for knowledge.

They were convinced by their knowledge of human nature, derived from history and their own experience, that nothing could preserve their posterity from the encroachments of the two systems of tyranny in opposition to which, as has been observed already, they erected their government in church and state; but knowledge diffused generally through the whole body of the people. Their civil and religious principles, therefore, conspired to prompt them to use every measure and take every precaution in their power to propagate and perpetuate knowledge. For this purpose they laid very early the foundations of colleges and invested them with ample privileges and emoluments; and it is

[8] Social Compact, page 164.

remarkable that they have left among their posterity so universal an affection and veneration for those seminaries and for liberal education that the meanest of the people contribute cheerfully to the support and maintenance of them every year, and that nothing is more generally popular than projections for the honor, reputation, and advantage of those seats of learning. But the wisdom and benevolence of our fathers rested not here. They made an early provision by law that every town consisting of so many families should be always furnished with a grammar school. They made it a crime for such a town to be destitute of a grammar schoolmaster for a few months and subjected it to a heavy penalty. So that the education of all ranks of people was made the care and expense of the public in a manner that I believe has been unknown to any other people ancient or modern.

The consequences of these establishments we see and feel every day. A native of America who cannot read and write is as rare an appearance as a Jacobite [e] or a Roman Catholic, that is, as rare as a comet or an earthquake. It has been observed, that we are all of us lawyers, divines, politicians, and philosophers. And I have good authorities to say that all candid foreigners who have passed through this country and conversed freely with all sorts of people here will allow that they have never seen so much knowledge and civility among the common people in any part of the world. It is true there has been among us a party for some years, consisting chiefly not of the descendants of the first settlers of this country but of high churchmen and high statesmen imported since, who affect to censure this provision for the education of our youth as a needless expense and an imposition upon the rich in favor of the poor and as an institution productive of idleness and vain speculation among the people, whose time and attention, it is said, ought to be devoted to labor, and not to public affairs or to examination into the conduct of their superiors. And certain officers of the crown and certain other missionaries of ignorance, foppery, servility, and slavery have been most inclined to countenance and increase the same party. Be it remembered, however, that liberty must at all hazards be supported. We have a right to it, derived from our Maker. But if we had not, our fathers have earned and bought it for us at the expense of their ease, their estates, their pleasure, and their blood. And liberty cannot be preserved without a general knowledge among the people, who have a right, from the frame of their nature, to knowledge, as their great Creator, who does nothing in vain, has given them understandings and a desire to know; but besides this, they have a right, an indisputable, unalienable, indefeasible, divine right to that most dreaded and envied kind of knowledge—I mean, of the characters and conduct of their rulers. Rulers are no more than attorneys, agents, and trustees for the people; and if the cause, the interest and trust, is insidiously betrayed or wantonly trifled away, the people have a right to revoke the authority that they themselves have deputed and to constitute abler and better agents, attorneys, and trustees. And the preservation of the means of knowledge among the lowest ranks is of more importance to the public than all the property of all the rich men in the country. It is even of more consequence to the rich themselves and to their posterity. The only question is whether it is a public emolument; and if it is, the rich ought undoubtedly to contribute in the same proportion as to all other public burdens—that is, in proportion to their wealth, which is secured by public expenses. But none of the means of information are more sacred or have been cherished with more tenderness and care by the settlers of America than the press. Care has been taken that the art of printing should be encouraged, and that it should be easy and cheap and safe for any person to communicate his thoughts to the public. And you, Messieurs printers,[9] whatever the tyrants of the earth may say of your paper, have done important service to your country by your readiness and freedom in publishing the speculations of the curious. The stale, impudent insinuations of slander and sedition with which the gormandizers of power have endeavored to discredit your paper are so much the more to your honor; for the jaws of power are always opened to devour, and her arm is always stretched out, if possible, to destroy the freedom of thinking, speaking, and writing. And if the public interest, liberty, and happiness have been in danger

[9] Edes and Gill, printers of the Boston Gazette.

from the ambition or avarice of any great man, whatever may be his politeness, address, learning, ingenuity, and, in other respects, integrity and humanity, you have done yourselves honor and your country service by publishing and pointing out that avarice and ambition. These vices are so much the more dangerous and pernicious for the virtues with which they may be accompanied in the same character, and with so much the more watchful jealousy to be guarded against.

Curse on such virtues, they've undone their country.

Be not intimidated, therefore, by any terrors, from publishing with the utmost freedom whatever can be warranted by the laws of your country; nor suffer yourselves to be wheedled out of your liberty by any pretenses of politeness, delicacy, or decency. These, as they are often used, are but three different names for hypocrisy, chicanery, and cowardice. Much less, I presume, will you be discouraged by any pretenses that malignants on this side the water will represent your paper as factious and seditious, or that the great on the other side the water will take offense at them. This dread of representation has had for a long time, in this province, effects very similar to what the physicians call a hydropho or dread of water. It has made us delirious; and we have rushed headlong into the water, till we are almost drowned, out of simple or phrensical fear of it. Believe me, the character of this country has suffered more in Britain by the pusillanimity with which we have borne many insults and indignities from the creatures of power at home and the creatures of those creatures here than it ever did or ever will by the freedom and spirit that has been or will be discovered in writing or action. Believe me, my countrymen, they have imbibed an opinion on the other side the water that we are an ignorant, a timid, and a stupid people; nay, their tools on this side have often the impudence to dispute your bravery. But I hope in God the time is near at hand when they will be fully convinced of your understanding, integrity and courage. But can anything be more ridiculous, were it not too provoking to be laughted at, than to pretend that offense should be taken at home for writings here? Pray, let them look at home. Is not the human understanding exhausted there? Are not reason, imagination, wit, passion, senses, and all, tortured to find out satire and invective against the characters of the vile and futile fellows who sometimes get into place and power? The most exceptionable paper that ever I saw here is perfect prudence and modesty in comparison of multitudes of their applauded writings. Yet the high regard they have for the freedom of the press indulges all. I must and will repeat it, your paper deserves the patronage of every friend to his country. And whether the defamers of it are arrayed in robes of scarlet or sable, whether they lurk and skulk in an insurance office, whether they assume the venerable character of a priest, the sly one of a scrivener, or the dirty, infamous, abandoned one of an informer, they are all the creatures and tools of the lust of domination.

The true source of our sufferings has been our timidity.

We have been afraid to think. We have felt a reluctance to examining into the grounds of our privileges and the extent in which we have an indisputable right to demand them against all the power and authority on earth. And many who have not scrupled to examine for themselves have yet for certain prudent reasons been cautious and diffident of declaring the result of their inquiries.

The cause of this timidity is perhaps hereditary and to be traced back in history as far as the cruel treatment the first settlers of this country received before their embarkation for America from the government at home. Everybody knows how dangerous it was to speak or write in favor of anything in those days but the triumphant system of religion and politics. And our fathers were particularly the objects of the persecutions and proscriptions of the times. It is not unlikely, therefore, that although they were inflexibly steady in refusing their positive assent to anything against their principles, they might have contracted habits of reserve and a cautious diffidence of asserting their opinions publicly. These habits they probably brought with them to America and have transmitted down to us. Or we may possibly account for this appearance by the great affection and veneration Americans have always entertained for the country from whence they sprang; or by the quiet temper for which they have been remarkable, no country having been less disposed to discontent than this; or by a sense they have that it is their duty to acquiesce under the administration of government, even when in many smaller matters grievous to them, and until the essentials of the great compact are destroyed or invaded. These peculiar causes might operate upon them; but without these we all know that human nature itself from indolence, modesty, humanity, or fear has always too much reluctance to a manly assertion of its rights. Hence, perhaps, it has happened that nine tenths of the species are groaning and gasping in misery and servitude.

But whatever the cause has been, the fact is certain, we have been excessively cautious of giving offense by complaining of grievances. And it is as certain that American governors, and their friends, and all the crown officers have availed themselves of this disposition in the people. They have prevailed on us to consent to many things which were grossly injurious to us and to surrender many others with voluntary tameness to which we had the clearest right. Have we not been treated, formerly, with abominable insolence by officers of the navy? I mean no insinuation against any gentleman now on this station, having heard no complaint of any one of them to his dishonor. Have not some generals from England treated us like servants, nay, more like slaves than like Britons? Have we not been under the most ignominious contribution, the most abject submission, the most supercilious insults, of some custom-house officers? Have we not been trifled with, brow-beaten, and trampled on by former governors in a manner which no King of England since James the Second has dared to indulge towards his subjects? Have we not raised up one family, in them placed an unlimited confidence, and been soothed and flattered and intimidated by their influence into a great part of this infamous tameness and submission? "These are serious and alarming questions, and deserve a dispassionate consideration."

This disposition has been the great wheel and the mainspring in the American machine of court politics. We have been told that "the word *rights* is an offensive expression"; "that the king, his ministry, and parliament, will not endure to hear Americans talk of their *rights*"; "that Britain is the mother and we the children, that a filial duty and submission is due from us to her," and that "we ought to doubt our own judgment and presume that she is right, even when she seems to us to shake the foundations of government"; that "Britain is immensely rich and great and powerful, has fleets and armies at her command which have been the dread and terror of the universe, and that she will force her own judgment into execution, right or wrong." But let me entreat you, sir, to pause. Do you consider yourself as a missionary of loyalty or of rebellion? Are you not representing your king, his ministry, and parliament as tyrants—imperious, unrelenting tyrants—by such reasoning as this? Is not this representing your most gracious sovereign as endeavoring to destroy the foundations of his own throne? Are you not representing every member of parliament as renouncing the transactions at Runing Mede (the meadow, near Windsor, where Magna Charta was signed), and as repealing in effect the bill of rights, when the Lords and Commons asserted and vindicated the rights of the people and their own rights and insisted on the king's assent to that assertion and vindication? Do you not represent them as forgetting that the Prince of Orange was created King William by the people on purpose that their rights might be eternal and inviolable? Is there not something extremely fallacious in the commonplace images of mother country and children colonies? Are we the children of Great Britain any more than the cities of London, Exeter, and Bath? Are we not brethren and fellow subjects with those in Britain, only under a somewhat different method of legislation and a totally different method of taxation? But admitting we are children, have not children a right to complain when their parents are attempting to break their limbs, to administer poison, or to sell them to enemies for slaves? Let me entreat you to consider, will the mother be pleased when you represent her as deaf to the cries of her children—when you compare her to the infamous miscreant who lately stood on the

gallows for starving her child—when you resemble her to Lady
Macbeth in Shakespeare (I cannot think of it without horror),
who

> Had given suck, and knew
> How tender 't was to love the babe that milked her,

but yet, who could

> Even while 't was smiling in her face,
> Have plucked her nipple from the boneless gums,
> And dashed the brains out.

Let us banish for ever from our minds, my countrymen, all
such unworthy ideas of the king, his ministry, and parliament.
Let us not suppose that all are become luxurious, effeminate,
and unreasonable on the other side the water as many designing
persons would insinuate. Let us presume, what is in fact true,
that the spirit of liberty is as ardent as ever among the body of
the nation though a few individuals may be corrupted. Let us
take it for granted that the same great spirit which once gave
Cæsar so warm a reception, which denounced hostilities against
John till Magna Charta was signed, which severed the head of
Charles the First from his body and drove James the Second
from his kingdom, the same great spirit (may heaven preserve it
till the earth shall be no more) which first seated the great
grandfather of his present most gracious majesty on the throne of
Britain—is still alive and active and warm in England; and that
the same spirit in America, instead of provoking the inhabitants
of that country, will endear us to them forever and secure their
good-will.

This spirit, however, without knowledge, would be little better
than a brutal rage. Let us tenderly and kindly cherish, therefore, the means of knowledge. Let us dare to read, think, speak,
and write. Let every order and degree among the people rouse
their attention and animate their resolution. Let them all become
attentive to the grounds and principles of government, ecclesiastical and civil. Let us study the law of nature; search into the
spirit of the British constitution; read the histories of ancient
ages; contemplate the great examples of Greece and Rome; set

before us the conduct of our own British ancestors who have defended for us the inherent rights of mankind against foreign and domestic tyrants and usurpers, against arbitrary kings and cruel priests, in short, against the gates of earth and hell. Let us read and recollect and impress upon our souls the views and ends of our own more immediate forefathers in exchanging their native country for a dreary, inhospitable wilderness. Let us examine into the nature of that power and the cruelty of that oppression which drove them from their homes. Recollect their amazing fortitude, their bitter sufferings—the hunger, the nakedness, the cold, which they patiently endured—the severe labors of clearing their grounds, building their houses, raising their provisions, amidst dangers from wild beasts and savage men before they had time or money or materials for commerce. Recollect the civil and religious principles and hopes and expectations which constantly supported and carried them through all hardships with patience and resignation. Let us recollect it was liberty, the hope of liberty for themselves and us and ours, which conquered all discouragements, dangers, and trials. In such researches as these, let us all in our several departments cheerfully engage—but especially the proper patrons and supporters of law, learning, and religion!

Let the pulpit resound with the doctrines and sentiments of religious liberty. Let us hear the danger of thraldom to our consciences from ignorance, extreme poverty, and dependence, in short, from civil and political slavery. Let us see delineated before us the true map of man. Let us hear the dignity of his nature, and the noble rank he holds among the works of God—that consenting to slavery is a sacrilegious breach of trust, as offensive in the sight of God as it is derogatory from our own honor or interest or happiness—and that God Almighty has promulgated from heaven, liberty, peace and good-will to man!

Let the bar proclaim "the laws, the rights, the generous plan of power" delivered down from remote antiquity, inform the world of the mighty struggles and numberless sacrifices made by our ancestors in defense of freedom. Let it be known that British liberties are not the grants of princes or parliaments but original rights, conditions of original contracts, coequal with prerogative and coeval with government; that many of our rights are inherent and essential, agreed on as maxims and established as preliminaries even before a parliament existed. Let them search for the foundations of British laws and government in the frame of human nature, in the constitution of the intellectual and moral world. There let us see that truth, liberty, justice, and benevolence are its everlasting basis; and if these could be removed, the superstructure is overthrown of course.

Let the colleges join their harmony in the same delightful concert. Let every declamation turn upon the beauty of liberty and virtue and the deformity, turpitude, and malignity of slavery and vice. Let the public disputations become researches into the grounds and nature and ends of government and the means of preserving the good and demolishing the evil. Let the dialogues and all the exercises become the instruments of impressing on the tender mind, and of spreading and distributing far and wide, the ideas of right and the sensations of freedom.

In a word, let every sluice of knowledge be opened and set aflowing. The encroachments upon liberty in the reigns of the first James and the first Charles, by turning the general attention of learned men to government, are said to have produced the greatest number of consummate statesmen which has ever been seen in any age or nation. The Brookes, Hampdens, Vanes, Seldens, Miltons, Nedhams, Harringtons, Nevilles, Sidneys, Lockes are all said to have owed their eminence in political knowledge to the tyrannies of those reigns. The prospect now before us in America ought in the same manner to engage the attention of every man of learning to matters of power and of right, that we may be neither led nor driven blindfolded to irretrievable destruction. Nothing less than this seems to have been meditated for us by somebody or other in Great Britain. There seems to be a direct and formal design on foot to enslave all America. This, however, must be done by degrees. The first step that is intended seems to be an entire subversion of the whole system of our fathers by the introduction of the canon and feudal law into America. The canon and feudal systems, though greatly mutilated in England, are not yet destroyed. Like the temples and palaces in which the great contrivers of them once worshipped and inhabited, they exist in ruins; and much of the domineering spirit of them still remains. The designs and labors of a certain society to introduce the former of them into America have been well exposed to the public by a writer of great abilities; [10] and the further attempts to the same purpose, that may be made by that society or by the ministry or parliament I leave to the conjectures of the thoughtful. But it seems very manifest from the Stamp Act itself that a design is formed to strip us in a great measure of the means of knowledge by loading the press, the colleges, and even an almanack and a newspaper, with restraints and duties; and to introduce the inequalities and dependencies of the feudal system by taking from the poorer sort of people all their little subsistence and conferring it on a set of stamp officers, distributors, and their deputies. But I must proceed no further at present. The sequel, whenever I shall find health and leisure to pursue it, will be a "disquisition of the policy of the stamp act." In the meantime, however, let me add: These are not the vapors of a melancholy mind, nor the effusions of envy, disappointed ambition, nor of a spirit of opposition to government, but the emanations of a heart that burns for its country's welfare. No one of any feeling, born and educated in this once happy country, can consider the numerous distresses, the gross indignities, the barbarous ignorance, the haughty usurpations, that we have reason to fear are meditating for ourselves, our children, our neighbors, in short, for all our countrymen and all their posterity, without the utmost agonies of heart and many tears.

[10] The late Rev. Dr. Mayhew.

II. INSTRUCTIONS OF THE TOWN OF BRAIN-TREE TO THEIR REPRESENTATIVE [1]

Concerning these "Instructions" John Adams wrote in his diary: "I prepared a draught of instructions at home, and carried them with me. The cause of the meeting was explained at some length, and the state and danger of the country pointed out; a committee was appointed to prepare instructions, of which I was nominated as one. We retired to Mr. Niles's house, my draught was produced, and unanimously adopted without amendment, reported to the town, and accepted without a dissenting voice." [2] The import of Adams' argument was simply that the Stamp Act was contrary to the English Constitution, even "directly repugnant to the Great Charter itself." The basis of the appeal was founded on the rights of Englishmen enshrined in the spirit of the common law, itself the embodiment of right reason. The thesis advanced here, though based on the English Constitution, differs from the argument found in the Novanglus papers which in the main are devoted to the nature of the British Empire.

BOSTON, 14 October [3]

We hear from Braintree that the freeholders and other inhabitants of that town, legally assembled on Tuesday, the twenty-fourth of September last, unanimously voted that instructions should be given their representative for his conduct in General Assembly on this great occasion. The substance of these instructions is as follows:

TO EBENEZER THAYER, ESQ.

Sir: In all the calamities which have ever befallen this country, we have never felt so great a concern or such alarming apprehensions as on this occasion. Such is our loyalty to the King, our veneration for both houses of Parliament, and our affection

[1] [III, 465–468.]
[2] [III, 153.]
[3] Printed from the *Boston Gazette*, of Monday, 14 October, 1765.

22

for all our fellow subjects in Britain that measures which discover any unkindness in that country towards us are the more sensibly and intimately felt. And we can no longer forbear complaining that many of the measures of the late ministry and some of the late acts of Parliament have a tendency, in our apprehension, to divest us of our most essential rights and liberties. We shall confine ourselves, however, chiefly to the act of Parliament commonly called the Stamp Act by which a very burthensome and, in our opinion, unconstitutional tax is to be laid upon us all, and we subjected to numerous and enormous penalties, to be prosecuted, sued for, and recovered at the option of an informer in a court of admiralty without a jury.

We have called this a burthensome tax because the duties are so numerous and so high and the embarrassments to business in this infant, sparsely-settled country so great that it would be totally impossible for the people to subsist under it if we had no controversy at all about the right and authority of imposing it. Considering the present scarcity of money, we have reason to think the execution of that act for a short space of time would drain the country of its cash, strip multitudes of all their property, and reduce them to absolute beggary. And what the consequence would be to the peace of the province from so sudden a shock and such a convulsive change in the whole course of our business and subsistence we tremble to consider. We further apprehend this tax to be unconstitutional. We have always understood it to be a grand and fundamental principle of the constitution that no freeman should be subject to any tax to which he has not given his own consent, in person or by proxy. And the maxims of the law, as we have constantly received them, are to the same effect, that no freeman can be separated from his property but by his own act or fault. We take it clearly, therefore, to be inconsistent with the spirit of the common law and of the essential fundamental principles of the British constitution that we should be subject to any tax imposed by the British Parliament, because we are not represented in that assembly in any sense, unless it be by a fiction of law, as insensible in theory as it would be injurious in practice if such a taxation should be grounded on it.

But the most grievous innovation of all is the alarming extension of the power of courts of admiralty. In these courts one judge presides alone! No juries have any concern there! The law and the fact are both to be decided by the same single judge, whose commission is only during pleasure, and with whom, as we are told, the most mischievous of all customs has become established, that of taking commissions on all condemnations, so that he is under a pecuniary temptation always against the subject. Now, if the wisdom of the mother country has thought the independence of the judges so essential to an impartial administration of justice as to render them independent of every power on earth—independent of the King, the Lords, the Commons, the people, nay, independent in hope and expectation of the heir-apparent, by continuing their commissions after a demise of the crown, what justice and impartiality are we at three thousand miles distance from the fountain to expect from such a judge of admiralty? We have all along thought the acts of trade in this respect a grievance; but the Stamp Act has opened a vast number of sources of new crimes which may be committed by any man and cannot but be committed by multitudes, and prodigious penalties are annexed, and all these are to be tried by such a judge of such a court! What can be wanting, after this, but a weak or wicked man for a judge, to render us the most sordid and forlorn of slaves—we mean the slaves of a slave of the servants of a minister of state? We cannot help asserting, therefore, that this part of the act will make an essential change in the constitution of juries, and it is directly repugnant to the Great Charter itself; for by that charter, "no amerciament shall be assessed but by the oath of honest and lawful men of the vicinage;" and, "no freeman shall be taken, or imprisoned, or disseized of his freehold, or liberties of free customs, nor passed upon, nor condemned, but by lawful judgment of his peers, or by the law of the land." So that this act will "make such a distinction and create such a difference between" the subjects in Great Britain and those in America as we could not have expected from the guardians of liberty in "both."

As these, sir, are our sentiments of this act, we, the freeholders and other inhabitants, legally assembled for this purpose, must enjoin it upon you to comply with no measures or proposals for countenancing the same or assisting in the execution of it, but by all lawful means, consistent with our allegiance to the King and relation to Great Britain, to oppose the execution of it till we can hear the success of the cries and petitions of America for relief.

We further recommend the most clear and explicit assertion and vindication of our rights and liberties to be entered on the public records, that the world may know in the present and all future generations that we have a clear knowledge and a just sense of them, and, with submission to Divine Providence, that we never can be slaves.[4]

Nor can we think it advisable to agree to any steps for the protection of stamped papers or stamp-officers. Good and wholesome laws we have already for the preservation of the peace; and we apprehend there is no further danger of tumult and disorder, to which we have a well-grounded aversion; and that any extraordinary and expensive exertions would tend to exasperate the people and endanger the public tranquility, rather than the contrary. Indeed, we cannot too often inculcate upon you our desires that all extraordinary grants and expensive measures may, upon all occasions, as much as possible be avoided. The public money of this country is the toil and labor of the people, who are under many uncommon difficulties and distresses at this time, so that all reasonable frugality ought to be observed. And we would recommend particularly the strictest care and the utmost firmness to prevent all unconstitutional draughts upon the public treasury.

[4] A Cambridge correspondent of the *Evening Post,* in October, 1765, enters into a comparison of these instructions with some of an opposite nature, coming from Marblehead and published at the same time, and picks out this paragraph, as "worthy to be wrote in letters of gold."

III. NOVANGLUS AND MASSACHUSETTENSIS
December, 1774 – April, 1775

In his *Diary* John Adams records the occasion for the publication of the Novanglus letters. He had returned from the Continental Congress [a] in the autumn of 1774 and found in the *Massachusetts Gazette and Post-Boy* a series of articles signed Massachusettensis ably defending the Tory point of view. The author was thought by him to be his old friend Jonathan Sewall, although it is now known to have been Daniel Leonard. "These papers were well written," wrote Adams, "abounded with wit, discovered good information, and were conducted with a subtlety of art and address wonderfully calculated to keep up the spirits of their party, to depress ours, to spread intimidation, and to make proselytes among those whose principles and judgment give way to their fears; and these compose at least one third of mankind. Week after week passed away, and these papers made a very visible impression on many minds. No answer appeared, and indeed some who were capable were too busy, and others too timorous. I began at length to think seriously of the consequences, and began to write under the signature of Novanglus, and continued every week in the *Boston Gazette*, till the 19th of April, 1775. . . . In New England, they had the effect of an antidote to the poison of Massachusettensis; and the battle of Lexington,[b] on the 19th of April, changed the instruments of warfare from the pen to the sword." [1]

In the Novanglus letters John Adams advances a thesis different from that put forth in his "Instructions for the Representative of Braintree," and this difference is significant. The Tory view so precisely stated by Daniel Leonard held that the authority of Parliament over the empire was complete, that the colonies were part of the empire, hence Parliament's authority extended fully over the colonies. It was impossible for him to conceive of the colonies as independent within the empire because "Two supreme or independent authorities cannot exist in the same state. . . . If, then, we are a part of the British empire, we must be subject to the supreme power of the state,

[1] [II, 405.]

which is vested in the estates of parliament, notwithstanding each of the colonies have legislative and executive powers of their own, delegated, or granted to them for the purposes of regulating their own internal police, which are subordinate to, and must necessarily be subject to the checks, control, and regulation of the supreme authority." [2] Adams met the issue squarely. "I agree that 'two supreme and independent authorities cannot exist in the same state,' any more than two supreme beings in one universe; and, therefore, I contend that our provincial legislatures are the only supreme authorities in our colonies. . . . I say we are not a part of the British empire. . . . Distinct states may be united under one king. And those states may be further cemented and united together by a treaty of commerce. This is the case. . . . We [the colonies] owe allegiance to the person of his majesty, King George III, whom God preserve." [3] In this fashion was the issue joined. Massachusettensis insisted the empire was just that, controlled by a sovereign parliament sitting at London; Novanglus held that the empire was a commonwealth of independent states cemented by a common allegiance to the King, with the several states regulating their internal affairs and the British Parliament deciding external imperial matters. Thus did Adams appreciate and prophesy the Commonwealth.

The Novanglus letters are addressed in each instance "To the Inhabitants of the Colony of Massachusetts Bay"; the Massachusettensis letters, "To the Inhabitants of the Province of Massachusetts Bay." In order to understand fully the nature of the controversy between John Adams and Daniel Leonard it is necessary to include letters representing each point of view. The letters are arranged in such a fashion that one may see an argument presented by the one writer and then answered by the other. Massachusettensis commences the argument by his letter of December 12, 1774, and continues in the same vein in his letter of December 26. This is answered by Novanglus in his letter of January 23, 1775. In the meantime Massachusettensis advances another thesis in his letter of January 9, 1775, which Novanglus counters on March 6, 1775, and so it goes.

[2] [January 9, 1775. Cf. p. 34f.]
[3] [IV, 105–114; passim.]

1. MASSACHUSETTENSIS

December 12, 1774

My Dear Countrymen: When a people, by what means soever, are reduced to such a situation that everything they hold dear as men and citizen is at stake, it is not only excusable, but even praiseworthy for an individual to offer to the public anything that he may think has a tendency to ward off the impending danger; nor should he be restrained from an apprehension that what he may offer will be unpopular, any more than a physician should be restrained from prescribing a salutary medicine through fear it might be unpalatable to his patient.

The press, when open to all parties and influenced by none, is a salutary engine in a free state, perhaps a necessary one to preserve the freedom of that state; but when a party has gained the ascendancy so far as to become the licensers of the press, either by an act of government or by playing off the resentment of the populace against printers and authors, the press itself becomes an engine of oppression or licentiousness, and is as pernicious to society as otherwise it would be beneficial. It is too true to be denied that ever since the origin of our controversy with Great Britain the press in this town has been much devoted to the partisans of liberty; they have been indulged in publishing what they pleased, *fas vel nefas*, ["permitted or not permitted"] while little has been published on the part of government. The effect this must have had upon the minds of the people in general is obvious; they must have formed their opinion upon a partial view of the subject and of course it must have been in some degree erroneous. In short, the changes have been rung so often upon oppression, tyranny, and slavery that, whether sleeping or waking, they are continually vibrating in our ears, and it is now high time to ask ourselves whether we have not been deluded by sound only.

My dear countrymen: let us divest ourselves of prejudice, take a view of our present wretched situation, contrast it with our

former happy one, carefully investigate the cause, and industri-
ously seek some means to escape the evils we now feel and prevent those that we have reason to expect.

. . . .

2. NOVANGLUS

January 23, 1775

My Friends: A writer under the signature of *Massachusettensis*
has addressed you in a series of papers on the great national
subject of the present quarrel between the British administration
and the Colonies. As I have not in my possession more than one
of his essays, and that is in the *Gazette* of December 26, I will
take the liberty in the spirit of candor and decency to bespeak
your attention upon the same subject.

There may be occasion to say very severe things before I shall
have finished what I propose in opposition to this writer, but
there ought to be no reviling. *Rem ipsam dic, mitte male loqui,*
which may be justly translated, "speak out the whole truth
boldly, but use no bad language."

It is not very material to inquire, as others have done, who is
the author of the speculations in question. If he is a disinterested
writer and has nothing to gain or to lose, to hope or to fear, for
himself more than other individuals of your community, but
engages in this controversy from the purest principles, the noblest
motives of benevolence to men, and of love to his country, he
ought to have no influence with you further than truth and
justice will support his argument. On the other hand, if he hopes
to acquire or preserve a lucrative employment, to screen himself
from the just detestation of his countrymen, or whatever other
sinister inducement he may have, so far as the truth of facts and
the weight of argument are in his favor, he ought to be duly
regarded.

He tells you, "that the temporal salvation of this province
depends upon an entire and speedy change of measures, which

must depend upon a change of sentiment respecting our own conduct and the justice of the British nation."

The task of effecting these great changes this courageous writer has undertaken in a course of publications in a newspaper. *Nil desperandum* is a good motto, and *nil admirari* is another. He is welcome to the first, and I hope will be willing that I should assume the last. The public, if they are not mistaken in their conjecture, have been so long acquainted with this gentleman and have seen him so often disappointed that if they were not habituated to strange things, they would wonder at his hopes at this time to accomplish the most unpromising project of his whole life. In the character of *Philanthrop,* he attempted to reconcile you to Mr. Bernard. But the only fruit of his labor was to expose his client to more general examination and consequently to more general resentment and aversion. In the character of *Philalethes,* he essayed to prove Mr. Hutchinson a patriot and his letters not only innocent but meritorious. But the more you read and considered, the more you were convinced of the ambition and avarice, the simulation and dissimulation, the hypocrisy and perfidy of that destroying angel.

This ill-fated and unsuccessful though persevering writer still hopes to change your sentiments and conduct, by which it is supposed that he means to convince you that the system of colony administration which has been pursued for these ten or twelve years past is a wise, righteous, and humane plan; that Sir Francis Bernard and Mr. Hutchinson, with their connections who have been the principal instruments of it, are your best friends; and that those gentlemen, in this province and in all the other colonies who have been in opposition to it, are from ignorance, error, or from worse and baser causes your worst enemies.

This is certainly an inquiry that is worthy of you; and I promise to accompany this writer in his ingenious labors to assist you in it. And I earnestly entreat you, as the result of all shall be, to change your sentiments or persevere in them as the evidence shall appear to you upon the most dispassionate and impartial consideration without regard to his opinion or mine.

He promises to avoid personal reflections, but to "penetrate the arcana" and "expose the wretched policy of the whigs." The cause of the whigs is not conducted by intrigues at a distant court but by constant appeals to a sensible and virtuous people; it depends entirely on their good-will and cannot be pursued a single step without their concurrence, to obtain which all their designs, measures, and means are constantly published to the collective body. The whigs, therefore, can have no arcana; but if they had, I dare say they were never so left as to communicate them to this writer; you will therefore be disappointed if you expect from him anything which is true but what has been as public as records and newspapers could make it.

I, on my part, may, perhaps, in a course of papers, penetrate arcana too, show the wicked policy of the tories, trace their plan from its first rude sketches to its present complete draught, show that it has been much longer in contemplation than is generally known—who were the first in it—their views, motives, and secret springs of action, and the means they have employed. This will necessarily bring before your eyes many characters, living and dead. From such a research and detail of facts it will clearly appear who were the aggressors and who have acted on the defensive from first to last; who are still struggling at the expense of their ease, health, peace, wealth, and preferment against the encroachments of the tories on their country, and who are determined to continue struggling at much greater hazards still and, like the Prince of Orange, are resolved never to see its entire subjection to arbitrary power but rather to die fighting against it in the last ditch. . . .

. . . .

3. MASSACHUSETTENSIS

January 9, 1775

My Dear Countrymen: Some of you may perhaps suspect that I have been wantonly scattering firebrands, arrows, and death to gratify a malicious and revengeful disposition. The truth is this:

I had seen many excellent detached pieces, but could see no pen at work to trace our calamity to its source and point out the many adventitious aids that conspired to raise it to its present height, though I impatiently expected it, being fully convinced that you wait only to know the true state of facts, to rectify whatever is amiss in the province without any foreign assistance. Others may be induced to think that I grudge the industrious poor of Boston their scantlings of charity. I will issue a brief in their favor. The opulent, be their political sentiments what they may, ought to relieve them from their sufferings; and those who, by former donations, have been the innocent cause of protracting their sufferings are under a tenfold obligation to assist them now; and at the same time to make the most explicit declarations that they did not intend to promote nor ever will join in rebellion. Great allowances are to be made for the crossings, windings, and tergiversations of a politician; he is a cunning animal, and as government is said to be founded in opinion, his tricks may be a part of the *arcana imperii* ["state secrets"]. Had our politicians confined themselves within any reasonable bounds, I never should have molested them; but when I became satisfied that many innocent, unsuspecting persons were in danger of being seduced to their utter ruin and the province of Massachusetts Bay in danger of being drenched with blood and carnage, I could restrain my emotions no longer; and having once broke the bands of natural reserve, was determined to probe the sore to the bottom, though I was sure to touch the quick. It is very foreign from my intentions to draw down the vengeance of Great Britain upon the Whigs;c they are too valuable a part of the community to lose—if they will permit themselves to be saved. I wish nothing worse to the highest of them than that they may be deprived of their influence till such time as they shall have changed their sentiments, principles, and measures.

Sedition has already been marked through its zigzag path to the present times. When the statute for regulating the government arrived, a match was put to the train, and the mine that had been long forming, sprung and threw the whole province into confusion and anarchy. The occurrences of the summer and autumn past are so recent and notorious that a particular detail of them is unnecessary. Suffice it to say that every barrier that civil government had erected for the security of property, liberty, and life was broken down; and law, constitution, and government trampled under foot by the rudest invaders. I shall not dwell upon these harsh notes much longer. I shall yet become an advocate for the leading Whigs; much must be allowed to men in their situation, forcibly actuated by the chagrin of disappointment, the fear of punishment, and the fascination of hope at the same time.

Perhaps the whole story of empire does not furnish another instance of a forcible opposition to government with so much apparent and little real cause, with such apparent probability without any possibility of success. The Stamp Act gave the alarm. The instability of the public councils from the Greenvillian Administration [d] to the appointment of the Earl of Hillsborough to the American department afforded as great a prospect of success as the heavy duties imposed by the Stamp Act did a color for the opposition. It was necessary to give the history of this matter in its course, offend whom it would, because those acts of government that are called the greatest grievances became proper and necessary through the misconduct of our politicians; and the justice of Great Britain towards us could not be made apparent without first pointing out that. I intend to consider the acts of the British government which are held up as the principal grievances and inquire whether Great Britain is chargeable with injustice in any one of them, but must first ask your attention to the authority of parliament. I suspect many of our politicians are wrong in their first principle—in denying that the constitutional authority of parliament extends to the colonies; if so, it must not be wondered at that their whole fabric is so ruinous. I shall not travel through all the arguments that have been adduced for and against this question, but attempt to reduce the substance of them to a narrow compass, after having taken a cursory view of the British constitution.

The security of the people from internal rapacity and violence and from foreign invasion is the end and design of government.

The simple forms of government are monarchy, aristocracy, and democracy; that is, where the authority of the state is vested in one, a few, or the many. Each of these species of government has advantages peculiar to itself and would answer the ends of government were the persons entrusted with the authority of the state always guided, themselves, by unerring wisdom and public virtue; but rulers are not always exempt from the weakness and depravity which make government necessary to society. Thus monarchy is apt to rush headlong into tyranny; aristocracy to beget faction and multiplied usurpation; and democracy, to degenerate into tumult, violence, and anarchy. A government formed upon these three principles in due proportion is the best calculated to answer the ends of government and to endure. Such a government is the British constitution, consisting of king, lords, and commons, which at once includes the principal excellences and excludes the principal defects of the other kinds of government. It is allowed both by Englishmen and foreigners to be the most perfect system that the wisdom of ages has produced. The distributions of power are so just and the proportions so exact as at once to support and control each other. An Englishman glories in being subject to, and protected by, such a government. The colonies are a part of the British empire. The best writers upon the law of nations tell us that when a nation takes possession of a distant country and settles there, that country, though separated from the principal establishment or mother country, naturally becomes a part of the state, equal with its ancient possessions. Two supreme or independent authorities cannot exist in the same state. It would be what is called *imperium in imperio,* the height of political absurdity. The analogy between the political and human body is great. Two independent authorities in a state would be like two distinct principles of volition and action in the human body, dissenting, opposing, and destroying each other. If, then, we are a part of the British empire, we must be subject to the supreme power of the state, which is vested in the estates of parliament—notwithstanding each of the colonies have legislative and executive powers of their own, delegated or granted to them for the purposes of regulating their own internal police, which are subordinate to and must necessarily be subject to the checks, control, and regulation of the supreme authority.

This doctrine is not new, but the denial of it is. It is beyond a doubt that it was the sense both of the parent country and our ancestors that they were to remain subject to parliament. It is evident from the charter itself; and this authority has been exercised by parliament from time to time, almost ever since the first settlement of the country and has been expressly acknowledged by our provincial legislatures. It is not less our interest than our duty to continue subject to the authority of parliament, which will be more fully considered hereafter. The principal argument against the authority of parliament is this: the Americans are entitled to all the privileges of an Englishman; it is the privilege of an Englishman to be exempt from all laws that he does not consent to in person or by representative. The Americans are not represented in parliament and therefore are exempt from acts of parliament, or in other words, not subject to its authority. This appears specious, but leads to such absurdities as demonstrate its fallacy. If the colonies are not subject to the authority of parliament, Great Britain and the colonies must be distinct states, as completely so as England and Scotland were before the union, or as Great Britain and Hanover e are now. The colonies in that case will owe no allegiance to the imperial crown and perhaps not to the person of the king, as the title to the crown is derived from an act of parliament made since the settlement of this province, which act respects the imperial crown only. Let us waive this difficulty and suppose allegiance due from the colonies to the person of the king of Great Britain. He then appears in a new capacity—of king of America—or rather in several new capacities: of king of Massachusetts, king of Rhode Island, king of Connecticut, etc. For if our connection with Great Britain by the parliament be dissolved, we shall have none among ourselves, but each colony become as distinct from the others as England was from Scotland before the union. Some have supposed that each state, having one and the same person for its king, is a sufficient connection. Were he an absolute monarch, it might be; but in a mixed government, it is no union at all. For as the king must govern each state by its parliament, those several parliaments would pursue the particular interest of its own state; and however well disposed the king might be to pursue a line of interest that was common to all, the checks and control that he would meet with would render it impossible. If the king of Great Britain has really these new capacities, they ought to be added to his titles; and another difficulty will arise—the prerogatives of these new crowns have never been defined or limited. Is the monarchical part of the several provincial constitutions to be nearer or more remote from absolute monarchy, in an inverted ratio to each one's approaching to or receding from a republic? But let us suppose the same prerogatives inherent in the several American crowns as are in the imperial crown of Great Britain; where shall we find the British constitution, that we all agree we are entitled to? We shall seek for it in vain in our provincial assemblies. They are but faint sketches of the estates of parliament. The houses of representatives, or Burgesses, have not all the powers of the house of commons; in the charter governments they have no more than what is expressly granted by their several charters. The first charters granted to this province did not empower the assembly to tax the people at all. Our council boards are as destitute of the constitutional authority of the house of lords as their several members are of the noble independence and splendid appendages of peerage. The house of peers is the bulwark of the British constitution, and through successive ages has withstood the shocks of monarchy and the sappings of democracy, and the constitution gained strength by the conflict. Thus the supposition of our being independent states or exempt from the authority of parliament destroys the very idea of our having a British constitution. The provincial constitutions, considered as subordinate, are generally well adapted to those purposes of government for which they were intended; that is, to regulate the internal police of the several colonies, but have no principle of stability within themselves. They may support themselves in moderate times, but would be merged by the violence of turbulent ones, and the several colonies become wholly monarchical or wholly republican were it not for the checks, controls, regulations, and supports of the supreme authority of the empire. Thus the argument that is drawn from their first principle of our being entitled to English liberties destroys the principle itself; it deprives us of the bill of rights and all the benefits resulting from the revolution of English laws and of the British constitution.

Our patriots have been so intent upon building up American rights that they have overlooked the rights of Great Britain and our own interest. Instead of proving that we were entitled to privileges that our fathers knew our situation would not admit us to enjoy, they have been arguing away our most essential rights. If there be any grievance, it does not consist in our being subject to the authority of parliament but in our not having an actual representation in it. Were it possible for the colonies to have an equal representation in parliament and were refused it upon proper application, I confess I should think it a grievance; but at present it seems to be allowed by all parties to be impracticable, considering the colonies are distant from Great Britain a thousand transmarine leagues. If that be the case, the right or privilege that we complain of being deprived of, is not withheld by Britain; but the first principles of government and the immutable laws of nature render it impossible for us to enjoy it. This is apparently the meaning of that celebrated passage in Governor Hutchinson's letter that rang through the continent, viz: "There must be an abridgment of what is called English liberties." He subjoins that he had never yet seen the projection whereby a colony, three thousand miles distant from the parent state, might enjoy all the privileges of the parent state and remain subject to it, or in words to that effect. The obnoxious sentence, taken detached from the letter, appears very unfriendly to the colonies; but considered in connection with the other parts of the letter, is but a necessary result from our situation. Allegiance and protection are reciprocal. It is our highest interest to continue a part of the British empire, and equally our duty to remain subject to the authority of parliament. Our own internal police may generally be regulated by our provincial legislatures, but in national concerns or where our own assemblies do not answer the ends of government with respect to ourselves, the ordinances or interposition of the great council of the nation is necessary. In this case the major must rule the minor. After many more centuries shall have rolled away long after we, who are now bustling upon the stage of life, shall have been received to the bosom of mother earth and our names are forgotten, the colonies may be so far increased as to have the balance of wealth, numbers, and power in their favor, the good of the empire make it necessary to fix the seat of government here; and some future George, equally the friend of mankind with him that now sways the British sceptre, may cross the Atlantic and rule Great Britain by an American parliament.

4. NOVANGLUS

March 6, 1775

Our rhetorical magician in his paper of January the 9th continues to *wheedle:* You want nothing but "to know the true state of facts, to rectify whatever is amiss." He becomes an advocate for the poor of Boston! is for making great allowance for the whigs. "The whigs are too valuable a part of the community to lose. He would not draw down the vengeance of Great Britain. He shall become an advocate for the leading whigs," etc. It is in vain for us to inquire after the *sincerity* or *consistency* of all this. It is agreeable to the precept of Horace:

> *Irritat, mulcet, falsis terroribus implet,*
> *Ut magus* [f] —

And that is all he desires.

After a long discourse, which has nothing in it but what has been answered already, he comes to a great subject indeed, the British constitution, and undertakes to prove that "the authority of parliament extends to the colonies."

Why will not this writer state the question fairly? The whigs allow that, from the necessity of a case not provided for by common law and to supply a defect in the British dominions, which there undoubtedly is, if they are to be governed only by that law, America has all along consented, still consents, and ever will consent that parliament, being the most powerful legislature in the dominions, should regulate the trade of the dominions. This is founding the authority of parliament to regulate our trade upon *compact* and *consent* of the colonies, not upon any principle of common or statute law, not upon any original principle of the English constitution, not upon the principle that parliament is the supreme and sovereign legislature over them in all cases whatsoever. The question is not, therefore, whether the authority of parliament extends to the colonies in any case, for it is admitted by the whigs that it does in that of commerce, but whether it extends in all cases.

We are then detained with a long account of the three simple forms of government and are told that "the British constitution, consisting of king, lords, and commons, is formed upon the principles of monarchy, aristocracy, and democracy, in due proportion; that it includes the principal excellences and excludes the principal defects of the other kinds of government—the most perfect system that the wisdom of ages has produced, and Englishmen glory in being subject to and protected by it."

Then we are told "that the colonies are a part of the British empire." But what are we to understand by this? Some of the colonies, most of them, indeed, were settled before the kingdom of Great Britain was brought into existence. The union of England and Scotland was made and established by act of parliament in the reign of Queen Anne, and it was this union and statute which erected the kingdom of Great Britain. The colonies were settled long before, in the reigns of the Jameses and Charleses. What authority over them had Scotland? Scotland, England, and the colonies were all under one king before that; the two crowns of England and Scotland united on the head of James I and continued united on that of Charles I, when our first charter was granted. Our charter being granted by him who was king of both nations to our ancestors, most of whom were *post nati,* born after the union of the two crowns, and consequently, as was adjudged in Calvin's case, free, natural subjects of Scotland as well as England—had not the king as good a right to have governed the colonies by his Scottish as by his English parliament, and to have granted our charters under the seal of Scotland as well as that of England?

But to wave this. If the English parliament were to govern us, where did they get the right without our consent to take the Scottish parliament into a participation of the government over us? When this was done, was the American share of the democracy of the constitution consulted? If not, were not the Americans deprived of the benefit of the democratical part of the constitution? And is not the democracy as essential to the English constitution as the monarchy or aristocracy? Should we have been more effectually deprived of the benefit of the British or English constitution, if one or both houses of parliament, or if our house and council, had made this union with the two houses of parliament in Scotland without the king?

If a new constitution was to be formed for the whole British dominions and a supreme legislature coextensive with it upon the general principles of the English constitution, an equal mixture of monarchy, aristocracy, and democracy, let us see what would be necessary. England has six millions of people, we will say; America had three. England has five hundred members in the house of commons, we will say; America must have two hundred and fifty. Is it possible she should maintain them there, or could they at such a distance know the state, the sense, or exigencies of their constituents? Ireland, too, must be incorporated and send another hundred or two of members. The territory in the East Indies and West India Islands must send members. And after all this, every navigation act, every act of trade must be repealed. America, and the East and West Indies, and Africa, too, must have equal liberty to trade with all the world that the favored inhabitants of Great Britain have now. Will the ministry thank Massachusettensis for becoming an advocate for such a union and incorporation of all the dominions of the king of Great Britain? Yet, without such a union, a legislature which shall be sovereign and supreme in all cases whatsoever and coextensive with the empire can never be established upon the general principles of the English constitution which Massachusettensis lays down, namely, an equal mixture of monarchy, aristocracy, and democracy. Nay, further, in order to comply with this principle, this new government, this mighty colossus which is to bestride the narrow world, must have a house of lords, consisting of Irish, East and West Indian, African, American, as well as English and Scottish noblemen; for the nobility ought to be scattered about all the dominions, as well as the representatives of the commons. If in twenty years more America should have six millions of inhabitants, as there is a boundless territory to fill up, she must have five hundred representatives. Upon these principles, if in forty years she should have twelve millions, a thousand, and if the inhabitants of the three kingdoms remain as they are, being already full of inhabitants, what will become of your supreme legislative? It will be translated, crown and all, to America. This is a sublime system for America. It will flatter those ideas of independence which the tories impute to them, if they have any such, more than any other plan of independence that I have ever heard projected.

"The best writers upon the law of nations tell us that when a nation takes possession of a distant country and settles there, that country, though separated from the principal establishment, or mother country, naturally becomes a part of the state, equal with its ancient possessions." We are not told who these "best writers" are. I think we ought to be introduced to them. But their meaning may be no more than that it is best they should be incorporated with the ancient establishment by contract, or by some new law and institution, by which the new country shall have equal right, powers, and privileges, as well as equal protection, and be under equal obligations of obedience, with the old. Has there been any such contract between Britain and the colonies? Is America incorporated into the realm? Is it a part of the realm? Is it a part of the kingdom? Has it any share in the legislative of the realm? The constitution requires that every foot of land should be represented in the third estate, the democratical branch of the constitution. How many millions of acres in

America, how many thousands of wealthy landholders, have no representatives there?

But let these "best writers" say what they will, there is nothing in the law of nations, which is only the law of right reason applied to the conduct of nations, that requires that emigrants from a state should continue, or be made, a part of the state.

The practice of nations has been different. The Greeks planted colonies and neither demanded nor pretended any authority over them; but they became distinct, independent commonwealths. The Romans continued their colonies under the jurisdiction of the mother commonwealth; but, nevertheless, they allowed them the privileges of cities. Indeed, that sagacious city seems to have been aware of difficulties similar to those under which Great Britain is now laboring. She seems to have been sensible of the impossibility of keeping colonies planted at great distances under the absolute control of her *senatus-consulta* [g]. . . .

. . . .

I have said that the practice of free governments alone can be quoted with propriety to show the sense of nations. But the sense and practice of nations is not enough. Their practice must be reasonable, just, and right, or it will not govern Americans.

Absolute monarchies, whatever their practice may be, are nothing to us; for, as Harrington observes, "Absolute monarchy, as that of the Turks, neither plants its people at home nor abroad otherwise than as tenants for life or at will; wherefore, its national and provincial government is all one."

I deny, therefore, that the practice of free nations or the opinions of the best writers upon the law of nations will warrant the position of Massachusettensis that "when a nation takes possession of a distant territory, that becomes a part of the state equally with its ancient possessions." The practice of free nations and the opinions of the best writers are in general on the contrary.

I agree that "two supreme and independent authorities cannot exist in the same state," any more than two supreme beings in one universe; and, therefore, I contend that our provincial legislatures are the only supreme authorities in our colonies. Parliament, notwithstanding this, may be allowed an authority supreme and sovereign over the ocean, which may be limited by the banks of the ocean or the bounds of our charters; our charters give us no authority over the high seas. Parliament has our consent to assume a jurisdiction over them. And here is a line fairly drawn between the rights of Britain and the rights of the colonies, namely, the banks of the ocean, or low-water mark, the line of division between common law and civil or maritime law. If this is not sufficient—if parliament are at a loss for any principle of natural, civil, maritime, moral, or common law on which to ground any authority over the high seas, the Atlantic especially, let the colonies be treated like reasonable creatures, and they will discover great ingenuity and modesty. The acts of trade and navigation might be confirmed by provincial laws and carried into execution by our own courts and juries, and in this case illicit trade would be cut up by the roots forever. I knew the smuggling tories in New York and Boston would cry out against this because it would not only destroy their profitable game of smuggling, but their whole place and pension system. But the whigs, that is, a vast majority of the whole continent, would not regard the smuggling tories. In one word, if public principles, and motives, and arguments were alone to determine this dispute between the two countries, it might be settled forever in a few hours; but the everlasting clamors of prejudice, passion, and private interest drown every consideration of that sort and are precipitating us into a civil war.

"If, then, we are a part of the British empire, we must be subject to the supreme power of the state, which is vested in the estates in parliament."

Here, again, we are to be conjured out of our senses by the magic in the words "British empire," and "supreme power of the state." But, however it may sound, I say we are not a part of the British empire; because the British government is not an empire. The governments of France, Spain, etc., are not empires but monarchies, supposed to be governed by fixed fundamental laws, though not really. The British government is still less entitled to the style of *an empire*. It is a limited monarchy. If Aristotle, Livy, and Harrington knew what a republic was, the British constitution is much more like a republic than an empire. They define a republic to be a *government of laws, and not of men.* If this definition be just, the British constitution is nothing more nor less than a republic in which the king is first magistrate. This office being hereditary and being possessed of such ample and splendid prerogatives is no objection to the government's being a republic, as long as it is bound by fixed laws which the people have a voice in making and a right to defend. An empire is a despotism, and an emperor a despot bound by no law or limitation but his own will; it is a stretch of tyranny beyond absolute monarchy. For, although the will of an absolute monarch is law, yet his edicts must be registered by parliaments. Even this formality is not necessary in an empire. There the maxim is *quod principi placuit legis habet vigorem,*[h] even without having that will and pleasure recorded. There are but three empires now in Europe, the German or Holy Roman, the Russian, and the Ottoman.

There is another sense, indeed, in which the word *empire* is used in which it may be applied to the government of Geneva or any other republic as well as to monarchy or despotism. In this sense it is synonymous with *government, rule,* or *dominion.* In this sense we are within the dominion, rule, or government of the king of Great Britain.

The question should be whether we are a part of the kingdom of Great Britain. This is the only language known in English laws. We are not then a part of the British kingdom, realm, or state; and therefore the supreme power of the kingdom, realm, or state is not, upon these principles, the supreme power of us. That "supreme power over America is vested in the estates in parliament" is an affront to us, for there is not an acre of American land represented there; there are no American estates in parliament.

To say that we "must be" subject seems to betray a consciousness that we are not by any law or upon any principles but those of mere power, and an opinion that we ought to be or that it is necessary that we should be. But if this should be admitted for argument's sake only, what is the consequence? The consequences that may fairly be drawn are these: that Britain has been imprudent enough to let colonies be planted, until they are become numerous and important, without ever having wisdom enough to concert a plan for their government consistent with her own welfare; that now it is necessary to make them submit to the authority of parliament; and, because there is no principle of law, or justice, or reason by which she can effect it, therefore she will resort to war and conquest—to the maxim, *delenda est Carthago*.[i] These are the consequences, according to this writer's idea. We think the consequences are that she has after one hundred and fifty years discovered a defect in her government which ought to be supplied by some just and reasonable means, that is, by the consent of the colonies; for metaphysicians and politicians may dispute forever but they will never find any other moral principle or foundation of rule or obedience than the consent of governors and governed. She has found out that the great machine will not go any longer without a new wheel. She will make this herself. We think she is making it of such materials and workmanship as will tear the whole machine to pieces. We are willing, if she can convince us of the necessity of such a wheel, to assist with artists and materials in making it, so that it may answer the end. But she says, we shall have no share in it, and if we will not let her patch it up as she pleases, her Massachusettensis and other advocates tell us, she will tear it to pieces herself by cutting our throats. To this kind of reasoning we can only answer that we will not stand still to be butchered. We will defend our lives as long as Providence shall enable us. . . .

.   .   .   .

. . . "If the colonies are not subject to the authority of parliament, Great Britain and the colonies must be distinct states, as completely so as England and Scotland were before the union, or as Great Britain and Hanover are now." There is no need of being startled at this consequence. It is very harmless. There is no absurdity at all in it. Distinct states may be united under one king. And those states may be further cemented and united together by a treaty of commerce. This is the case. We have by our own express consent contracted to observe the Navigation Act and by our implied consent, by long usage and uninterrupted acquiescence, have submitted to the other acts of trade, however grievous some of them may be. This may be compared to a treaty of commerce by which those distinct states are cemented together in perpetual league and amity. And if any further ratifications of this pact or treaty are necessary, the colonies would readily enter into them provided their other liberties were inviolate.

That "the colonies owe no allegiance to any imperial crown," provided such a crown involves in it a house of lords and a house of commons, is certain. Indeed, we owe no allegiance to any crown at all. We owe allegiance to the person of his majesty, King George III, whom God preserve. But allegiance is due universally, both from Britons and Americans, to the person of the king, not to his crown; to his natural, not his politic capacity, as I will undertake to prove hereafter, from the highest authorities and the most solemn adjudications which were ever made within any part of the British dominions.

If his majesty's title to the crown is "derived from an act of parliament, made since the settlement of these colonies," it was not made since the date of our charter. Our charter was granted by King William and Queen Mary, three years after the revolution; and the oaths of allegiance are established by a law of the province. So that our allegiance to his majesty is not due by virtue of any act of a British parliament but by our own charter and province laws. It ought to be remembered that there was a revolution here, as well as in England, and that we, as well as the people of England, made an original, express contract with King William.

If it follows from thence that he appears "king of Massachusetts, king of Rhode Island, king of Connecticut, etc." this is no absurdity at all. He will appear in this light, and does appear so, whether parliament has authority over us or not. He is king of Ireland, I suppose, although parliament is allowed to have authority there. As to giving his majesty those titles, I have no objection at all; I wish he would be graciously pleased to assume them.

The only proposition in all this writer's long string of pretended absurdities which he says follows from the position that we are distinct states is this: That "as the king must govern each state by its parliament, those several parliaments would pursue the particular interest of its own state, and however well disposed the king might be to pursue a line of interest that was common to all, the checks and control that he would meet with would render it impossible." Every argument ought to be allowed its full weight; and therefore candor obliges me to acknowledge that here lies all the difficulty that there is in this whole controversy. There has been from first to last on both sides of the Atlantic an idea, an apprehension, that it was necessary there should be some superintending power to draw together all the wills and unite all the strength of the subjects in all the dominions, in case of war and in the case of trade. The necessity of this in case of trade has been so apparent that, as has often been said, we have consented that parliament should exercise such a power. In case of war it has by some been thought necessary. But in fact and experience it has not been found so. What though the proprietary colonies, on account of disputes with the proprietors, did not come in so early to the assistance of the general cause in the last war as they ought, and perhaps one of them not at all? The inconveniences of this were small in comparison of the absolute ruin to the liberties of all which must follow the submission to parliament in all cases, which would be giving up all the popular limitations upon the government. These inconveniences fell chiefly upon New England. She was necessitated to greater exertions; but she had rather suffer these again and again than others infinitely greater. However, this subject has been so long in contemplation that it is fully understood now in all the colonies, so that there is no danger in case of another war of any colony's failing of its duty.

But, admitting the proposition in its full force, that it is absolutely necessary there should be a supreme power coextensive with all the dominions, will it follow that parliament, as now constituted, has a right to assume this supreme jurisdiction? By no means.

A union of the colonies might be projected and an American legislature, for if America has three millions of people and the whole dominions twelve millions, she ought to send a quarter part of all the members to the house of commons, and instead of holding parliaments always at Westminster, the haughty members for Great Britain must humble themselves, one session in four, to cross the Atlantic and hold the parliament in America.

There is no avoiding all inconveniences in human affairs. The greatest possible or conceivable would arise from ceding to parliament power over us without a representation in it. The next greatest would accrue from any plan that can be devised for a representation there. The least of all would arise from going on as we began and fared well for one hundred and fifty years by letting parliament regulate trade, and our own assemblies all other matters.

As to "the prerogatives not being defined, or limited," it is as much so in the colonies as in Great Britain, and as well understood and as cheerfully submitted to in the former as the latter.

But "where is the British constitution, that we all agree we are entitled to?" I answer, if we enjoy and are entitled to more liberty than the British constitution allows, where is the harm? Or if we enjoy the British constitution in greater purity and perfection than they do in England, as is really the case, whose fault is this? Not ours.

We may find all the blessings of this constitution "in our provincial assemblies." Our houses of representatives have, and ought to exercise, every power of the house of commons. The first charter to this colony is nothing to the present argument, but it did grant a power of taxing the people, implicitly, though not in express terms. It granted all the rights and liberties of Englishmen, which include the power of taxing the people.

"Our council boards" in the royal governments "are destitute of the noble independence and splendid appendages of peerage." Most certainly they are the meanest creatures and tools in the political creation, dependent every moment for their existence on the tainted breath of a prime minister. But they have the authority of the house of lords in our little models of the English constitution; and it is this which makes them so great a grievance. The crown has really two branches of our legislature in its power. Let an act of parliament pass at home, putting it in the power of the king to remove any peer from the house of lords at his pleasure, and what will become of the British constitution? It will be overturned from the foundation. Yet we are perpetually insulted by being told that making our council by mandamus brings us nearer to the British constitution. In this province by charter, the council certainly hold their seats for the year, after being chosen and approved, independent of both the other branches. For their creation they are equally obliged to both the other branches, so that there is little or no bias in favor of either; if any, it is in favor of the prerogative. In short, it is not easy without an hereditary nobility to constitute a council more independent, more nearly resembling the house of lords, than the council of this province has ever been by charter.

But perhaps it will be said that we are to enjoy the British constitution in our supreme legislature, the parliament, not in our provincial legislatures. To this I answer, if parliament is to be our supreme legislature, we shall be under a complete oligarchy or aristocracy, not the British constitution, which this writer himself defines a mixture of monarchy, aristocracy, and democracy. For king, lords, and commons will constitute one great oligarchy, as they will stand related to America, as much as the decemvirs did in Rome; with this difference for the worse, that our rulers are to be three thousand miles off. The definition of an oligarchy is a government by a number of grandees over whom the people have no control. The States of Holland were once chosen by the people frequently, then chosen for life; now they are not chosen by the people at all. When a member dies, his place is filled up, not by the people he is to represent, but by the States. Is not this depriving the Hollanders of a free constitution and subjecting them to an aristocracy or oligarchy? Will not the government of America be like it? Will not representatives be chosen for them by others whom they never saw nor heard of? If our provincial constitutions are in any respect imperfect and want alteration, they have capacity enough to discern it and power enough to effect it without the interposition of parliament. There never was an American constitution attempted by parliament before the Quebec bill and Massachusetts bill. These are such *samples* of what they may, and probably will be, that few Americans are in love with them. However, America will never allow that parliament has any authority to alter their constitution at all. She is wholly penetrated with a sense of the necessity of resisting it at all hazards. And she would resist it if the constitution of the Massachusetts had been altered as much for *the better* as it is for the worse. The question we insist on most is, not whether the alteration is for the better or not, but whether parliament has any right to make any alteration at all. And it is the universal sense of America that it has none.

We are told, that "the provincial constitutions have no principle of stability within themselves." This is so great a mistake that there is not more order or stability in any government upon the globe than there ever has been in that of Connecticut. The same may be said of the Massachusetts and Pennsylvania, and, indeed, of the others very nearly. "That these constitutions, in turbulent times, would become wholly monarchical or wholly republican," they must be such times as would have a similar effect upon the constitution at home. But in order to avoid the danger of this, what is to be done? Not give us an English constitution, it seems, but make sure of us at once by giving us constitutions wholly monarchical, annihilating our houses of representatives first, by taking from them the support of government, etc., and then making the council and judges wholly dependent on the crown.

That a representation in parliament is impracticable we all agree; but the consequence is that we must have a representation in our supreme legislatures here. This was the consequence that was drawn by kings, ministers, our ancestors, and the whole nation more than a century ago when the colonies were first settled and continued to be the general sense until the last peace; and it must be the general sense again soon, or Great Britain will lose her colonies.

"This is apparently the meaning of that celebrated passage in Governor Hutchinson's letter, that rung through the continent, namely, 'There must be an abridgment of what is called English liberties.'" But all the art and subtlety of Massachusettensis will never vindicate or excuse that expression. According to this writer, it should have been "there is an abridgment of English liberties, and it cannot be otherwise." But every candid reader must see that the letter writer had more than that in his *view* and in his *wishes*. In the same letter, a little before, he says, "what marks of resentment the parliament will show, whether they will be upon the province in general or particular persons, is extremely uncertain; but that they will be placed somewhere is most certain; and I add, *because I think it ought to be so*."[4] Is it possible to read this without thinking of the Port Bill, the Charter Bill, and the resolves for sending persons to England by the statute of Henry VIII to be tried? But this is not all: "This is most certainly a crisis," says he, etc. "If no measure shall have been taken to secure this dependence (that is, the dependence which a colony ought to have upon the parent state), it is all over with us." "The friends of government will be utterly disheartened; and the friends of anarchy will be afraid of nothing, be it ever so extravagant." But this is not all: "I never think of the measures necessary for the peace and good order of the colonies without pain." "There must be an abridgment of what are called English liberties." What could he mean? Anything less than depriving us of trial by jury? Perhaps he wanted an act of parliament to try persons here for treason, by a court of admiralty. Perhaps an act that the province should be governed by a governor and a mandamus council without a house of representatives. But to put it out of all doubt that his meaning was much worse than Massachusettensis endeavors to make it, he explains himself in a subsequent part of the letter: "I wish," says he, "the good of the colony, *when I wish to see some further restraint of liberty*." Here it is rendered certain that he is pleading for a further restraint of liberty, not explaining the restraint he apprehended the constitution had already laid us under.

My indignation at this letter has sometimes been softened by

[4] These extracts are taken from the most significant of the letters obtained in England and sent out by Dr. Franklin, which betrayed the real policy of Governor Hutchinson. See the *Diary*, Vol. II, 318f.

compassion. It carries on the face of it evident marks of *madness*. It was written in such a transport of passions, *ambition* and *revenge* chiefly, that his reason was manifestly overpowered. The vessel was tost in such a hurricane that she could not feel her helm. Indeed he seems to have had a confused consciousness of this himself. "Pardon me this excursion," says he; "it really proceeds from the state of mind into which our perplexed affairs often throw me."

"It is our highest interest to continue a part of the British empire and equally our duty to remain subject to the authority of parliament," says Massachusettensis.

We are a part of the British dominions, that is, of the King of Great Britain, and it is our interest and duty to continue so. It is equally our interest and duty to continue subject to the authority of parliament in the regulation of our trade as long as she shall leave us to govern our internal policy, and to give and grant our own money, and no longer.

This letter concludes with an agreeable flight of fancy. The time may not be so far off, however, as this writer imagines, when the colonies may have the balance of numbers and wealth in their favor. But when that shall happen, if we should attempt to rule her by an American parliament without an adequate representation in it, she will infallibly resist us by her arms.

5. MASSACHUSETTENSIS

January 16, 1775

My Dear Countrymen: Had a person some fifteen years ago undertaken to prove that the colonies were a part of the British empire or dominion, and as such subject to the authority of the British parliament, he would have acted as ridiculous a part as to have undertaken to prove a self-evident proposition. Had any person denied it, he would have been called a fool or madman. At this wise period, individuals and bodies of men deny it, notwithstanding in doing it they subvert the fundamentals of government, deprive us of British liberties, and build up absolute monarchy in the colonies, for our charters suppose regal authority in the grantor. If that authority be derived from the British crown, it presupposes this territory to have been a part of the British dominion, and as such subject to the imperial sovereign. If that authority was vested in the person of the king in a different capacity, the British constitution and laws are out of the question; and the king must be absolute as to us, as his prerogatives have never been circumscribed. Such must have been the sovereign authority of the several kings who have granted American charters previous to the several grants. There is nothing to detract from it at this time in those colonies that are destitute of charters, and the charter governments must severally revert to absolute monarchy, as their charters may happen to be forfeited by the grantees not fulfilling the conditions of them, as every charter contains an express or implied condition.

It is curious indeed to trace the denial and oppugnation to the supreme authority of the state. When the Stamp Act was made, the authority of parliament to impose internal taxes was denied; but their right to impose external ones—or in other words, to lay duties upon goods and merchandise, was admitted. When the act was made imposing duties upon tea, etc., a new distinction was set up: that the parliament had a right to lay duties upon merchandise for the purpose of regulating trade, but not for the purpose of raising a revenue; that is, the parliament had good right and lawful authority to lay the former duty of a shilling on the pound, but had none to lay the present duty of three-pence. Having got thus far safe, it was only taking one step more to extricate ourselves entirely from their fangs and become independent states that our patriots most heroically resolved upon and flatly denied that parliament had a right to make any laws whatever that should be binding upon the colonies. There is no possible medium between absolute independence and subjection to the authority of parliament. He must be blind indeed that cannot see our dearest interest in the latter, notwithstanding many pant after the former. Misguided men! Could they once overtake their wish, they would be convinced of the madness of the pursuit.

My dear countrymen, it is of the last importance that we settle this point clearly in our minds: it will serve as a sure test, certain criterion, and invariable standard to distinguish the friends from the enemies of our country, patriotism from sedition, loyalty from rebellion. To deny the supreme authority of the state is a high misdemeanor, to say no worse of it; to oppose it by force is an overt act of treason punishable by confiscation of estate and most ignominious death. The realm of England is an appropriate term for the ancient realm of England, in contradistinction to Wales and other territories that have been annexed to it. These as they have been severally annexed to the crown, whether by conquest or otherwise, became a part of the empire and subject to the authority of parliament, whether they send members to parliament or not, and whether they have legislative powers of their own or not.

Thus Ireland, who has perhaps the greatest possible subordinate legislature and sends no members to the British parliament, is bound by its acts when expressly named. Guernsey and Jersey are no part of the realm of England, nor are they represented in parliament, but are subject to its authority: and, in the same predicament are the American colonies and all the other dispersions of the empire. Permit me to request your attention to this subject a little longer; I assure you it is as interesting and important as it is dry and unentertaining.

Let us now recur to the first charter of this province, and we shall find irresistible evidence that our being part of the empire, subject to the supreme authority of the state, bound by its laws, and entitled to its protection were the very terms and conditions by which our ancestors held their lands and settled the province. Our charter, like all other American charters, are under the great seal of England; the grants are made by the king for his heirs and *successors*; the several tenures to be of the king, his heirs and *successors*; in like manner are the reservations. It is apparent the king acted in his royal capacity as king of England, which necessarily supposes the territory granted to be a part of the English dominions, holden of the crown of England.

The charter, after reciting several grants of the territory to Sir Henry Roswell and others, proceeds to incorporation in these words: "And for as much as the good and prosperous success of the plantations of the said parts of New England aforesaid, intended by the said Sir Henry Roswell and others to be speedily set upon, cannot but chiefly depend, next under the blessing of almighty God and the support of our royal authority, upon the good government of the same, to the end that the *affairs of business* which from time to time shall happen and arise concerning the said lands and the plantations of the same may be the better managed and ordered, we have further hereby, of our especial grace, certain knowledge and mere motion given, granted and confirmed, and for us, our heirs and successors, do give, grant, and confirm unto our said trusty and well beloved subjects, Sir Henry Roswell, etc., and all such others as shall hereafter be admitted and made free of *the company and society hereafter mentioned,* shall from time to time and at all times forever hereafter be by virtue of these presents *one body corporate, politic in fact and name, by the name of the governor and company of the Massachusetts Bay,ʲ in New England;* and them by the name of the governor and company of the Massachusetts Bay, in New England, one body politic and corporate in deed, fact and name. We do for us, our heirs, and successors make, ordain, constitute, and confirm by these presents, and that by that name they shall have perpetual succession, and that by that name they and their successors shall be capable and enabled as well *to implead and to be impleaded and to prosecute, demand and answer and be answered unto all and singular suits, causes, quarrels and actions of what kind or nature soever; and also to have, take, possess, acquire and purchase any lands, tenements and hereditaments, or any goods or chattels, the same to lease, grant, demise, aleine, bargain, sell and dispose of as our liege people of this our realm of England, or any other corporation or body politic of the same may do.*" I would beg leave to ask one simple question: whether this looks like a distinct state or independent empire? Provision is then made for electing a governor, deputy governor, and eighteen assistants. After which, is this clause: "We do for us, our heirs and successors, give and grant to the said governor and company and their successors, that the governor or, in his absence, the deputy governor of the said company, for the time being, and such of the assistants or freemen of the said company as shall be present, or the greater number of them so assembled, whereof the governor or deputy governor and six of the assistants, at the least to be seven, shall have full power and authority to choose, nominate and appoint such and so many others as they shall think fit and shall be willing to accept the same to be free of the said company and body, and them into the same to admit and to elect and constitute such officers as they shall think fit and requisite for the ordering, managing and dispatching of the affairs of the said governor and company and their successors, and to make *laws and ordinances for the good and welfare of the said company* and for the government and ordering of the said lands and plantations and the people inhabiting and to inhabit the same as to them from time to time shall be thought meet: *So as such laws and ordinances be not contrary or repugnant to the laws and statutes of this our realm of England.*"

Another clause is this: "And for their further encouragement, of our especial grace and favor, we do by these presents, for us, our heirs, and successors, yield and grant to the said governor and company and their successors, and every of them, their factors and assigns, that they and every of them shall be free and quit from all taxes, subsidies, and customs in New England for the space of seven years and from all taxes and impositions for the space of twenty-one years upon all goods and merchandise at any time or times hereafter, either upon importation thither or exportation from thence into our realm of England or into other of our dominions, by the said governor and company and their successors, their deputies, factors, and assigns, etc."

The exemption from taxes for seven years in one case and twenty-one years in the other plainly indicates that after their expiration this province would be liable to taxation. Now I would ask by what authority those taxes were to be imposed? It could not be by the governor and company, for no such power was delegated or granted to them; and besides it would have been absurd and nugatory to exempt them from their own taxation, supposing them to have had the power, for they might have exempted themselves. It must therefore be by the king or parliament; it could not be by the king alone, for as king of England, the political capacity in which he granted the charter, he had no such power, exclusive of the lords and commons. Consequently it must have been by the parliament. This clause in the charter is as evident a recognition of the authority of the parliament over this province as if the words "acts of parliament" had been inserted as they were in the Pennsylvania charter. There was no session of parliament after the grant of our charter until the year 1640. In 1642 the House of Commons passed a resolve "that for the better advancement of the plantations in New England, and the encouragement of the planters to proceed in their undertaking, their exports and imports should be freed and discharged from all customs, subsidies, taxations and duties until the further order of the house"; which was gratefully received and recorded in the archives of our predecessors. This transaction shows very clearly in what sense our connection with England was then understood. It is true that in some arbitrary reigns attempts were made by the servants of the crown to exclude the two Houses of Parliament from any share of the authority over the colonies. They also attempted to render the king absolute in England, but the parliament always rescued the colonies, as well as England, from such attempts.

I shall recite but one more clause of this charter, which is this: "And further our will and pleasure is, and we do hereby for us, our heirs and successors ordain, declare and grant to the said governor and company and their successors, that all and every of the subjects of us, our heirs and successors which shall go to and inhabit within the said land and premises hereby mentioned to be granted, and every of their children which shall happen to be born there, or on the seas in going thither, or returning from thence, shall have and enjoy *all liberties and immunities of free and natural subjects, within any of the dominions* of us, our heirs or successors, to all intents, constructions and purposes whatsoever, as if they and every of them were born within the realm of England." It is upon this or a similar clause in the charter of William and Mary that our patriots have built up the stupendous fabric of American independence. They argue from it a total exemption from parliamentary authority because we are not represented in parliament.

I have already shown that the supposition of our being exempt from the authority of parliament is pregnant with the grossest absurdities. Let us now consider this clause in connection with the other parts of the charter. It is a rule of law, founded in reason and common sense, to construe each part of an instrument so as the whole may hang together and be consistent with itself. If we suppose this clause to exempt us from the authority of parliament, we must throw away all the rest of the charter, for every other part indicates the contrary as plainly as words can do it; and what is still worse, this clause becomes *felo de se* [suicide] and destroys itself; for if we are not annexed to the crown, we are aliens, and no charter, grant, or other act of the crown can naturalize us or entitle us to the liberties and immunities of Englishmen. It can be done only by act of parliament. An alien is one born in a strange country out of the allegiance of the king and is under many disabilities though residing in the realm. As Wales, Jersey, Guernsey, Ireland, the foreign plantations, etc. were severally annexed to the crown, they became parts of one and the same empire, the natives of which are equally free as though they had been born in that territory which was the ancient realm. As our patriots depend upon this clause, detached from the charter, let us view it in that light. If a person born in England removes to Ireland and settles there, he is then no longer represented in the British parliament, but he and his posterity are, and will ever be subject to the authority of the British parliament. If he removes to Jersey, Guernsey, or any other parts of the British dominions that send no members to parliament, he will still be in the same predicament. So that the inhabitants of the American colonies do in fact enjoy all the liberties and immunities of natural born subjects. We are entitled to no greater privileges than those that are born within the realm; and they can enjoy no other than we do when they reside out of it. Thus, it is evident that this clause amounts to no more than the royal assurance that we are a part of the British empire, are not aliens, but natural born subjects, and as such bound to obey the supreme power of the state and entitled to protection from it. To avoid prolixity, I shall not remark particularly upon other parts of this charter, but observe in general that whoever reads it with attention will meet with irresistible evidence in every part of it, that our being a part of the English dominions, subject to the English crown, and within the jurisdiction of parliament, were the terms upon which our ancestors settled this colony and the very tenures by which they held their estates.

No lands within the British dominions are perfectly allodial; they are held mediately or immediately of the king, and upon forfeiture revert to the crown. My dear countrymen, you have, many of you, been most falsely and wickedly told by our patriots that Great Britain was meditating a land tax and seeking to deprive us of our inheritance; but had all the malice and subtilty of men and devils been united, a readier method to effect it could not have been devised than the late denials of the authority of parliament and forcible oppositions to its acts. Yet, this has been planned and executed chiefly by persons of desperate fortunes.

6. NOVANGLUS

March 13, 1775

It has often been observed by me, and it cannot be too often repeated, that *colonization* is *casus omissus* [k] at common law. There is no such title known in that law. By common law I mean that system of customs, written and unwritten, which was known and in force in England in the time of King Richard I. This continued to be the case down to the reign of Elizabeth and King James I. In all that time the laws of England were confined to the realm and within the four seas. There was no provision made in this law for governing colonies beyond the Atlantic or beyond the four seas by authority of parliament; no, nor for the king to grant charters to subjects to settle in foreign countries. It was the king's prerogative to prohibit the emigration of any of his subjects by issuing his writ *ne exeat regno*.[1] And, there-fore, it was in the king's power to permit his subjects to leave the kingdom. "It is a high crime to disobey the king's lawful com-mands or prohibitions, as not returning from beyond sea upon the king's letters to that purpose, for which the offender's lands shall be seized until he return; and when he does return, he shall be fined, etc.; or going beyond sea against the king's will, expressly signified, either by the writ *ne exeat regno,* or under the great or privy seal, or signet, or by proclamation."[5] When a subject left the kingdom by the king's permission, and if the nation did not remonstrate against it, by the nation's permission too, at least connivance, he carried with him as a man all the rights of nature. His allegiance bound him to the king and en-titled him to protection. But how? Not in France; the King of England was not bound to protect him in France. Nor in America. Nor in the dominions of Louis. Nor of Sassacus, or Massachu-setts. He had a right to protection and the liberties of England upon his return there, not otherwise. How, then, do we New Englandmen derive our laws? I say, not from parliament, not from common law, but from the law of nature and the compact made with the king in our charters. Our ancestors were entitled to the common law of England when they emigrated, that is, to just so much of it as they pleased to adopt, and no more. They were not bound or obliged to submit to it unless they chose it. By a positive principle of the common law they were bound, let them be in what part of the world they would, to do nothing against the allegiance of the king. But no kind of provision was ever made by common law for punishing or trying any man, even for treason committed out of the realm. He must be tried in some county of the realm by that law, the county where the overt act was done, or he could not be tried at all. Nor was any provision ever made until the reign of Henry VIII for trying treasons committed abroad, and the acts of that reign were made on purpose to catch Cardinal Pole.

So that our ancestors, when they emigrated, having obtained permission of the king to come here and being never com-

[5] Hawkins' *Pleas of the Crown,* Ch. XXII, § 4.

manded to return into the realm, had a clear right to have erected in this wilderness a British constitution, or a perfect democracy, or any other form of government they saw fit. They, indeed, while they lived, could not have taken arms against the King of England without violating their allegiance; but their children would not have been born within the king's allegiance, would not have been natural subjects, and consequently not entitled to protection or bound to the king.

Massachusettensis seems possessed of these ideas and attempts in the most awkward manner to get rid of them. He is conscious that America must be a part of the realm before it can be bound by the authority of parliament and, therefore, is obliged to suggest that we are annexed to the realm and to endeavor to confuse himself and his readers by confounding the realm with the empire and dominions.

But will any man soberly contend that America was ever annexed to the realm? to what realm? When New England was settled, there was a realm of England, a realm of Scotland, and a realm of Ireland. To which of these three realms was New England annexed? To the realm of England, it will be said. But by what law? No territory could be annexed to the realm of England but by an act of parliament. Acts of parliament have been passed to annex Wales, etc., to the realm; but none ever passed to annex America. But if New England was annexed to the realm of England, how came she annexed to the realm of, or kingdom of Great Britain? The two realms of England and Scotland were by the act of union incorporated into one kingdom by the name of Great Britain; but there is not one word about America in that act.

Besides, if America was annexed to the realm, or a part of the kingdom, every act of parliament that is made would extend to it, named or not named. But everybody knows that every act of parliament and every other record constantly distinguishes between this kingdom and his majesty's other dominions. Will it be said that Ireland is annexed to the realm or a part of the kingdom of Great Britain? Ireland is a distinct kingdom or realm by itself, notwithstanding British parliament claims a right of binding it in all cases and exercises it in some. And even so, the Massachusetts is a realm, New York is a realm, Pennsylvania another realm, to all intents and purposes, as much as Ireland is or England or Scotland ever were. The King of Great Britain is the sovereign of all these realms.

This writer says "that in denying that the colonies are annexed to the realm and subject to the authority of parliament, individuals and bodies of men subvert the fundamentals of government, deprive us of British liberties, and build up absolute monarchy in the colonies."

This is the first time that I ever heard or read that the colonies are annexed to the realm. It is utterly denied that they are and that it is possible they should be without an act of parliament and acts of the colonies. Such an act of parliament cannot be produced nor any such law of any one colony. Therefore, as this writer builds the whole authority of parliament upon this fact, namely, that the colonies are annexed to the realm, and as it is certain they never were so annexed, the consequence is that his whole superstructure falls.

When he says that they subvert the fundamentals of government, he begs the question. We say that the contrary doctrines subvert the fundamentals of government. When he says that they deprive us of British liberties, he begs the question again. We say that the contrary doctrine deprives us of English liberties; as to British liberties, we scarcely know what they are, as the liberties of England and Scotland are not precisely the same to this day. English liberties are but certain rights of nature reserved to the citizen by the English constitution, which rights cleaved to our ancestors when they crossed the Atlantic and would have inhered in them if, instead of coming to New England, they had gone to Otaheite [Tahiti] or Patagonia, even although they had taken no patent or charter from the king at all. These rights did not adhere to them the less, for their purchasing patents and charters in which the king expressly stipulates with them that they and their posterity should forever enjoy all those rights and liberties.

The human mind is not naturally the clearest atmosphere; but the clouds and vapors which have been raised in it by the artifices of temporal and spiritual tyrants have made it impossible to see objects in it distinctly. Scarcely anything is involved in more systematical obscurity than the rights of our ancestors when they arrived in America. How, in common sense, came the dominions of King Philip, King Massachusetts, and twenty other sovereigns, independent princes here to be within the allegiance of the Kings of England, James and Charles? America was no more within the allegiance of those princes by the common law of England or by the law of nature than France and Spain were. Discovery, if that was incontestable, could give no title to the English king by common law or by the law of nature to the lands, tenements, and hereditaments of the native Indians here. Our ancestors were sensible of this and, therefore, honestly purchased their lands of the natives. They might have bought them to hold allodially if they would.

But there were two ideas which confused them and have continued to confuse their posterity, one derived from the feudal, the other from the canon law. By the former of these systems, the prince, the general, was supposed to be sovereign lord of all the lands conquered by the soldiers in his army; and upon this principle, the King of England was considered in law as sovereign lord of all the land within the realm. If he had sent an army here to conquer King Massachusetts and it had succeeded, he would have been sovereign lord of the land here upon these principles; but there was no rule of the common law that made the discovery of the country by a subject a title to that country in the prince. But conquest would not have annexed the country to the realm nor have given any authority to the parliament. But there was another mist cast before the eyes of the English nation from another source. The pope claimed a sovereign propriety in, as well as authority over, the whole earth. As head of the Christian church and vicar of God, he claimed this authority over all Christendom; and, in the same character, he claimed a right to all the countries and possessions of heathens and infidels, a right divine to exterminate and destroy them at his discretion in order to propagate the Catholic faith. When King Henry VIII and his parliament threw off the authority of the pope, stripped his holiness of his supremacy, and invested it in himself by an act of parliament, he and his courtiers seemed to think that all the rights of the holy see were transferred to him; and it was a union of these two (the most impertinent and fantastical ideas that ever got into a human pericranium, namely, that, as feudal sovereign and supreme head of the church together, a king of England had a right to all the lands his subjects could find not possessed by any Christian state or prince, though possessed by heathen or infidel nations) which seems to have deluded the nation about the time of the settlement of the colonies. But none of these ideas gave or inferred any right in parliament over the new countries conquered or discovered; and, therefore, denying that the colonies are a part of the realm and that as such they are subject to parliament by no means deprives us of English liberties. Nor does it "build up absolute monarchy in the colonies." For, admitting these notions of the common and feudal law to have been in full force and that the king was absolute in America when it was settled, yet he had a right to enter into a contract with his subjects and stipulate that they should enjoy all the rights and liberties of Englishmen forever in consideration of their undertaking to clear the wilderness, propagate Christianity, pay a fifth part of ore, etc. Such a contract as this has been made with all the colonies, royal governments as well as charter ones. For the commissions to the governors contain the plan of the government and the contract between the king and subject in the former as much as the charters in the latter.

Indeed, this was the reasoning, and upon these feudal and *catholic* principles, in the time of some of the predecessors of Massachusettensis. This was the meaning of Dudley when he asked, "Do you think that English liberties will follow you to the ends of the earth?" His meaning was that English liberties were confined to the realm, and out of that the king was absolute. But this was not true, for an English king had no right to be absolute over Englishmen out of the realm any more than in it; and they were released from their allegiance as soon as he deprived them of their liberties.

But "our charters suppose regal authority in the grantor."
True, they suppose it, whether there was any or not. "If that
authority be derived from the British (he should have said English) crown, it presupposes this territory to have been a part of
the British (he should have said English) dominion and as such
subject to the imperial sovereign." How can this writer show
this authority to be derived from the English crown, including in
the idea of it lords and commons? Is there the least color for
such an authority but in the popish and feudal ideas before
mentioned? And do these popish and feudal ideas include parliament? Was parliament, were lords and commons parts of the
head of the church; or was parliament, that is, lords and commons, part of the sovereign feudatory? Never. But why was this
authority derived from the English any more than the Scottish
or Irish crown? It is true, the land was to be held in socage like
the manor of East Greenwich; but this was compact, and it
might have been as well to hold as they held in Glasgow or
Dublin.

But, says this writer, "if that authority was vested in the person
of the king in a different capacity, the British constitution and
laws are out of the question and the king must be absolute as to
us as his prerogatives have never been limited." Not the prerogatives limited in our charters, when in every one of them all the
rights of Englishmen are secured to us? Are not the rights of
Englishmen sufficiently known, and are not the prerogatives of
the king among those rights?

As to those colonies which are destitute of charters, the commissions to their governors have ever been considered as equivalent securities, both for property, jurisdiction, and privileges, with
charters; and as to the power of the crown being absolute in
those colonies, it is absolute nowhere. There is no fundamental
or other law that makes a king of England absolute anywhere
except in conquered countries; and an attempt to assume such a
power by the fundamental laws forfeits the prince's right even
to the limited crown.

As to "the charter governments reverting to absolute monarchy,
as their charters may happen to be forfeited by the grantees not

fulfilling the conditions of them," I answer, if they could be forfeited and were actually forfeited, the only consequence would be that the king would have no power over them at all. He would not be bound to protect the people, nor, that I can see, would the people here, who were born here, be by any principle of common law bound even to allegiance to the king. The connection would be broken between the crown and the natives of the country.

It has been a great dispute whether charters granted within the realm can be forfeited at all. It was a question debated with infinite learning in the case of the charter of London. It was adjudged forfeited in an arbitrary reign; but afterwards, after the revolution, it was declared in parliament not forfeited and by an act of parliament made incapable of forfeiture. The charter of Massachusetts was declared forfeited too. So were other American charters. The Massachusetts alone were tame enough to give it up. But no American charter will ever be decreed forfeited again; or if any should, the decree will be regarded no more than a vote of the lower house of the Robinhood society. The court of chancery has no authority without the realm; by common law, surely it has none in America. What! the privileges of millions of Americans depend on the discretion of a lord chancellor? God forbid! The passivity of this colony in receiving the present charter in lieu of the first is, in the opinion of some, the deepest stain upon its character. There is less to be said in excuse for it than the witchcraft or hanging the Quakers. A vast party in the province were against it at the time and thought themselves betrayed by their agent. It has been a warning to their posterity and one principal motive with the people never to trust any agent with power to concede away their privileges again. It may as well be pretended that the people of Great Britain can forfeit their privileges, as the people of this province. If the contract of state is broken, the people and king of England must recur to nature. It is the same in this province. We shall never more submit to decrees in chancery or acts of parliament annihilating charters or abridging English liberties.

Whether Massachusettensis was born as a politician in the

year 1764, I know not; but he often writes as if he knew nothing of that period. In his attempt to trace the denial of the supreme authority of the parliament, he commits such mistakes as a man of age at that time ought to blush at. He says that "when the Stamp Act was made, the authority of parliament to impose external taxes or, in other words, to lay duties upon goods and merchandise was admitted," and that when the Tea Act was made, "a new distinction was set up, that parliament had a right to lay duties upon merchandise for the purpose of regulating trade but not for the purpose of raising a revenue." This is a total misapprehension of the declared opinions of people at those times. The authority of parliament to lay taxes for a revenue has been always generally denied. And their right to lay duties to regulate trade has been denied by many who have ever contended that trade should be regulated only by prohibitions. . . .

. . . .

This writer sneers at the distinction between a right to lay the former duty of a shilling on the pound of tea and the right to lay the threepence. But is there not a real difference between laying a duty to be paid in England upon exportation and to be paid in America upon importation? Is there not a difference between parliament's laying on duties within their own realm, where they have undoubted jurisdiction, and laying them out of their realm, nay, laying them on in our realm, where we say they have no jurisdiction? Let them lay on what duties they please in England, we have nothing to say against that.

"Our patriots most heroically resolved to become independent states and flatly denied that parliament had a right to make any laws whatever that should be binding upon the colonies."

Our scribbler, more heroically still, is determined to show the world that he has courage superior to all regard to modesty, justice, or truth. Our patriots have never determined or desired to be independent states if a voluntary cession of a right to regulate their trade can make them dependent even on parliament, though they are clear in theory that by the common law and the English constitution parliament has no authority over them. None of the patriots of this province of the present age have ever denied that parliament has a right from our voluntary cession to make laws which shall bind the colonies so far as their commerce extends.

"There is no possible medium between absolute independence and subjection to the authority of parliament." If this is true, it may be depended upon that all North America are as fully convinced of their independence, their absolute independence, as they are of their own existence and as fully determined to defend it at all hazards as Great Britain is to defend her independence against foreign nations. But it is not true. An absolute independence on parliament in all internal concerns and cases of taxation is very compatible with an absolute dependence on it in all cases of external commerce.

"He must be blind indeed that cannot see our dearest interest in the latter (that is, in an absolute subjection to the authority of parliament), notwithstanding many pant after the former" (that is, absolute independence). The man who is capable of writing, in cool blood, that our interest lies in an absolute subjection to parliament is capable of writing or saying anything for the sake of his pension. A legislature that has so often discovered a want of information concerning us and our country; a legislature interested to lay burdens upon us; a legislature, two branches of which, I mean the lords and commons, neither love nor fear us! Every American of fortune and common sense must look upon his property to be sunk downright one half of its value the moment such an absolute subjection to parliament is established.

That there are any who pant after "independence" (meaning by this word a new plan of government over all America unconnected with the crown of England or meaning by it an exemption from the power of parliament to regulate trade) is as great a slander upon the province as ever was committed to writing. The patriots of this province desire nothing new; they wish only to keep their old privileges. They were for one hundred and fifty years allowed to tax themselves and govern their internal concerns as they thought best. Parliament governed their trade as they thought fit. This plan they wish may continue forever. But it is honestly confessed, rather than become subject to the absolute authority of parliament in all cases of taxation and internal policy, they will be driven to throw off that of regulating trade.

"To deny the supreme authority of the state is a high misdemeanor; to oppose it by force, an overt act of treason." True; and therefore, Massachusettensis, who denies the king represented by his governor, his majesty's council by charter, and house of representatives, to be the supreme authority of this province, has been guilty of a high misdemeanor; and those ministers, governors ,and their instruments who have brought a military force here and employed it against that supreme authority are guilty of ——, and ought to be punished with ——. I will be more mannerly than Massachusettensis. . . .

. . . .

From the conquest of Lewellyn to this statute of James is near three hundred and fifty years, during all which time the Welsh were very fond of being incorporated and enjoying the English laws; the English were desirous that they should be; yet the crown would never suffer it to be completely done because it claimed an authority to rule it by discretion. It is conceived, therefore, that there cannot be a more complete and decisive proof of anything than this instance is that a country may be subject to the crown of England, the imperial crown, and yet not annexed to the realm, nor subject to the authority of parliament.

The word *crown*, like the word *throne*, is used in various figurative senses; sometimes it means the kingly office, the head of the commonwealth, but it does not always mean the political capacity of the king; much less does it include in the idea of it lords and commons. It may as well be pretended that the house of commons includes or implies a king. Nay, it may as well be pretended that the mace includes the three branches of the legislature.

By the feudal law, a person or a country might be subject to a king, a feudal sovereign three several ways.

1. It might be subject to his person, and in this case it would continue so subject, let him be where he would, in his dominions or without. 2. To his crown, and in this case subjection was

due to whatsoever person or family wore that crown and would
follow it, whatever revolutions it underwent. 3. To his crown and
realm of state, and in this case it was incorporated as one body
with the principal kingdom; and if that was bound by a parliament, diet, or cortes, so was the other.

It is humbly conceived that the subjection of the colonies by
compact and law is of the second sort.

7. MASSACHUSETTENSIS

April 3, 1775

My Dear Countrymen: The advocates for the opposition to
parliament often remind us of the rights of the people, repeat
the Latin adage *vox populi vox Dei*, and tell us that government
in the *dernier* resort is in the people; they chime away melodiously,
and to render their music more ravishing, tell us that these are
revolution[ary] principles. I hold the rights of the people as
sacred and revere the principles that have established the succession to the imperial crown of Great Britain in the line of the
illustrious house of Brunswick, but [I also hold] that the difficulty lies in applying them to the cause of the Whigs, *hic labor
hoc opus est.*[m] For admitting that the collective body of the people
that are subject to the British Empire have an inherent right to
change their form of government or race of kings, it does not
follow that the inhabitants of a single province, or of a number
of provinces, or any given part under a majority of the whole
empire have such a right. By admitting that the less may rule
or sequester themselves from the greater, we unhinge all government. Novanglus has accused me of traducing the people of this
province. I deny the charge. Popular demagogues always call
themselves the people, and when their own measures are censured, cry out: the people—the people are abused and insulted.
He says that I once entertained different sentiments from those
now advanced. I did not write to exculpate myself. If through
ignorance, inadvertence, or design I have heretofore contributed

in any degree to the forming that destructive system of politics that is now in vogue, I was under the greater obligation thus publicly to expose its errors and point out its pernicious tendency. He suggests that I write from sordid motives. I despise the imputation. I have written my real sentiments not to serve a party (for, as he justly observes, I have sometimes quarreled with my friends), but to serve the public; nor would I injure my country to inherit all the treasures that avarice and ambition sigh for. Fully convinced that our calamities were chiefly created by the leading Whigs, and that a persevering in the same measures that gave rise to our troubles would complete our ruin, I have written freely. It is painful to me to give offense to an individual, but I have not spared the ruinous policy of my brother or my friend; they are both far advanced. Truth, from its own energy, will finally prevail; but to have a speedy effect it must sometimes be accompanied with severity. The terms Whig and Tory have been adopted according to the arbitrary use of them in this province, but they rather ought to be reversed; an American Tory is a supporter of our excellent constitution and an American Whig is a subverter of it.

Novanglus abuses me for saying that the Whigs aim at independence. The writer from Hampshire county is my advocate. He frankly asserts the independence of the colonies without any reserve and is the only consistent writer I have met with on that side of the question. For by separating us from the king as well as the parliament, he is under no necessity of contradicting himself. Novanglus strives to hide the inconsistencies of his hypothesis under a huge pile of learning. Surely he is not to learn that arguments drawn from obsolete maxims raked out of the ruins of the feudal system, or from principles of absolute monarchy, will not conclude to the present constitution of government. When he has finished his essays, he may expect some particular remarks upon them. I should not have taken the trouble of writing these letters had I not been satisfied that real and permanent good would accrue to this province, and indeed to all the colonies, from a speedy change of measures. Public justice and generosity are no less characteristic of the English than their private honesty and hospitality. The total repeal of the Stamp Act and the partial repeal of the act imposing duties on paper, etc., may convince us that the nation has no disposition to injure us. We are blessed with a king that reflects honor upon a crown. He is so far from being avaricious that he has relinquished a part of his revenue, and so far from being tyrannical that he has generously surrendered part of his prerogative for the sake of freedom. His court is so far from being tinctured with dissipation that the palace is rather an academy of the literati, and the royal pair are as exemplary in every private virtue as they are exalted in their stations. We have only to cease contending with the supreme legislature respecting its authority, with the king respecting his prerogatives, and with Great Britain respecting our subordination; to dismiss our illegal committees, disband our forces, despise the thraldom of *arrogant congresses,* and submit to constitutional government, to be happy.

Many appear to consider themselves as *procul a Jove a fulmine procul;* [n] and because we never have experienced any severity from Great Britain, think it impossible that we should. The English nation will bear much from its friends; but whoever has read its history must know that there is a line that cannot be passed with impunity. It is not the fault of our patriots if that line be not already passed. They have demanded of Great Britain more than she can grant consistent with honor, her interest, or our own and are now brandishing the sword of defiance.

Do you expect to conquer in war? War is no longer a simple but an intricate science, not to be learned from books or two or three campaigns, but from long experience. You need not be told that his majesty's generals, Gage and Haldimand, are possessed of every talent requisite to great commanders, matured by long experience in many parts of the world, and stand high in military fame; that many of the officers have been bred to arms from their infancy, and a large proportion of the army *now* here have already reaped immortal honors in the iron harvest of the field. Alas! My friends, you have nothing to oppose to this force, but a militia unused to service, impatient of command, and destitute of resources. Can your officers depend upon the privates, or the

privates upon the officers? Your war can be but little more than
mere tumultuary rage. And besides, there is an awful disparity
between troops that fight the battles of their sovereign and those
that follow the standard of rebellion. These reflections may arrest
you in an hour that you think not of and come too late to serve
you. Nothing short of a miracle could gain you one battle; but
could you destroy all the British troops that are now here and
burn the men of war that command our coast, it would be but
the beginning of sorrow; and yet without a decisive battle, one
campaign would ruin you. This province does not produce its
necessary provision when the husbandman can pursue his calling
without molestation. What then must be your condition when
the demand shall be increased and the resource in a manner cut
off? Figure to yourselves what must be your distress should your
wives and children be driven from such places as the king's troops
shall occupy into the interior parts of the province and they, as
well as you, be destitute of support. I take no pleasure in painting
these scenes of distress. The Whigs affect to divert you from
them by ridicule; but should war commence, you can expect nothing but its severities. Might I hazard an opinion—but few of
your leaders ever intended to engage in hostilities, but they may
have rendered inevitable what they intended for intimidation.
Those that unsheath the sword of rebellion may throw away
the scabbard they cannot be treated with while in arms; and if
they lay them down they are in no other predicament than conquered rebels. The conquered in other wars do not forfeit the
rights of men, nor all the rights of citizens. Even their bravery
is rewarded by a generous victor; far different is the case of a
routed rebel host. My dear countrymen, you have before you, at
your election, peace or war, happiness or misery. May the God of
our forefathers direct you in the way that leads to peace and
happiness before your feet stumble on the dark mountains, before
the evil days come, wherein you shall say we have no pleasure
in them.

8. NOVANGLUS [6]

April 17, 1775

We now come to Jersey and Guernsey, which Massachusettensis says, "are no part of the realm of England, nor are they represented in parliament, but are subject to its authority." A little knowledge of this subject will do us no harm; and, as soon as we shall acquire it, we shall be satisfied how these islands came to be subject to the authority of parliament. It is either upon the principle that the king is absolute there and has a right to make laws for them by his mere will, and, therefore, may express his will by an act of parliament or an edict at his pleasure, or it is an usurpation. If it is an usurpation, it ought not to be a precedent for the colonies, but it ought to be reformed, and they ought to be incorporated into the realm by act of parliament and their own act. Their situation is no objection to this. Ours is an insurmountable obstacle.

Thus we see that in every instance which can be found the observation proves to be true that, by the common law, the laws of England, the authority of parliament, and the limits of the realm were confined within seas. That the kings of England had frequently foreign dominions, some by conquest, some by marriage, and some by descent. But in all those cases the kings were either absolute in those dominions or bound to govern them according to their own respective laws and by their own legislative and executive councils. That the laws of England did not extend there, and the English parliament pretended no jurisdic-

[6] [IV, 169f, 173–177. This is the last letter by John Adams to appear in print. The following note, first published in the edition of 1819 (Hews and Goss), indicates why the exchange of letters was terminated:

"Hostilities at Lexington, between Great Britain and her colonies, commenced on the nineteenth of April, two days succeeding the publication of the last essay. Several others were written, and sent to the printers of the Boston Gazette, which were probably lost amidst the confusion occasioned by that event."]

tion there nor claimed any right to control the king in his government of those dominions. And from this extensive survey of all the foregoing cases there results a confirmation of what has been so afore said, that there is no provision in the common law, in English precedents, in the English government or constitution, made for the case of the colonies. It is not a conquered but a discovered country. It came not to the king by descent but was explored by the settlers. It came not by marriage to the king but was purchased by the settlers of the savages. It was not granted by the king of his grace, but was dearly, very dearly earned by the planters in the labor, blood, and treasure which they expended to subdue it to cultivation. It stands upon no grounds, then, of law or policy, but what are found in the law of nature, and their express contracts in their charters, and their implied contracts in the commissions to governors and terms of settlement.

. . . .

Massachusettensis then comes to the first charter of this province [Massachusetts Bay], and he tells us that in it we shall find irresistible evidence that our being a part of the empire, subject to the supreme authority of the state, bound by its laws and subject to its protection were the very terms and conditions by which our ancestors held their lands and settled the province. This is roundly and warmly said, but there is more zeal in it than knowledge. As to our being part of the empire, it could not be the British empire, as it is called, because that was not then in being, but was created seventy or eighty years afterwards. It must be the English empire, then; but the nation was not then polite enough to have introduced into the language of the law, or common parlance, any such phrase or idea. Rome never introduced the terms Roman empire until the tragedy of her freedom was completed. Before that, it was only the republic or the city. In the same manner the realm, or the kingdom, or the dominions of the king were the fashionable style in the age of the first charter. As to being subject to the supreme authority of the state, the prince who granted that charter thought it resided in himself, without any such troublesome tumults as lords and commons; and before the granting that charter had dissolved his parliament and determined never to call another, but to govern without. It is not very likely, then, that he intended our ancestors should be governed by parliament or bound by its laws. As to being subject to its protection, we may guess what ideas king and parliament had of that, by the protection they actually afforded to our ancestors. Not one farthing was ever voted or given by the king or his parliament, or any one resolution taken about them. As to holding their lands, surely they did not hold their lands of lords and commons. If they agreed to hold their lands of the king, this did not subject them to English lords and commons any more than the inhabitants of Scotland, holding their lands of the same king, subjected them. But there is not a word about the empire, the supreme authority of the state being bound by its laws or obliged for its protection in that whole charter. But "our charter is in the royal style." What then? Is that the parliamentary style? The style is this: "Charles, by the grace of God, King of England, Scotland, France, and Ireland, Defender of the Faith," etc. Now, in which capacity did he grant that charter, as King of France, or Ireland, or Scotland, or England? He governed England by one parliament, Scotland by another. Which parliament were we to be governed by? And Ireland by a third; and it might as well be reasoned that America was to be governed by the Irish parliament as by the English. But it was granted "under the great seal of England." True; but this seal runneth not out of the realm, except to mandatory writs, and when our charter was given, it was never intended to go out of the realm. The charter and the corporation were intended to abide and remain within the realm and be like other corporations there. But this affair of the seal is a mere piece of imposition.

In Moore's Reports, in the case of the union of the realm of Scotland with England, it is resolved by the judges that "the seal is alterable by the king at his pleasure, and he might make one seal for both kingdoms (of England and Scotland); for seals, coin, and leagues are of absolute prerogative to the king without parliament, not restrained to any assent of the people"; and in determining how far the great seal does command out of England, they made this distinction:

That the great seal was current for remedials, which groweth on complaint of the subject, and thereupon writs are addressed under the great seal of England; which writs are limited, their precinct to be within the places of the jurisdiction of the court that was to give the redress of the wrong. And therefore writs are not to go into Ireland, or the Isles, nor Wales, nor the counties palatine, because the king's courts here have not power to hold pleas of lands or things there. But the great seal hath a power preceptory to the person, which power extendeth to any place where the person may be found . . .

This authority plainly shows that the great seal of England has no more authority out of the realm, except to mandatory or preceptory writs (and surely the first charter was no preceptory writ) than the privy seal, or the great seal of Scotland, or no seal at all. In truth, the seal and charter were intended to remain within the realm and be of force to a corporation there; but the moment it was transferred to New England, it lost all its legal force, by the common law of England; and as this translation of it was acquiesced in by all parties, it might well be considered as good evidence of a contract between the parties, and in no other light, but not a whit the better or stronger for being under the great seal of England. But "the grants are made by the king, for his heirs and successors." What then? So the Scots held their lands of him who was then king of England, his heirs and successors, and were bound to allegiance to him, his heirs and successors; but it did not follow from thence that the Scots were subject to the English parliament. So the inhabitants of Aquitain, for ten descents, held their lands, and were tied by allegiance to him who was king of England, his heirs and successors, but were under no subjection to English lords and commons.

Heirs and successors of the king are supposed to be the same persons, and are used as synonymous words in the English law. There is no positive artificial provision made by our laws, or the British constitution, for revolutions. All our positive laws suppose that the royal office will descend to the eldest branch of the male line or, in default of that, to the eldest female, etc., forever, and that the succession will not be broken. It is true that nature, necessity, and the great principles of self-preservation have often overruled the succession. But this was done without any positive instruction of law. Therefore, the grants being by the king, for his heirs and successors, and the tenures being of the king, his heirs and successors, and the reservation being to the king, his heirs and successors, are so far from proving that we were to be part of an empire as one state, subject to the supreme authority of the English or British state and subject to its protection, that they do not so much as prove that we are annexed to the English crown. And all the subtilty of the writers on the side of the ministry has never yet proved that America is so much as annexed to the crown, much less to the realm. "It is apparent the king acted in his royal capacity, as king of England." This I deny. The laws of England gave him no authority to grant any territory out of the realm. Besides, there is no color for his thinking that he acted in that capacity but his using the great seal of England; but if the king is absolute in the affair of the seal, and may make or use any seal that he pleases, his using that seal which had been commonly used in England is no certain proof that he acted as king of England; for it is plain he might have used the English seal in the government of Scotland, and in that case it will not be pretended that he would have acted in his royal capacity as king of England. But his acting as king of England "necessarily supposes the territory granted to be a part of the English dominions, and holden of the crown of England." Here is the word "dominions" systematically introduced instead of the word "realm." There was no English dominions but the realm. And I say that America was not any part of the English realm or dominions. And therefore, when the king granted it, he could not act as king of England, by the laws of England. As to the "territory being holden of the crown, there is no such thing in nature or art." Lands are holden according to the original notices of feuds, of the natural person of the lord. Holding lands, in feudal language, means no more than the relation between lord and tenant. The reciprocal duties of these are all personal. Homage, fealty, etc., and all other services are personal to the lord; protection, etc. is personal to the tenant. And therefore no homage, fealty, or other services can ever be rendered to the body politic, the political capacity, which is not corporated but only a frame in the mind, an idea. No lands here, or in England, are held of the crown, meaning by it the political capacity; they are all held of the royal person, the natural person of the king. Holding lands, etc. of the crown is an impropriety of expression; but it is often used; and when it is, it can have no other sensible meaning than this, that we hold lands of that person, whoever he is, who wears the crown; the law supposes he will be a right, natural heir of the present king forever.

Massachusettensis then produces a quotation from the first charter to prove several points. It is needless to repeat the whole, but the parts chiefly relied on are italicized. It makes the company a body politic in fact and name, etc., and enables it "to sue and be sued." Then the writer asks, "whether this looks like a distinct state or independent empire?" I answer, no. And that it is plain and uncontroverted that the first charter was intended only to erect a corporation within the realm; and the governor and company were to reside within the realm; and their general courts were to be held there. Their agents, deputies, and servants only were to come to America. And if this had taken place, nobody ever doubted but they would have been subject to parliament. But this intention was not regarded on either side, and the company came over to America and brought their charter with them. And as soon as they arrived here, they got out of the English realm, dominions, state, empire, call it by what name you will, and out of the legal jurisdiction of parliament. The king might, by his writ or proclamation, have commanded them to return, but he did not.

THE POLITICAL SYSTEM

I. THE PLAN

THOUGHTS ON GOVERNMENT[1]

This brief essay represents the very essence of John Adams' political system. Though it was dashed off quickly as a letter to a friend, it obviously was the result of years of study, reflection, and experience. Adams deviated little in his later writings from the principles laid down here. In this piece we find his insistence on republican (representative democratic) government, on frequent elections, on a tripartite legislature composed of a lower house, an upper house, and a single executive armed with a strong veto power and constituting an integral part of the legislature itself, on a strong and independent judiciary, and finally on laws for the liberal education of youth. These few pages alone would establish Adams as one of the keenest students of government in America at the time and even unelaborated are worth our study today.

In later years Adams recorded specifically the occasion for these *Thoughts on Government*. To John Taylor of Caroline County, Virginia, he wrote: "In January, 1776, six months before the Declaration of Independence, Mr. Wythe of Virginia passed an evening with me at my chambers. In the course of conversation upon the necessity of independence, Mr. Wythe, observing that the greatest obstacle in the way of a declaration of it was the difficulty of agreeing upon a government for our future regulation, I replied that each colony should form a government for itself, as a free and independent State. 'Well,' said Mr. Wythe, 'what plan would you institute or advise for any one of the States?' My answer was, 'It is a thing I have not thought much of, but I will give you the first ideas that occur to me:' and I went on to explain to him off-hand in short-hand my first thoughts. Mr. Wythe appeared to think more of them than I did and requested me to put down in writing what I had then said, I agreed and, accordingly, that night and the next morning wrote it and sent it in a letter to him. This letter he sent to R. H. Lee, who came and

[1] [*Works* IV, 193–200.]

asked my leave to print it. I said it was not fit to be printed nor worth printing; but, if he thought otherwise, he might, provided he would suppress my name. He went accordingly to Dunlap and had it printed under the title of *Thoughts on Government, in a Letter from a Gentleman to his Friend.*" [2]

The printed pamphlet excited interest and may have been influential. Patrick Henry wrote Adams that he was exceedingly happy to get it and that he was "not without hopes it may produce good here where there is among most of our opulent families a strong bias to aristocracy." [3] Also on request from John Penn of North Carolina, Adams supplied his views on government to the legislative body of that colony and these views in the main reproduce those of this piece. At a much later date this second version was inserted by John Taylor in his *An Inquiry into the Principles and Policy of the Government of the United States,* and this prompted Adams' letter referred to above.

That Adams' views well represented the climate of opinion may be seen from the comments made to him and by the exceedingly interesting parallel which obtains between these views and the Virginia Plan advanced by the Virginia Delegation to the Constitutional Convention in 1787.[a]

My dear Sir: If I was equal to the task of forming a plan for the government of a colony, I should be flattered with your request and very happy to comply with it because, as the divine science of politics is the science of social happiness, and the blessings of society depend entirely on the constitutions of government, which are generally institutions that last for many generations, there can be no employment more agreeable to a benevolent mind than a research after the best.

Pope flattered tyrants too much when he said,

> For forms of government let fools contest,
> That which is best administered is best.
> [Essay on Man]

Nothing can be more fallacious than this. But poets read history to collect flowers, not fruits; they attend to fanciful images, not the effects of social institutions. Nothing is more certain from

[2] [X, 95.]
[3] [IV, 201.]

the history of nations and nature of man than that some forms of government are better fitted for being well administered than others.

We ought to consider what is the end of government before we determine which is the best form. Upon this point all speculative politicians will agree that the happiness of society is the end of government, as all divines and moral philosophers will agree that the happiness of the individual is the end of man. From this principle it will follow that the form of government which communicates ease, comfort, security, or, in one word, happiness to the greatest number of persons and in the greatest degree is the best.

All sober inquirers after truth, ancient and modern, pagan and Christian, have declared that the happiness of man, as well as his dignity, consists in virtue. Confucius, Zoroaster, Socrates, Mahomet, not to mention authorities really sacred, have agreed in this.

If there is a form of government, then, whose principle and foundation is virtue, will not every sober man acknowledge it better calculated to promote the general happiness than any other form?

Fear is the foundation of most governments; but it is so sordid and brutal a passion and renders men in whose breasts it predominates so stupid and miserable that Americans will not be likely to approve of any political institution which is founded on it.

Honor is truly sacred but holds a lower rank in the scale of moral excellence than virtue. Indeed, the former is but a part of the latter and consequently has not equal pretensions to support a frame of government productive of human happiness.

The foundation of every government is some principle or passion in the minds of the people. The noblest principles and most generous affections in our nature, then, have the fairest chance to support the noblest and most generous models of government.

A man must be indifferent to the sneers of modern Englishmen to mention in their company the names of Sidney, Harrington, Locke, Milton, Nedham, Neville, Burnet, and Hoadly. No small fortitude is necessary to confess that one has read them. The wretched condition of this country, however, for ten or fifteen years past has frequently reminded me of their principles and reasonings. They will convince any candid mind that there is no good government but what is republican. That the only valuable part of the British constitution is so because the very definition of a republic is "an empire of laws, and not of men." That, as a republic is the best of governments, so that particular arrangement of the powers of society or, in other words, that form of government which is best contrived to secure an impartial and exact execution of the laws is the best of republics.

Of republics there is an inexhaustible variety because the possible combinations of the powers of society are capable of innumerable variations.

As good government is an empire of laws, how shall your laws be made? In a large society inhabiting an extensive country, it is impossible that the whole should assemble to make laws. The first necessary step, then, is to depute power from the many to a few of the most wise and good. But by what rules shall you choose your representatives? Agree upon the number and qualifications of persons who shall have the benefit of choosing or annex this privilege to the inhabitants of a certain extent of ground.

The principal difficulty lies, and the greatest care should be employed, in constituting this representative assembly. It should be in miniature an exact portrait of the people at large. It should think, feel, reason, and act like them. That it may be the interest of this assembly to do strict justice at all times, it should be an equal representation, or, in other words, equal interests among the people should have equal interests in it. Great care should be taken to effect this and to prevent unfair, partial, and corrupt elections. Such regulations, however, may be better made in times of greater tranquility than the present; and they will spring up themselves naturally when all the powers of government come to be in the hands of the people's friends. At present, it will be safest to proceed in all established modes to which the people have been familiarized by habit.

A representation of the people in one assembly being obtained, a question arises whether all the powers of government—legislative, executive, and judicial—shall be left in this body? I think a people cannot be long free, nor ever happy, whose government is in one assembly. My reasons for this opinion are as follow:

1. A single assembly is liable to all the vices, follies, and frailties of an individual—subject to fits of humor, starts of passion, flights of enthusiasm, partialities, or prejudice—and consequently productive of hasty results and absurd judgments. And all these errors ought to be corrected and defects supplied by some controlling power.

2. A single assembly is apt to be avaricious and in time will not scruple to exempt itself from burdens which it will lay without compunction on its constituents.

3. A single assembly is apt to grow ambitious and after a time will not hesitate to vote itself perpetual. This was one fault of the Long Parliament,[b] but more remarkably of Holland, whose assembly first voted themselves from annual to septennial, then for life, and after a course of years, that all vacancies happening by death or otherwise should be filled by themselves without any application to constituents at all.

4. A representative assembly, although extremely well qualified and absolutely necessary as a branch of the legislative, is unfit to exercise the executive power for want of two essential properties, secrecy and dispatch.

5. A representative assembly is still less qualified for the judicial power because it is too numerous, too slow, and too little skilled in the laws.

6. Because a single assembly, possessed of all the powers of government, would make arbitrary laws for their own interest, execute all laws arbitrarily for their own interest, and adjudge all controversies in their own favor.

But shall the whole power of legislation rest in one assembly? Most of the foregoing reasons apply equally to prove that the legislative power ought to be more complex, to which we may add that if the legislative power is wholly in one assembly and the executive in another or in a single person, these two powers will oppose and encroach upon each other until the contest shall end in war, and the whole power, legislative and executive, be usurped by the strongest.

The judicial power, in such case, could not mediate or hold the balance between the two contending powers because the legislative would undermine it. And this shows the necessity, too, of giving the executive power a negative upon the legislative; otherwise this will be continually encroaching upon that.

To avoid these dangers, let a distinct assembly be constituted as a mediator between the two extreme branches of the legislature, that which represents the people and that which is vested with the executive power.

Let the representative assembly then elect by ballot, from among themselves or their constituents or both, a distinct assembly which, for the sake of perspicuity, we will call a council. It may consist of any number you please, say twenty or thirty, and should have a free and independent exercise of its judgment and consequently a negative voice in the legislature.

These two bodies, thus constituted and made integral parts of the legislature, let them unite and by joint ballot choose a governor, who, after being stripped of most of those badges of domination called prerogatives, should have a free and independent exercise of his judgment and be made also an integral part of the legislature. This, I know, is liable to objections; and, if you please, you may make him only president of the council, as in Connecticut. But as the governor is to be invested with the executive power with consent of council, I think he ought to have a negative upon the legislative. If he is annually elective, as he ought to be, he will always have so much reverence and affection for the people, their representatives and counsellors, that, although you give him an independent exercise of his judgment, he will seldom use it in opposition to the two houses, except in cases the public utility of which would be conspicuous; and some such cases would happen.

In the present exigency of American affairs, when by an act of Parliament we are put out of the royal protection and consequently discharged from our allegiance, and it has become necessary to assume government for our immediate security, the governor, lieutenant-governor, secretary, treasurer, commissary, attorney-general should be chosen by joint ballot of both houses. And these and all other elections, especially of representatives and counsellors, should be annual, there not being in the whole circle of the sciences a maxim more infallible than this, "where annual elections end, there slavery begins."

These great men, in this respect, should be once a year—

> Like bubbles on the sea of matter borne,
> They rise, they break, and to that sea return.

This will teach them the great political virtues of humility, patience, and moderation, without which every man in power becomes a ravenous beast of prey.

This mode of constituting the great offices of state will answer very well for the present; but if by experiment it should be found inconvenient, the legislature may at its leisure devise other methods of creating them; by elections of the people at large, as in Connecticut; or it may enlarge the term for which they shall be chosen to seven years, or three years, or for life; or make any other alterations which the society shall find productive of its ease, its safety, its freedom, or, in one word, its happiness.

A rotation of all offices, as well as of representatives and counsellors, has many advocates and is contended for with many plausible arguments. It would be attended no doubt with many advantages; and if the society has a sufficient number of suitable characters to supply the great number of vacancies which would be made by such a rotation, I can see no objection to it. These persons may be allowed to serve for three years and then be excluded three years, or for any longer or shorter term.[c]

Any seven or nine of the legislative council may be made a quorum for doing business as a privy council, to advise the governor in the exercise of the executive branch of power and in all acts of state.

The governor should have the command of the militia and of all your armies. The power of pardons should be with the governor and council.

Judges, justices, and all other officers, civil and military, should be nominated and appointed by the governor with the advice and consent of council, unless you choose to have a government more popular; if you do, all officers, civil and military, may be chosen by joint ballot of both houses; or, in order to preserve the independence and importance of each house, by ballot of one house, concurred in by the other. Sheriffs should be chosen by the freeholders of counties; so should registers of deeds and clerks of counties.

All officers should have commissions under the hand of the governor and seal of the colony.

The dignity and stability of government in all its branches, the morals of the people, and every blessing of society depend so much upon an upright and skillful administration of justice that the judicial power ought to be distinct from both the legislative and executive, and independent upon both, that so it may be a check upon both, as both should be checks upon that. The judges, therefore, should be always men of learning and experience in the laws, of exemplary morals, great patience, calmness, coolness, and attention. Their minds should not be distracted with jarring interests; they should not be dependent upon any man, or body of men. To these ends, they should hold estates for life in their offices; or, in other words, their commissions should be during good behavior and their salaries ascertained and established by law. For misbehavior the grand inquest of the colony, the house of representatives, should impeach them before the governor and council, where they should have time and opportunity to make their defense; but, if convicted, should be removed from their offices and subjected to such other punishment as shall be thought proper.

A militia law requiring all men, or with very few exceptions besides cases of conscience, to be provided with arms and ammunition, to be trained at certain seasons; and requiring counties, towns, or other small districts to be provided with public stocks of ammunition and entrenching utensils and with some settled plans for transporting provisions after the militia, when marched to defend their country against sudden invasions; and requiring certain districts to be provided with field-pieces, companies of matrosses, and perhaps some regiments of light-horse is always a wise institution, and in the present circumstances of our country indispensable.

Laws for the liberal education of youth, especially of the lower class of people, are so extremely wise and useful that to a humane and generous mind no expense for this purpose would be thought extravagant.

The very mention of sumptuary laws will excite a smile. Whether our countrymen have wisdom and virtue enough to submit to them, I know not; but the happiness of the people might be greatly promoted by them, and a revenue saved sufficient to carry on this war forever. Frugality is a great revenue, besides curing us of vanities, levities, and fopperies, which are real antidotes to all great, manly, and warlike virtues.

But must not all commissions run in the name of a king? No. Why may they not as well run thus, "The colony of —— to A. B. greeting," and be tested by the governor?

Why may not writs, instead of running in the name of the king, run thus, "The colony of —— to the sheriff," etc., and be tested by the chief justice?

Why may not indictments conclude, "against the peace of the colony of —— and the dignity of the same?"

A constitution founded on these principles introduces knowledge among the people and inspires them with a conscious dignity becoming freemen; a general emulation takes place which causes good humor, sociability, good manners, and good morals to be general. That elevation of sentiment inspired by such a government makes the common people brave and enterprising. That ambition which is inspired by it makes them sober, industrious, and frugal. You will find among them some elegance, perhaps, but more solidity; a little pleasure, but a great deal of business; some politeness, but more civility. If you compare such a country with the regions of domination, whether monarchical or aristocratical, you will fancy yourself in Arcadia or Elysium.

If the colonies should assume governments separately, they should be left entirely to their own choice of the forms; and if a continental constitution should be formed, it should be a congress containing a fair and adequate representation of the colonies, and its authority should sacredly be confined to these cases, namely: war, trade, disputes between colony and colony, the post office, and the unappropriated lands of the crown, as they used to be called.

These colonies, under such forms of government and in such a union, would be unconquerable by all the monarchies of Europe.

You and I, my dear friend, have been sent into life at a time when the greatest lawgivers of antiquity would have wished to live. How few of the human race have ever enjoyed an opportunity of making an election of government—more than of air, soil, or climate—for themselves or their children! When, before the present epocha, had three millions of people full power and a fair opportunity to form and establish the wisest and happiest government that human wisdom can contrive? I hope you will avail yourself and your country of that extensive learning and indefatigable industry which you possess to assist her in the formation of the happiest governments and the best character of a great people. For myself, I must beg you to keep my name out of sight; for this feeble attempt, if it should be known to be mine, would oblige me to apply to myself those lines of the immortal John Milton in one of his sonnets:

> I did but prompt the age to quit their clogs
> By the known rules of ancient liberty,
> When straight a barbarous noise environs me
> Of owls and cuckoos, asses, apes, and dogs.

II. THE MODEL

THE CONSTITUTION OF MASSACHUSETTS, 1780 [1]

The following piece consists of excerpts from a proposed constitution in large part drawn up by John Adams when he was a member of the Massachusetts Constitutional Convention of 1779–1780. The circumstances surrounding the adoption of this constitution serve to put it in historical context. The last session of the General Court of Massachusetts [a] under the Crown Government was held in June 1774. Commencing in October, 1774, an interim Provincial Congress [b] acted as the governing body, but it lacked constitutional sanction. Therefore in 1778, this body requested the people to grant it authority to formulate a new constitution, which request was granted, though few persons bothered to vote. The resulting constitution when submitted to the voters was rejected. The following year the voters agreed to establish a popularly elected constitutional convention, which drew up a constitution that was accepted at the polls in June of 1780. Adams was elected by the citizens of Braintree to represent his town at the convention and was in attendance from its opening on the first of September until the eleventh of November when he embarked on his second mission to Europe. In a letter to Mr. Edmund Jenings he summarized his role in this way: "I was chosen by my native town into the convention two or three days after my arrival. I was, by the convention, put upon the committee; by the committee, upon the sub-committee; so that I had the honor to be principal engineer. The committee made some alterations, as, I am informed, the convention have made a few others, in the report; but the frame and essence and substance is preserved." [2]

The Declaration of Rights was drawn up by Adams alone and little altered by the convention. This declaration reaffirmed the principles of the Declaration of Independence—popular

[1] [Works IV, 219–259 passim.]
[2] [IV, 216.]

sovereignty, government instituted by contract for the public good, and the right of revolution—and restated the liberties guaranteed by the Virginia Bill of Rights.^c At the same time Adams recognized "the duty of all men in society, publicly, and at stated seasons to worship the Supreme Being." The famous Article XXX of this Constitution was not written by him, but represented an addition of the convention. As finally accepted, this article read: "XXX. In the government of this commonwealth, the legislative department shall never exercise the executive and judicial powers, or either of them; the executive shall never exercise the legislative and judicial powers, or either of them; the judicial shall never exercise the legislative and executive powers, or either of them, to the end it may be a government of laws and not of men." The Adams' draft read simply: "XXX. The judicial department of the state ought to be separate from, and independent of, the legislative and executive powers."

The form of government suggested by Adams followed rather naturally the older colonial form, in much the same way that the Constitution of the United States created in 1787 followed colonial form. His principal regrets about the constitution concerned the executive branch. During the course of the convention he wrote Benjamin Rush, "If the committee had boldly made the legislative consist of three branches, I should have been better pleased." [3] By this he meant that in weakening the governor's power in the matter of the absolute veto and also in some phases of his appointive authority the convention had not sufficiently integrated the executive into the whole scheme of balanced government. A legislature consisting of three branches meant in his mind a strong independent executive with a full veto power on the acts of a bicameral legislative body, a wise and selective upper house and a rather large and popularly elected lower house. Despite those misgivings, however, Adams was reasonably well satisfied, for he wrote: "There never was an example of such precautions as are taken by this wise and jealous people in the formation of their government. None was ever made so perfectly upon the principle of the people's rights and equality. It is Locke, Sidney, and Rousseau and deMably reduced to practice, in the first instance. I wish every step of their progress printed and preserved." [4] After the constitution had been adopted and he had reflected on it at length, he expressed his approval by writing, "I take a vast satisfaction in the general approbation of the Massachusetts Constitution.

[3] [IX, 507.]
[4] [IV, 216.]

If the people are as wise and honest in the choice of their rulers as they have been in framing a government, they will be happy, and I shall die content with the prospect of my children, who, if they cannot be well under such a form and such an administration, will not deserve to be at all." [5]

Since we are primarily interested in the broad outlines of the constitution as drafted by Adams, changes of detail made by the convention and explained in the *Works*, Volume IV, are not included. The text below is the Report made by the convention committee, prepared for that committee by Adams. Passages enclosed by brackets were erased by the convention; passages in italics underwent change; and blanks indicate later insertions by the convention.

Agreed upon by the Committee,—to be laid before the CONVENTION OF DELEGATES, *assembled at* CAMBRIDGE, *on the first day of September, 1779; and continued by adjournment to the twenty-eighth day of October following.*

PREAMBLE

The end of the institution, maintenance, and administration of government is to secure the existence of the body politic, to protect it and to furnish the individuals who compose it with the power of enjoying, in safety and tranquility, their natural rights and the blessings of life; and whenever these great objects are not obtained, the people have a right to alter the government and to take measures necessary for their safety, happiness, and prosperity.

The body politic is formed by a voluntary association of individuals. It is a social compact by which the whole people covenants with each citizen and each citizen with the whole people, that all shall be governed by certain laws for the common good. It is the duty of the people, therefore, in framing a Constitution of Government, to provide for an equitable mode of making laws, as well as for an impartial interpretation and a faithful execution of them, that every man may, at all times, find his security in them.

We, therefore, [the delegates of] the people of Massachusetts,

[5] [IX, 509.]

[in general convention assembled for the express and sole purpose of framing a constitution or form of government to be laid before our constituents according to their instructions] acknowledging with grateful hearts the goodness of the great Legislator of the universe in affording *to this people* in the course of His providence an opportunity *of entering into an original, explicit, and solemn compact with each other, deliberately and peaceably, without fraud, violence, or surprise;* and of forming a new constitution of civil government for *themselves* and [their] posterity; and devoutly imploring His direction in *a design so interesting* [to them and their posterity,] do, [by virtue of the authority vested in us by our constituents] agree upon   the following *Declaration of Rights and Frame of Government* as the CONSTITUTION OF THE COMMONWEALTH OF MASSACHUSETTS.

CHAPTER I

A DECLARATION OF THE RIGHTS OF THE INHABITANTS OF THE COMMONWEALTH OF MASSACHUSETTS

ART. I. All men are born [equally] free and *independent,* and have certain natural, essential, and unalienable rights, among which may be reckoned the right of enjoying and defending their lives and liberties; that of acquiring, possessing, and protecting [their] property; in fine, that of seeking and obtaining their safety and happiness.[6]

II. It is the —— duty of all men in society, publicly, and at stated seasons, to worship the SUPREME BEING, the great Creator and Preserver of the universe. And no subject shall be hurt, molested, or restrained, in his person, liberty, or estate, for worshipping GOD in the manner —— most agreeable to the dictates of his own conscience; or, for his religious profession or sentiments, provided he does not disturb the public peace or obstruct others in their religious worship. . . .

IV. The people of this commonwealth have the sole and exclusive right of governing themselves as a free, sovereign, and inde-

---

[6] "equal." The language of this article, as reported, is nearly the same with that of the first article of the Bill of Rights of Virginia.

pendent state; and do, and forever hereafter shall, exercise and enjoy every power, jurisdiction, and right, which *are* not, or may not hereafter be, by them expressly delegated to the United States of America, in congress assembled.

V. All power residing originally in the people and being derived from them, the several magistrates and officers of government vested with authority, whether legislative, executive, or judicial, are their substitutes and agents and are at all times accountable to them.[7]

VI. No man, nor corporation or association of men, have any other title to obtain advantages or particular and exclusive privileges distinct from those of the community than what arises from the consideration of services rendered to the public; and this title, being in nature neither hereditary nor transmissible to children, or descendants, or relations by blood, the idea of a man born a magistrate, lawgiver, or judge, is absurd and unnatural.[8]

VII. Government is instituted for the common good, for the protection, safety, prosperity, and happiness of the people and not for the profit, honor, or private interest of any one man, family, or class of men. Therefore, the people alone have an incontestable, unalienable, and indefeasible right to institute government and to reform, alter, or totally change the same, when their protection, safety, prosperity, and happiness require it.[9]

VIII. In order to prevent those who are vested with authority from becoming oppressors, the people have a right, at such periods and in such manner as *may be delineated in* their frame of government, to cause their public officers to return to private life, and to fill up vacant places by certain and regular elections.——

IX. All elections ought to be free, and all the [male] inhabitants of this commonwealth, having *sufficient qualifications,* have an equal right to elect officers and to be elected for public employments.

X. Each individual of the society has a right to be protected by

[7] This is an amplification of the second article of the Virginia Bill of Rights.
[8] The fourth article of the Virginia Bill amplified.
[9] The third article of Virginia expanded.

it in the enjoyment of his life, liberty, and property, according to standing laws. He is obliged, consequently, to contribute his share to the expense of this protection, and to give his personal service, or an equivalent, when necessary. But no part of the property of any individual can, with justice, be taken from him or applied to public uses without his own consent or that of the representative body of the people. In fine, the people of this commonwealth are not controllable by any other laws than those to which their constitutional representative body have given their consent.

XI. Every subject of the commonwealth ought to find a certain remedy, by having recourse to the laws, for all injuries or wrongs which he may receive in his person, property, or character. He ought to obtain right and justice freely and without being obliged to purchase it, completely, and without any denial, promptly, and without delay, conformably to the laws. . . .

. . . XXX. [XXXI.] *The judicial department of the state ought to be separate from, and independent of, the legislative and executive powers.*

CHAPTER II

The Frame of Government

The people inhabiting the territory *heretofore* called the Province of Massachusetts Bay do hereby solemnly and mutually agree with each other to form themselves into a free, sovereign, and independent body politic, or State, by the name of THE COMMONWEALTH OF MASSACHUSETTS.

In the government of the Commonwealth of Massachusetts the legislative, executive, and judicial power shall be placed in separate departments, to the end that it might be a government of laws and not of men.

SECTION I

ART. I. The department of legislation shall be formed by two branches: A SENATE and HOUSE OF REPRESENTATIVES, each of which shall have a negative on the other.

They shall assemble *once,* on the last Wednesday in May, and at such other times as they shall judge necessary, [every year] —— and shall be styled THE GENERAL COURT OF MASSACHUSETTS.

[And the first magistrate shall have a negative upon all the laws, that he may have power to preserve the independence of the executive and judicial departments.] . . .

IV. [III.] And further, full power and authority are hereby given and granted to the said general court from time to time to make, ordain, and establish all manner of wholesome and reasonable orders, laws, statutes and ordinances, directions and instructions, either with penalties or without; so as the same be not repugnant or contrary to this constitution, as they shall judge to be for the good and welfare of this commonwealth, and for the government and ordering thereof, and of the subjects of the same, and for the necessary support and defense of the government thereof; . . .

SECTION II

Senate

I. There shall be annually elected by the freeholders and other inhabitants of this commonwealth, qualified as in this constitution is provided, forty persons to be counsellors and senators for the year ensuing their election, to be chosen [in and] by the inhabitants of the districts into which the commonwealth may from time to time be divided by the general court for that purpose. . . .

II. The senate shall be the first branch of the legislature. . . .

SECTION III

House of Representatives

I. There shall be in the legislature of this commonwealth a representation of the people annually elected and founded *in* equality. . . .

V. The members of the house of representatives shall be

chosen annually in the month of May, ten days at least before the last Wednesday of that month, [from among the wisest, most prudent, and virtuous of the freeholders.]

VI. The house of representatives shall be the grand inquest of this commonwealth, and all impeachments made by them shall be heard and tried by the senate.

VII. All money bills shall originate in the house of representatives, but the senate may propose or concur with amendments as on other bills.

VIII. The house of representatives shall have power to adjourn themselves, provided such adjournment shall not exceed two days at a time.

IX. Not less than sixty members of the house of representatives shall constitute a quorum for doing business.

X. The house of representatives shall —— choose their own speaker, appoint their own officers, and settle the rules and orders of proceeding in their own house. They shall have authority to punish by imprisonment every person —— who shall be guilty of disrespect to the house, in its presence, by any disorderly or contemptuous behavior; *or by threatening or ill treating any of its members; or, in a word, by obstructing its deliberations; every person guilty of a breach of its privileges, in making arrests for debts, or by assaulting one of its members during his attendance at any session, or on the road, whether he be going to the house or returning home; in assaulting any one of its officers, or in disturbing him in the execution of any order or procedure of the house; in assaulting or troubling any witness or other person ordered to attend the house, in his way in going or returning, or in rescuing any person arrested by order of the house.*

XI. The senate shall have the same powers in the like cases, and the governor and council shall have the same authority to punish in like cases—provided that no imprisonment on the warrant or order of the governor, council, senate, or house of representatives, for either of the above described offences, be for a term exceeding thirty days.

CHAPTER II [III]

EXECUTIVE POWER

SECTION I

Governor

ART. I. There shall be a supreme executive magistrate who shall be styled THE GOVERNOR OF THE COMMONWEALTH OF MASSACHUSETTS and whose title shall be HIS EXCELLENCY.

II. The governor shall be chosen annually; and no person shall be eligible to this office unless, at the time of his election, he shall have been an inhabitant of this commonwealth for seven years next preceding, and unless he shall at the same time be seised in his own right of a freehold within the commonwealth, of the value of one thousand pounds, and unless he shall [10] be of the Christian religion. . . .

VII. [VIII.] The governor of this commonwealth, for the time being, shall be the commander in chief of the army and navy and of all the military forces of the state by sea and land; and shall have full power, by himself or by any [chief] commander, or other officer or officers [to be appointed by him] from time to time to train, instruct, exercise, and govern the militia and navy; and for the special defense and safety of the commonwealth to assemble in martial array and put in warlike posture, the inhabitants thereof. . . .

[XI.] [All officers of the militia shall be appointed by the governor with the advice and consent of the council, he first nominating them seven days at least before the appointment. . . .]

XIII. [XV.] As the public good requires that the governor should not be under the undue influence of any of the members of the general court by a dependence on them for his support, that he should, in all cases, act with freedom for the benefit of the

---

[10] [The convention added: "declare himself to." This requirement was annulled by the convention of 1820.]

public; that he should not have his attention necessarily diverted from that object to his private concerns; and that he should maintain the dignity of the commonwealth, in the character of its chief magistrate, it is necessary that he should have an honorable stated salary of a fixed and permanent value, amply sufficient for those purposes and established by standing laws; and it shall be among the first acts of the general court, after the commencement of this constitution, to establish such salary by law accordingly.

Permanent and honorable salaries shall also be established by law for the justices of the *superior* court.

And if it shall be found that any of the salaries aforesaid, so established, are insufficient, they shall from time to time be enlarged, as the general court shall judge proper. . . .

SECTION III

Council and the Manner of Settling Elections by the Legislature
[Oaths to be Taken, etc.]

I. There shall be a council for advising the governor in the executive part of government to consist of nine persons besides the lieutenant governor, whom the governor, for the time being, shall have full power and authority, from time to time, at his discretion, to assemble and call together. And the governor, with the said counsellors, or five of them at least, shall and may, from time to time, hold and keep a council for the ordering and directing the affairs of the commonwealth, according to the laws of the land. . . .

CHAPTER III [IV]

JUDICIARY POWER

ART. 1. The tenure that all commission officers *by law hold* in their offices shall be expressed in their respective commissions. All judicial officers, duly appointed, commissioned, and sworn, shall hold their offices during good behavior —— provided, nevertheless, the governor, with consent of the council, may remove them upon the address of both houses of the legislature. [And all other officers appointed by the governor and council shall hold their offices during pleasure.] . . .

CHAPTER V (VI)

SECTION II

The Encouragement of Literature, etc.

Wisdom and knowledge, as well as virtue, diffused generally among the body of the people, being necessary for the preservation of their rights and liberties, and as these depend on spreading the opportunities and advantages of education in the various parts of the country and among the different orders of the people, it shall be the duty of legislators and magistrates in all future periods of this commonwealth to cherish the interests of literature and sciences and all seminaries of them—especially the university at Cambridge,[d] public schools and grammar schools in the towns—to encourage private societies and public institutions, rewards and immunities for the promotion of agriculture, arts, sciences, commerce, trades, manufactures, and a natural history of the country; to countenance and inculcate the principles of humanity and general benevolence, public and private charity, industry and frugality, honesty and punctuality in their dealings, sincerity, good humor, and all social affections and generous sentiments among the people.[11] . . .

[11] This feature of the constitution of Massachusetts is peculiar, and in one sense original with Mr. Adams. The recognition of the obligation of a state to promote a higher and more extended policy than is embraced in the protection of the temporal interests and political rights of the individual, however understood among enlightened minds, had not at that time been formally made a part of the organic law. Those clauses, since inserted in other state constitutions, which, with more or less of fullness, acknowledge the same principle, are all manifestly taken from this source. . . . C. F. A.

III. THE DEFENSE

I. A DEFENCE OF THE CONSTITUTIONS OF GOVERNMENT OF THE UNITED STATES OF AMERICA

In October of 1786, John Adams embarked upon his most ambitious treatise on government and completed it some fourteen months later in December, 1787. It was a three-volume work entitled: *A Defence of the Constitutions of Government of the United States of America against the attack of M. Turgot, in his letter to Dr. Price, dated the twenty-second of March, 1778.* At the time Adams was serving as the first United States Minister to Great Britain, where the work was composed, printed and published. Volume I was reprinted in both Philadelphia and New York in 1787, while the Federal Constitutional Convention [a] was assembling. It was on the whole favorably received and was said by some of the members of this Convention to have been of influence in the formation of the Constitution of the United States. The immediate occasion for publication, as we see from the title, was M. Turgot's attack on the constitutions of the American states as unreasonable imitations of the usages of England. Turgot lamented the fact that authority had not been more centralized and objected particularly to an unwarranted separation of powers, a poor copy of the British system. In the *Defence* not only was Adams replying to these strictures, but also he was directing his remarks to his own countrymen, for he had been disturbed by Shays's Rebellion [b] in Massachusetts. "The commotion in New England alarmed me so much that I have thrown together some hasty speculations upon the subject of government, which you will soon see." [1] Furthermore he feared that some of the states might consciously accept and adopt the simple, centralizing schemes of Dr. Franklin and Tom Paine.[c] Adams records the circumstances well in his own words. "In 1780, when I arrived in France, I carried a printed copy of

[1] [IX, 551.]

the report of the Grand Committee of the Massachusetts Convention, which I had drawn up; and this became an object of speculation. Mr. Turgot, the Duke de la Rochefoucauld, and Mr. Condorcet, and others admired Mr. Franklin's Constitution and reprobated mine. Mr. Turgot, in a letter to Dr. Price, printed in London, censured the American Constitution as adopting three branches, in imitation of the Constitution of Great Britain. The intention was to celebrate Franklin's Constitution and condemn mine. I understood it and undertook to defend my Constitution, and it cost me three volumes. . . . At the same time, every western wind brought us news of town and county meetings in Massachusetts, adopting Mr. Turgot's ideas, condemning my Constitution, reprobating the office of governor and the assembly of the Senate as expensive, useless, and pernicious, and not only proposing to toss them off, but rising in rebellion against them. . . . In this view I wrote my defense of the American Constitutions. I had only the Massachusetts Constitution in view, and such others as agreed with it in the distribution of the legislative power into three branches, in separating the executive from the legislative power, and the judiciary power from both. These three volumes had no relation to the Constitution of the United States. That was not in existence, and I scarcely knew that such a thing was in contemplation till I received it at the moment my third volume was about to issue from the press." [2]

The theme of John Adams' political philosophy embodied in the *Defence* is simply stated.[3] ". . . power is always abused when unlimited and unbalanced. . . ." Simple unchecked government is always despotic, whether it be government by a monarch, by aristocrats, or by the mass of people. All are equally intolerant, cruel, bloody, oppressive, tyrannical. The only sound and lasting government is one so balanced that ambition is made to counteract ambition, power to check power. The great art of lawgiving consists in balancing the poor against the rich in the legislature, and in constituting the legislative a perfect balance against the executive power, at the same time that no individual or party can become its rival. The essence of a free government consists in an effectual control of rivalries. The executive and the legislative powers are natural rivals; and if each has not an effectual control over the other, the weaker will ever be the lamb in the paws of the wolf. The nation which will not adopt an equilibrium of

[2] [IX, 623.]
[3] [VI, 73.]

power must adopt a despotism. There is no other alternative."[4] Each of the three branches, executive, upper house and lower house, acts as a check on the other. Each is independent and absolute, and exercises an absolute veto or negative to every law. There can be no stability or freedom without balance, and there can be no balance without three separate powers. Two powers in opposition beget rivalry, discord, bloodshed; a third power must act as mediator, so that each is checked and balanced in turn by the other two.

In the concluding chapter of the third volume Adams himself recognized that the work had been prepared hastily and without organization. "The preceding has been produced upon the spur of a particular occasion," he wrote, "which made it necessary to write and publish with precipitation, or it might have been useless to have published at all. The whole has been done in the midst of other occupations, in so much hurry that scarce a moment could be spared to correct the style, adjust the method, pare off excrescences, or even obliterate repetitions, in all which respects it stands in need of an apology."[5] In a sense the work is a dialogue between the authors quoted and John Adams, who inserted his trenchant comments at will. So true is this and so inadequate the citation that at times it is difficult to separate Adams from the writer being employed. A great deal of the three volumes consists simply of quotations *in extenso*. All this tends to make for difficult reading, except the reader can never anticipate when Adams is going to add his own cogent and provocative comments. The selections chosen are designed to illustrate both the methodology and substance of John Adams' *Defence*.

The three volumes of the *Defence* are to be found in Adams' *Works*, Volumes IV, V, and VI. Our selections are taken from the first volume of the *Defence* found in the *Works*, Volume IV, and from the third volume of the *Defence* found in the *Works*, Volumes V and VI, though only that portion of the third Volume contained in the *Works*, VI, is employed here.

PREFACE

The arts and sciences, in general, during the three or four last centuries have had a regular course of progressive improvement. The inventions in mechanic arts, the discoveries in natural phi-

[4] [VI, 280.]
[5] [VI, 217.]

losophy, navigation, and commerce, and the advancement of civilization and humanity have occasioned changes in the condition of the world and the human character which would have astonished the most refined nations of antiquity. A continuation of similar exertions is every day rendering Europe more and more like one community, or single family. Even in the theory and practice of government, in all the simple monarchies considerable improvements have been made. The checks and balances of republican governments have been in some degree adopted at the courts of princes. By the erection of various tribunals to register the laws and exercise the judicial power—by indulging the petitions and remonstrances of subjects until by habit they are regarded as rights—a control has been established over ministers of state and the royal councils, which, in some degree, approaches the spirit of republics. Property is generally secure and personal liberty seldom invaded. The press has great influence, even where it is not expressly tolerated; and the public opinion must be respected by a minister, or his place becomes insecure. Commerce begins to thrive; and if religious toleration were established, personal liberty a little more protected by giving an absolute right to demand a public trial in a certain reasonable time, and the states were invested with a few more privileges, or rather restored to some that have been taken away, these governments would be brought to as great a degree of perfection, they would approach as near to the character of governments of laws and not of men, as their nature will probably admit of. In so general a refinement, or more properly a reformation of manners and improvement in science, is it not unaccountable that the knowledge of the principles and construction of free governments, in which the happiness of life, and even the further progress of improvement in education and society, in knowledge and virtue, are so deeply interested, should have remained at a full stand for two or three thousand years?

According to a story in Herodotus, the nature of monarchy, aristocracy, and democracy, and the advantages and inconveniences of each were as well understood at the time of the neighing of the horse of Darius as they are at this hour. A variety of mixtures of these simple species were conceived and attempted with various success by the Greeks and Romans. Representations instead of collections of the people; a total separation of the executive from the legislative power, and of the judicial from both; and a balance in the legislature by three independent, equal branches are perhaps the only three discoveries in the constitution of a free government since the institution of Lycurgus. Even these have been so unfortunate that they have never spread: the first has been given up by all the nations, excepting one, which had once adopted it; and the other two, reduced to practice, if not invented, by the English nation, have never been imitated by any other except their own descendants in America.

While it would be rash to say that nothing further can be done to bring a free government in all its parts still nearer to perfection, the representations of the people are most obviously susceptible of improvement. The end to be aimed at in the formation of a representative assembly seems to be the sense of the people, the public voice. The perfection of the portrait consists in its likeness. Numbers, or property, or both should be the rule; and the proportions of electors and members an affair of calculation. The duration should not be so long that the deputy should have time to forget the opinions of his constituents. Corruption in elections is the great enemy of freedom. Among the provisions to prevent it, more frequent elections and a more general privilege of voting are not all that might be devised. Dividing the districts, diminishing the distance of travel, and confining the choice to residents would be great advances towards the annihilation of corruption. The modern aristocracies of Holland, Venice, Bern, etc., have tempered themselves with innumerable checks by which they have given a great degree of stability to that form of government; and though liberty and life can never be there enjoyed so well as in a free republic, none is perhaps more capable of profound sagacity. We shall learn to prize the checks and balances of a free government and even those of the modern aristocracies if we recollect the miseries of Greece, which arose from its ignorance of them. The only balance attempted against the ancient kings was a body of nobles; and the consequences were perpetual alternations of rebellion and tyranny and the butchery of thousands upon every revolution from one to the other. When kings were abolished, aristocracies tyrannized; and then no balance was attempted but between aristocracy and democracy. This, in the nature of things, could be no balance at all, and therefore the pendulum was forever on the swing.

It is impossible to read in Thucydides his account of the factions and confusions throughout all Greece, which were introduced by this want of an equilibrium, without horror. "During the few days that Eurymedon, with his troops, continued at Corcyra, the people of that city extended the massacre to all whom they judged their enemies. The crime alleged was their attempt to overturn the democracy. Some perished merely through private enmity; some by the hands of the borrower on account of the money they had lent. Every kind of death, every dreadful act was perpetrated. Fathers slew their children; some were dragged from altars; some were butchered at them; numbers, immured in temples, were starved. The contagion spread through the whole extent of Greece; factions raged in every city, the licentious many contending for the Athenians and the aspiring few for the Lacedæmonians. The consequence was seditions in cities with all their numerous and tragical incidents."

"Such things ever will be," says Thucydides, "so long as human nature continues the same." But if this nervous historian had known a balance of three powers, he would not have pronounced the distemper so incurable but would have added—*so long as parties in cities remain unbalanced.* He adds—"Words lost their signification; brutal rashness was fortitude; prudence, cowardice; modesty, effeminacy; and being wise in everything, to be good for nothing: the hot temper was manly valor; calm deliberation, plausible knavery; he who boiled with indignation was trustworthy; and he who presumed to contradict was ever suspected. Connection of blood was less regarded than transient acquaintance; associations were not formed for mutual advantage consistent with law, but for rapine against all law; trust was only communication of guilt; revenge was more valued than never to have suffered an injury; perjuries were masterpieces of cunning;

the dupes only blushed, the villains most impudently triumphed.

"The source of all these evils was a thirst of power, from rapacious and ambitious passions. The men of large influence, some contending for the just equality of the democratical and others for the fair decorum of aristocratical government, by artful sounds embarrassed those communities for their own private lucre by the keenest spirit, the most daring projects, and most dreadful machinations. Revenge, not limited by justice or the public welfare, was measured only by such retaliation as was judged the sweetest—by capital condemnations, by iniquitous sentences, and by glutting the present rancor of their hearts with their own hands. The pious and upright conduct was on both sides disregarded; the moderate citizens fell victims to both. Seditions introduced every species of outrageous wickedness into the Grecian manners. Sincerity was laughed out of countenance; the whole order of human life was confounded; the human temper, too apt to transgress in spite of laws, now having gained the ascendant over law, seemed to glory that it was too strong for justice and an enemy to all superiority."

Mr. Hume has collected from Diodorus Siculus alone a few massacres which happened in only sixty of the most polished years of Greece:—"From Sybaris, 500 nobles banished; of Chians, 600 citizens; at Ephesus, 340 killed, 1000 banished; of Cyrenians, 500 nobles killed, all the rest banished; the Corinthians killed 120, banished 500; Phæbidas banished 300 Bœotians. Upon the fall of the Lacedæmonians, democracies were restored in many cities and severe vengeance taken of the nobles; the banished nobles, returning, butchered their adversaries at Phialæ, in Corinth, in Megara, in Phliasia, where they killed 300 of the people; but these, again revolting, killed above 600 of the nobles, and banished the rest. In Arcadia, 1400 banished, besides many killed; the banished retired to Sparta and Pallantium; the latter were delivered up to their countrymen and all killed. Of the banished from Argos and Thebes, there were 500 in the Spartan army. The people before the usurpation of Agathocles had banished 600 nobles; afterwards that tyrant, in concurrence with the people, killed 4000 nobles and banished 6000, and killed 4000 people at Gela; his brother banished 8000 from Syracuse. The inhabitants of Ægesta, to the number of 40,000, were killed, man, woman, and child, for the sake of their money; all the relations of the Libyan army, fathers, brothers, children, killed; 7000 exiles killed after capitulation. These numbers, compared with the population of those cities, are prodigious; yet Agathocles was a man of character and not to be suspected of wanton cruelty contrary to the maxims of his age." [6]

Such were the fashionable outrages of unbalanced parties. In the name of human and divine benevolence, is such a system as this to be recommended to Americans in this age of the world? Human nature is as incapable now of going through revolutions with temper and sobriety, with patience and prudence, or without fury and madness, as it was among the Greeks so long ago. The latest revolution that we read of was conducted, at least on one side, in the Grecian style, with laconic energy; and with a little Attic salt, at least, without too much patience, foresight, and prudence on the other. Without three orders and an effectual balance between them in every American constitution, it must be destined to frequent unavoidable revolutions; though they are delayed a few years, they must come in time. The United States are large and populous nations in comparison with the Grecian commonwealths or even the Swiss cantons; and they are growing every day more disproportionate and therefore less capable of being held together by simple governments. Countries that increase in population so rapidly as the States of America did, even during such an impoverishing and destructive war as the last was, are not to be long bound with silken threads; lions, young or old, will not be bound by cobwebs. It would be better for America, it is nevertheless agreed, to ring all the changes with the whole set of bells and go through all the revolutions of the Grecian States, rather than establish an absolute monarchy among them, notwithstanding all the great and real improvements which have been made in that kind of government.

The objection to it is not because it is supported by nobles

[6] "On the Populousness of Ancient Nations." Hume's *Essays*, Vol. I, 477, note BB.

and a subordination of ranks; for all governments, even the most democratical, are supported by a subordination of offices and of ranks too. None ever existed without it but in a state of anarchy and outrage, in a contempt of law and justice, no better than no government. But the nobles in the European monarchies support them more by opposing than promoting their ordinary views. The kings are supported by their armies; the nobles support the crown, as it is in full possession of the gift of all employments; but they support it still more by checking its ministers and preventing them from running into abuses of power and wanton despotism; otherwise the people would be pushed to extremities and insurrections. It is thus that the nobles reconcile the monarchical authority to the obedience of the subjects; but take away the standing armies and leave the nobles to themselves, and in a few years they would overturn every monarchy in Europe and erect aristocracies.

It is become a kind of fashion among writers to admit, as a maxim, that if you could be always sure of a wise, active, and virtuous prince, monarchy would be the best of governments. But this is so far from being admissible that it will forever remain true that a free government has a great advantage over a simple monarchy. The best and wisest prince, by means of a freer communication with his people and the greater opportunities to collect the best advice from the best of his subjects, would have an immense advantage in a free state over a monarchy. A senate consisting of all that is most noble, wealthy, and able in the nation, with a right to counsel the crown at all times, is a check to ministers and a security against abuses such as a body of nobles who never meet and have no such right can never supply. Another assembly composed of representatives chosen by the people in all parts gives free access to the whole nation and communicates all its wants, knowledge, projects, and wishes to government; it excites emulation among all classes, removes complaints, redresses grievances, affords opportunities of exertion to genius, though in obscurity, and gives full scope to all the faculties of man; it opens a passage for every speculation to the legislature, to administration, and to the public; it gives a universal

energy to the human character, in every part of the state, such
as never can be obtained in a monarchy.

There is a third particular which deserves attention both from
governments and people. In a simple monarchy the ministers of
state can never know their friends from their enemies; secret
cabals undermine their influence and blast their reputation. This
occasions a jealousy, ever anxious and irritated, which never
thinks the government safe without an encouragement of in-
formers and spies throughout every part of the state, who inter-
rupt the tranquility of private life, destroy the confidence of
families in their own domestics and in one another, and poison
freedom in its sweetest retirements. In a free government, on the
contrary, the ministers can have no enemies of consequence but
among the members of the great or little council, where every
man is obliged to take his side and declare his opinions upon
every question. This circumstance alone to every manly mind
would be sufficient to decide the preference in favor of a free
government. Even secrecy, where the executive is entire in one
hand, is as easily and surely preserved in a free governmnt as in
a simple monarchy; and as to dispatch, all the simple monarchies
of the whole universe may be defied to produce greater or more
numerous examples of it than are to be found in English history.
An Alexander or a Frederic, possessed of the prerogatives only of
a king of England and leading his own armies, would never find
himself embarrassed or delayed in any honest enterprise. He
might be restrained, indeed, from running mad and from making
conquests to the ruin of his nation merely for his own glory; but
this is no argument against a free government.

There can be no free government without a democratical
branch in the constitution. Monarchies and aristocracies are in
possession of the voice and influence of every university and
academy in Europe. Democracy, simple democracy, never had
a patron among men of letters. Democratical mixtures in government have lost almost all the advocates they ever had out of
England and America. Men of letters must have a great deal of
praise and some of the necessaries, conveniences, and ornaments
of life. Monarchies and aristocracies pay well and applaud liber-

ally. The people have almost always expected to be served gratis and to be paid for the honor of serving them; and their applauses and adorations are bestowed too often on artifices and tricks, on hypocrisy and superstition, on flattery, bribes, and largesses. It is no wonder then that democracies and democratical mixtures are annihilated all over Europe except on a barren rock, a paltry fen, an inaccessible mountain, or an impenetrable forest. The people of England, to their immortal honor, are hitherto an exception; but, to the humiliation of human nature, they show very often that they are like other men. The people in America have now the best opportunity and the greatest trust in their hands that Providence ever committed to so small a number since the transgression of the first pair; if they betray their trust, their guilt will merit even greater punishment than other nations have suffered and the indignation of Heaven. If there is one certain truth to be collected from the history of all ages, it is this: that the people's rights and liberties and the democratical mixture in a constitution can never be preserved without a strong executive, or, in other words, without separating the executive from the legislative power. If the executive power or any considerable part of it is left in the hands either of an aristocratical or a democratical assembly, it will corrupt the legislature as necessarily as rust corrupts iron or as arsenic poisons the human body; and when the legislature is corrupted, the people are undone.

The rich, the well-born, and the able acquire an influence among the people that will soon be too much for simple honesty and plain sense in a house of representatives. The most illustrious of them must, therefore, be separated from the mass and placed by themselves in a senate; this is, to all honest and useful intents, an ostracism. A member of a senate of immense wealth, the most respected birth, and transcendent abilities has no influence in the nation in comparison of what he would have in a single representative assembly. When a senate exists, the most powerful man in the state may be safely admitted into the house of representatives because the people have it in their power to remove him into the senate as soon as his influence becomes dangerous. The senate becomes the great object of ambition and the richest and the most sagacious wish to merit an advancement to it by services to the public in the house. When he has obtained the object of his wishes, you may still hope for the benefits of his exertions without dreading his passions; for the executive power being in other hands, he has lost much of his influence with the people and can govern very few votes more than his own among the senators.

It was the general opinion of ancient nations that the Divinity alone was adequate to the important office of giving laws to men. The Greeks entertained this prejudice throughout all their dispersions; the Romans cultivated the same popular delusion; and modern nations, in the consecration of kings and in several superstitious chimeras of divine right in princes and nobles, are nearly unanimous in preserving remnants of it. Even the venerable magistrates of Amersfort devoutly believe themselves God's vice-regents. Is it that obedience to the laws can be obtained from mankind in no other manner? Are the jealousy of power and the envy of superiority so strong in all men that no considerations of public or private utility are sufficient to engage their submission to rules for their own happiness? Or is the disposition to imposture so prevalent in men of experience that their private views of ambition and avarice can be accomplished only by artifice? It was a tradition in antiquity that the laws of Crete were dictated to Minos by the inspiration of Jupiter. This legislator and his brother Rhadamanthus were both his sons; once in nine years they went to converse with their father, to propose questions concerning the wants of the people; and his answers were recorded as laws for their government. The laws of Lacedæmon were communicated by Apollo to Lycurgus; and, lest the meaning of the deity should not have been perfectly comprehended or correctly expressed, they were afterwards confirmed by his oracle at Delphos. Among the Romans Numa was indebted for those laws which procured the prosperity of his country to his conversations with Egeria. The Greeks imported these mysteries from Egypt and the East, whose despotisms from the remotest antiquity to this day have been founded in the same solemn empiricism, their emperors and nobles being all descended from their gods. Woden and Thor were divinities too; and their posterity ruled a thousand years in the north by the strength of a like credulity. Manco Capac was the child of the sun, the visible deity of the Peruvians, and transmitted his divinity, as well as his earthly dignity and authority, through a line of Incas. And the rudest tribes of savages in North America have certain families from which their leaders are always chosen under the immediate protection of the god War. There is nothing in which mankind have been more unanimous; yet nothing can be inferred from it more than this, that the multitude have always been credulous and the few are always artful.

The United States of America have exhibited, perhaps, the first example of governments erected on the simple principles of nature; and if men are now sufficiently enlightened to disabuse themselves of artifice, imposture, hypocrisy, and superstition, they will consider this event as an era in their history. Although the detail of the formation of the American governments is at present little known or regarded either in Europe or in America, it may hereafter become an object of curiosity. It will never be pretended that any persons employed in that service had interviews with the gods or were in any degree under the inspiration of Heaven, more than those at work upon ships or houses, or laboring in merchandise or agriculture; it will forever be acknowledged that these governments were contrived merely by the use of reason and the senses, as Copley painted Chatham; West, Wolf; and Trumbull, Warren and Montgomery; as Dwight, Barlow, Trumbull, and Humphries composed their verse, and Belknap and Ramsay history; as Godfrey invented his quadrant, and Rittenhouse his planetarium; as Boylston practised inoculation, and Franklin electricity; as Paine exposed the mistakes of Raynal, and Jefferson those of Buffon, so unphilosophically borrowed from the despicable dreams of De Pau.[7] Neither the people nor their conventions, committees, or subcommittees considered legislation in any other light than as ordinary arts and sciences, only more important. Called without expectation and compelled without previous inclination, though undoubtedly at the best period

[7] *Recherches philosophiques sur les Américains.*

of time, both for England and America, suddenly to erect new systems of laws for their future government, they adopted the method of a wise architect in erecting a new palace for the residence of his sovereign. They determined to consult Vitruvius, Palladio, and all other writers of reputation in the art; to examine the most celebrated buildings, whether they remain entire or in ruins; to compare these with the principles of writers; and to inquire how far both the theories and models were founded in nature or created by fancy; and when this was done, so far as their circumstances would allow, to adopt the advantages and reject the inconveniences of all. Unembarrassed by attachments to noble families, hereditary lines and successions, or any considerations of royal blood, even the pious mystery of holy oil had no more influence than that other one of holy water. The people were universally too enlightened to be imposed on by artifice; and their leaders, or more properly followers, were men of too much honor to attempt it. Thirteen governments thus founded on the natural authority of the people alone, without a pretense of miracle or mystery, and which are destined to spread over the northern part of that whole quarter of the globe, are a great point gained in favor of the rights of mankind. The experiment is made and has completely succeeded; it can no longer be called in question whether authority in magistrates and obedience of citizens can be grounded on reason, morality, and the Christian religion, without the monkery of priests or the knavery of politicians. As the writer was personally acquainted with most of the gentlemen in each of the states who had the principal share in the first draughts, the following work was really written to lay before the public a specimen of that kind of reading and reasoning which produced the American constitutions.

It is not a little surprising that all this kind of learning should have been unknown to any illustrious philosopher and statesman, and especially one who really was what he has been often called, "a well of science." But if he could be unacquainted with it or it could have escaped his memory, we may suppose millions in America have occasion to be reminded of it. The writer has long seen with anxiety the facility with which philosophers of greatest name have undertaken to write of American affairs without knowing anything of them and have echoed and reëchoed each other's visionary language. Having neither talents, leisure, nor inclination to meet such champions in the field of literary controversy, he little thought of venturing to propose to them any questions. Circumstances, however, have lately occurred which seem to require that some notice should be taken of one of them. If the publication of these papers should contribute anything to turn the attention of the younger gentlemen of letters in America to this kind of inquiry, it will produce an effect of some importance to their country. The subject is the most interesting that can engage the understanding or the heart; for whether the end of man, in this stage of his existence, be enjoyment, or improvement, or both, it can never be attained so well in a bad government as a good one. . . .

If Cicero and Tacitus could revisit the earth and learn that the English nation had reduced the great idea [8] to practice and brought it nearly to perfection by giving each division a power to defend itself by a negative; had found it the most solid and durable government, as well as the most free; had obtained by means of it a prosperity among civilized nations in an enlightened age like that of the Romans among barbarians; and that the Americans, after having enjoyed the benefits of such a constitution a century and a half, were advised by some of the greatest philosophers and politicians of the age to renounce it and set up the governments of ancient Goths and modern Indians—what would they say? That the Americans would be more reprehensible than the Cappadocians, if they should listen to such advice.

It would have been much to the purpose to have inserted a more accurate investigation of the form of government of the ancient Germans and modern Indians; in both, the existence of

---

[8] "Id enim tenetote, quod initio dixi, nisi aequabilis haec in civitate compensatio sit et juris et officii et muneris, ut et potestatis satis in magistratibus, et auctoritatis in principum consilio, et libertatis in populo sit, non posse hunc incommutabilem rei publicae conservari statum." *De Republica.*d

the three divisions of power is marked with a precision that excludes all controversy. The democratical branch especially is so determined that the real sovereignty resided in the body of the people and was exercised in the assembly of king, nobles, and commons together. These institutions really collected all authority into one center of kings, nobles and people. But, small as their numbers and narrow as their territories were, the consequence was confusion; each part believed it governed the whole; the chiefs thought they were sovereigns; the nobles believed the power to be in their hands; and the people flattered themselves that all depended upon them. Their purposes were well enough answered, without coming to an explanation, so long as they were few in number and had no property; but when spread over large provinces of the Roman empire, now the great kingdoms of Europe, and grown populous and rich, they found the inconvenience of each not knowing its place. Kings, nobles, and people claimed the government in turn; and after all the turbulence, wars, and revolutions which compose the history of Europe for so many ages, we find simple monarchies established everywhere. Whether the system will now become stationary and last forever by means of a few further improvements in monarchical government, we know not; or whether still further revolutions are to come. The most probable, or rather the only probable change is the introduction of democratical branches into those governments. If the people should ever aim at more, they will defeat themselves; as they will, indeed, if they aim at this by any other than gentle means and by gradual advances, by improvements in general education, and by informing the public mind.

The systems of legislators are experiments made on human life and manners, society and government. Zoroaster, Confucius, Mithras, Odin, Thor, Mahomet, Lycurgus, Solon, Romulus, and a thousand others may be compared to philosophers making experiments on the elements. Unhappily, political experiments cannot be made in a laboratory, nor determined in a few hours. The operation, once begun, runs over whole quarters of the globe and is not finished in many thousands of years. The experiment of Lycurgus lasted seven hundred years but never spread beyond the limits of Laconia. The process of Solon expired in one century;

that of Romulus lasted but two centuries and a half; but the Teutonic institutions, described by Caesar and Tacitus, are the most memorable experiment, merely political, ever yet made in human affairs. They have spread all over Europe and have lasted eighteen hundred years. They afford the strongest argument that can be imagined in support of the position assumed in these volumes. Nothing ought to have more weight with America to determine her judgment against mixing the authority of the one, the few, and the many confusedly in one assembly than the widespread miseries and final slavery of almost all mankind in consequence of such an ignorant policy in the ancient Germans. What is the ingredient which in England has preserved the democratical authority? The balance, and that only. The English have in reality blended together the feudal institutions with those of the Greeks and Romans and out of all have made that noble composition which avoids the inconveniences and retains the advantages of both.

The institutions now made in America will not wholly wear out for thousands of years. It is of the last importance, then, that they should begin right. If they set out wrong, they will never be able to return, unless it be by accident, to the right path. After having known the history of Europe and of England in particular, it would be the height of folly to go back to the institutions of Woden and of Thor, as the Americans are advised to do. If they had been counselled to adopt a single monarchy at once, it would have been less mysterious.

Robertson, Hume, and Gibbon have given such admirable accounts of the feudal institutions and their consequences that it would have been, perhaps, more discreet to have referred to them without saying anything more upon the subject. To collect together the legislation of the Indians would take up much room but would be well worth the pains. The sovereignty is in the nation, it is true, but the three powers are strong in every tribe; and their royal and aristocratical dignities are much more generally hereditary, from the popular partiality to particular families and the superstitious opinion that such are favorites of the God of War, than late writers upon this subject have allowed.

GROSVENOR SQUARE, January 1, 1787.

PRELIMINARY OBSERVATIONS

Three writers in Europe of great abilities, reputation, and learning—M. Turgot, the Abbé de Mably, and Dr. Price—have turned their attention to the constitutions of government in the United States of America and have written and published their criticisms and advice. They all had the most amiable characters and unquestionably the purest intentions. They all had experience in public affairs and ample information respecting the nature of man, the necessities of society, and the science of government.

There are in the productions of all of them, among many excellent things, some sentiments, however, that it will be difficult to reconcile to reason, experience, the constitution of human nature, or to the uniform testimony of the greatest statesmen, legislators, and philosophers of all enlightened nations, ancient and modern.

M. Turgot, in his letter to Dr. Price, confesses, "that he is not satisfied with the constitutions which have hitherto been formed for the different states of America." He observes, "that by most of them the customs of England are imitated, without any particular motive. Instead of collecting all authority into one center, that of the nation, they have established different bodies, a body of representatives, a council, and a governor, because there is in England a house of commons, a house of lords, and a king. They endeavor to balance these different powers as if this equilibrium, which in England may be a necessary check to the enormous influence of royalty, could be of any use in republics founded upon the equality of all the citizens, and as if establishing different orders of men was not a source of divisions and disputes."

There has been, from the beginning of the revolution in America, a party in every state who have entertained sentiments similar to these of M. Turgot. Two or three of them have established governments upon his principle; and, by advices from Boston, certain committees of counties have been held and other conventions proposed in the Massachusetts with the express purpose of deposing the governor and senate as useless and expensive branches of the constitution; and as it is probable that the publication of M. Turgot's opinion has contributed to excite such discontents among the people, it becomes necessary to examine it, and, if it can be shown to be an error, whatever veneration the Americans very justly entertain for his memory, it is to be hoped they will not be misled by his authority.

M. Turgot is offended because the customs of England are imitated in most of the new constitutions in America without any particular motive. But if we suppose English customs to be neither good nor evil in themselves and merely indifferent; and the people by their birth, education, and habits were familiarly attached to them—would not this be a motive particular enough for their preservation rather than to endanger the public tranquility or unanimity by renouncing them? If those customs were wise, just, and good, and calculated to secure the liberty, property, and safety of the people as well or better than any other institutions, ancient or modern, would M. Turgot have advised the nation to reject them merely because it was at that time justly incensed against the English government? What English customs has it retained which may with any propriety be called evil? M. Turgot has instanced only one, namely, "that a body of representatives, a council, and a governor have been established because there is in England a house of commons, a house of lords, and a king." It was not so much because the legislature in England consisted of three branches, that such a division of power was adopted by the states, as because their own assemblies had ever been so constituted. It was not so much from attachment by habit to such a plan of power that it was continued as from conviction that it was founded in nature and reason.

M. Turgot seems to be of a different opinion and is for "collecting all authority into one center, the nation." It is easily understood how all authority may be collected into "one center" in a despot or monarch; but how it can be done when the center is to be the nation is more difficult to comprehend. Before we attempt to discuss the notions of an author, we should be careful to ascertain his meaning. It will not be easy, after the most anxious research, to discover the true sense of this extraordinary passage. If after the pains of "collecting all authority into one center," that center is to be the nation, we shall remain exactly where we began and no collection of authority at all will be made. The nation will be the authority, and the authority the nation. The center will be the circle, and the circle the center. When a number of men, women, and children are simply congregated together there is no political authority among them; nor any natural authority but that of parents over their children. To leave the women and children out of the question for the present, the men will all be equal, free, and independent of each other. Not one will have any authority over any other. The first "collection" of authority must be an unanimous agreement to form themselves into a *nation, people, community,* or *body politic* and to be governed by the majority of suffrages or voices. But even in this case, although the authority is collected into one center, that center is no longer the nation but the majority of the nation. Did M. Turgot mean that the people of Virginia, for example, half a million of souls scattered over a territory of two hundred leagues square, should stop here and have no other authority by which to make or execute a law or judge a cause but by a vote of the whole people and the decision of a majority! Where is the plain large enough to hold them; and what are the means, and how long would be the time, necessary to assemble them together?

A simple and perfect democracy never yet existed among men. If a village of half a mile square and one hundred families is capable of exercising all the legislative, executive, and judicial powers in public assemblies of the whole by unanimous votes or by majorities, it is more than has ever yet been proved in theory or experience. In such a democracy, for the most part, the moderator would be king, the town-clerk legislator and judge, and the constable sheriff; and, upon more important occasions, committees would be only the counsellors of both the former and commanders of the latter.

Shall we suppose, then, that M. Turgot intended that an assembly of representatives should be chosen by the nation and vested with all the powers of government; and that this assembly should be the center in which all the authority was to be collected and should be virtually deemed the nation? After long reflection I have not been able to discover any other sense in his words, and this was probably his real meaning. To examine this system in detail may be thought as trifling an occupation as the labored reasonings of Sidney and Locke to show the absurdity of Filmer's superstitious notions appeared to Mr. Hume to be in his enlightened day. Yet the mistakes of great men and even the absurdities of fools, when they countenance the prejudices of numbers of people, especially in a young country and under new governments, cannot be too fully confuted. I shall not then esteem my time misspent in placing this idea of M. Turgot in all its lights, in considering the consequences of it, and in collecting a variety of authorities against it.

OF MODERN DEMOCRATIC REPUBLICS

RECAPITULATION

As we have taken a cursory view of those countries in Europe where the government may be called, in any reasonable construction of the word, republican, let us now pause a few moments and reflect upon what we have seen.

Among every people and in every species of republics, we have constantly found *a first magistrate, a head, a chief,* under various denominations, indeed, and with different degrees of authority, with the title of stadtholder, burgomaster, avoyer, doge, gonfaloniero, president, syndic, mayor, alcalde, capitaneo, governor, or king; in every nation we have met with a distinguished officer. If there is no example, then, in any free government any more than in those which are not free of a society without a principal personage, we may fairly conclude that the body politic cannot subsist, any more than the animal body, without a head. If M. Turgot had made any discovery which had escaped the penetration of all the legislators and philosophers who have lived before him, he ought at least to have communicated it to the world for their improvement; but as he has never hinted at any such invention, we may safely conclude that he had none and, therefore, that the Americans are not justly liable to censure for instituting *governors*.

In every form of government we have seen a *senate* or *little council*, a composition, generally, of those officers of state who have the most experience and power and of a few other members selected from the highest ranks and most illustrious reputations. On these lesser councils, with the first magistrate at their head, generally rests the principal burden of administration, a share in the legislative as well as executive and judicial authority of government. The admission of such senates to a participation of these three kinds of power has been generally observed to produce in the minds of their members an ardent aristocratical ambition, grasping equally at the prerogatives of the first magistrate and the privileges of the people and ending in the nobility of a few families and a tyrannical oligarchy. But in those states where the senates have been debarred from all executive power and confined to the legislative, they have been observed to be firm barriers against the encroachments of the crown and often great supporters of the liberties of the people. The Americans, then, who have carefully confined their senates to the legislative power, have done wisely in adopting them.

We have seen in every instance another and a larger assembly, composed of the body of the people in some little states, of representatives chosen by the people in others, of members appointed by the senate and supposed to represent the people in a third sort, and of persons appointed by themselves or the senate in certain aristocracies to prevent them from becoming oligarchies. The Americans, then, whose assemblies are the most adequate, proportional, and equitable representations of the people that are known in the world, will not be thought mistaken in appointing houses of representatives.

In every republic—in the smallest and most popular, in the larger and more aristocratical, as well as in the largest and most monarchical—we have observed a multitude of curious and ingenious inventions to balance, in their turn, all those powers, to check the passions peculiar to them, and to control them from rushing into those exorbitancies to which they are most addicted.

The Americans will then be no longer censured for endeavoring to introduce an equilibrium which is much more profoundly meditated and much more effectual for the protection of the laws than any we have seen, except in England. We may even question whether that is an exception.

In every country we have found a variety of *orders* with very great distinctions. In America there are different orders of *offices,* but none of *men.* Out of office, all men are of the same species and of one blood; there is neither a greater nor a lesser nobility. Why, then, are the Americans accused of establishing different orders of men? To our inexpressible mortification we must have observed that the people have preserved a share of power or an existence in the government in no country out of England except upon the tops of a few inaccessible mountains, among rocks and precipices, in territories so narrow that you may span them with a hand's breadth, where, living unenvied, in extreme poverty, chiefly upon pasturage, destitute of manufactures and commerce, they still exhibit the most charming picture of life and the most dignified character of human nature.[11]

Wherever we have seen a territory somewhat larger, arts and sciences more cultivated, commerce flourishing, or even agriculture improved to any great degree, an aristocracy has risen up in a course of time, consisting of a few rich and honorable families who have united with each other against both the people and the first magistrate, who have wrested from the former by art and by force all their participation in the government and have even inspired them with so mean an esteem of themselves and so deep a veneration and strong attachment to their rulers as to believe and confess them a superior order of beings.

We have seen these noble families, although necessitated to have a head, extremely jealous of his influence, anxious to reduce his power, and to constrain him to as near a level as possible with themselves, always endeavoring to establish a rotation by which they may all equally be entitled in turn to the preëminence, and likewise anxious to preserve to themselves as large a share

[11] [Reference is to the republic of San Marino.]

as possible of power in the executive and judicial, as well as the legislative departments of the state.

These patrician families have also appeared in every instance to be equally jealous of each other and to have contrived by blending lot and choice, by mixing various bodies in the elections to the same offices, and even by a resort to the horrors of an inquisition, to guard against the sin that so easily besets them, of being wholly influenced and governed by a junto or oligarchy of a few among themselves.

We have seen no one government in which is a distinct separation of the legislative from the executive power and of the judicial from both, or in which any attempt has been made to balance these powers with one another, or to form an equilibrium between the one, the few, and the many, for the purpose of enacting and executing equal laws by common consent for the general interest, excepting in England.

Shall we conclude from these melancholy observations that human nature is incapable of liberty, that no honest equality can be preserved in society, and that such forcible causes are always at work as must reduce all men to a submission to despotism, monarchy, oligarchy, or aristocracy?

By no means. We have seen one of the first nations in Europe, possessed of ample and fertile territories at home and extensive dominions abroad, of a commerce with the whole world, immense wealth, and the greatest naval power which ever belonged to any nation, which has still preserved the power of the people by the equilibrium we are contending for, by the trial by jury, and by constantly refusing a standing army. The people of England alone, by preserving their share in the legislature at the expense of the blood of heroes and patriots, have enabled their king to curb the nobility without giving him a standing army.

After all, let us compare every constitution we have seen with those of the United States of America, and we shall have no reason to blush for our country. On the contrary, we shall feel the strongest motives to fall upon our knees in gratitude to heaven for having been graciously pleased to give us birth and education in that country and for having destined us to live under her laws! We shall have reason to exult if we make our comparison with England and the English constitution. Our people are undoubtedly sovereign; all the landed and other property is in the hands of the citizens; not only their representatives but their senators and governors are annually chosen; there are no hereditary titles, honors, offices, or distinctions; the legislative, executive, and judicial powers are carefully separated from each other; the powers of the one, the few, and the many are nicely balanced in the legislatures; trials by jury are preserved in all their glory, and there is no standing army; the *habeas corpus* is in full force; the press is the most free in the world. Where all these circumstances take place, it is unnecessary to add that the laws alone can govern.

OPINIONS OF PHILOSOPHERS

DR. SWIFT

The authority of legislators and philosophers, in support of the system we contend for, is not difficult to find. The greatest lights of humanity, ancient and modern, have approved it, which renders it difficult to explain how it comes in this enlightened age to be called in question, as it certainly has been, by others as well as M. Turgot. I shall begin with one who, though seldom quoted as a legislator, appears to have considered this subject and to have furnished arguments enough forever to determine the question. Dr. Swift observes,[12] "that the best legislators of all ages agree in this, that the absolute power, which originally is in the whole body, is 'a trust too great to be committed to any one man or assembly'; and, therefore, in their several institutions of government, power, in the last resort, was always placed by them in balance among the one, the few, and the many; 'and

[12] *A Discourse of the Contests and Dissensions between the Nobles and Commons of Athens and Rome, with the Consequences they had upon both those States.*

Much of the substance of this, the best of all the political tracts of Dean Swift, is given in the text.—C. F. A.

it will be an eternal rule in politics among every free people that there is a balance of power to be carefully held by every state within itself.' . . ."

"The true meaning of a balance of power is best conceived by considering what the nature of a balance is. It supposes three things—first, the part which is held, together with the hand that holds it; and then the two scales with whatever is weighed therein. . . . In a state within itself, the balance must be held by a third hand, who is to deal the remaining power with the utmost exactness into the several scales. . . . The balance may be held by the weakest, who, by his address and conduct, removing from either scale and adding of his own, may keep the scales duly poised.

"When the balance is broken by mighty weights fallen into either scale, the power will never continue long in equal division between the two remaining parties; but, till the balance is fixed anew, will run entirely into one." This is made to appear by the examples of the Decemviri in Rome, the Ephori in Sparta, the four hundred in Athens, the thirty in Athens, and the Dominatio Plebis in Carthage and Argos. . . .

It is "an error to think it an uncontrollable maxim that power is always safer lodged in many hands than in one; for if these many hands be made up only from one of those three divisions, it is plain, from the examples produced and easy to be paralleled in other ages and countries, that they are as capable of enslaving the nation and of acting all manner of tyranny and oppression as it is possible for a single person to be, though we should suppose their number not only to be of four or five hundred but above three thousand.

"In order to preserve a balance in a mixed state, the limits of power deposited with each party ought to be ascertained and generally known. The defect of this is the cause that introduces those strugglings in a state about prerogative and liberty, about encroachments of the few upon the rights of the many, and of the many upon the privileges of the few, which ever did, and ever will, conclude in a tyranny—first, either of the few or the many, but at last, infallibly, of a *single person*; for, whichever of the three divisions in a state is upon the scramble for more power than its own (as one or other of them generally is), unless due care be taken by the other two, upon every new question that arises, they will be sure to decide in favor of themselves, talk much of inherent right; they will nourish up a dormant power and reserve privileges *in petto* to exert upon occasions, to serve expedients, and to urge upon necessities; they will make large demands and scanty concessions, ever coming off considerable gainers. Thus, at length, the balance is broken and tyranny let in, from which door of the three it matters not.

"The desires of men are not only exorbitant but endless; they grasp at all and can form no scheme of perfect happiness with less. Ever since men have been united into governments, the hopes and endeavors after universal monarchy have been bandied among them. . . . The Athenians, the Spartans, the Thebans, and the Achaians several times aimed at the universal monarchy of Greece; the commonwealths of Carthage and Rome affected the universal monarchy of the then known world. In like manner has absolute power been pursued by the several parties of each particular state; wherein single persons have met with most success though the endeavors of the few and the many have been frequent enough; yet, being neither so uniform in their designs nor so direct in their views, they neither could manage nor maintain the power they had got but were deceived by the popularity and ambition of some single person. So that it will be always a wrong step in policy for the nobles and commons to carry their endeavors after power so far as to overthrow the balance.

"With all respect for popular assemblies be it spoken, it is hard to recollect one folly, infirmity, or vice to which a single man is subject and from which a body of commons, either collective or represented, can be wholly exempt. . . . Whence it comes to pass that in their results have sometimes been found the same spirit of cruelty and revenge, of malice and pride; the same blindness, and obstinacy, and unsteadiness; the same ungovernable rage and anger; the same injustice, sophistry, and fraud that ever lodged in the breast of any individual.

"When a child grows easy and content by being humored, and when a lover becomes satisfied by small compliances without further pursuits, then expect to find popular assemblies content with small concessions. If there could one single example be brought from the whole compass of history of any one popular assembly who after beginning to contend for power ever sat down quietly with a certain share, or of one that ever knew, or proposed, or declared what share of power was their due, then might there be some hopes that it were a matter to be adjusted by reasonings, conferences, or debates.

"A usurping populace is its own dupe, a mere under-worker, and a purchaser in trust for some single tyrant, whose state and power they advance to their own ruin with as blind an instinct as those worms that die with weaving magnificent habits for beings of a superior order to their own.

"The people are much more dexterous at pulling down and setting up than at preserving what is fixed; and they are not fonder of seizing more than their own than they are of delivering it up again to the *worst bidder*, with their own into the bargain. For although in their corrupt notions of divine worship they are apt to multiply their gods; yet their earthly devotion is seldom paid to above one idol at a time, of their own creation, whose oar they pull with less murmuring and much more skill than when they *share the leading* or even *hold the helm*."

It will be perceived by the style that it is Dr. Swift that has been speaking; otherwise the reader might have been deceived and imagined that I was entertaining him with further reflections upon the short account previously given in these letters of the modern republics. There is not an observation here that is not justified by the history of every government we have considered. How much more maturely had this writer weighed the subject than M. Turgot! Perhaps there are not to be found in any library so many accurate ideas of government, expressed with so much perspicuity, brevity, and precision. . . .

RECAPITULATION

. . Let us now return to M. Turgot's idea of a government consisting in a single assembly. He tells us our republics are "founded on the equality of all the citizens, and, therefore, 'orders' and 'equilibriums' are unnecessary and occasion disputes." But what are we to understand here by equality? Are the citizens to be all of the same age, sex, size, strength, stature, activity, courage, hardiness, industry, patience, ingenuity, wealth, knowledge, fame, wit, temperance, constancy, and wisdom? Was there, or will there ever be, a nation whose individuals were all equal in natural and acquired qualities, in virtues, talents, and riches? The answer of all mankind must be in the negative. It must then be acknowledged that in every state, in the Massachusetts, for example, there are inequalities which God and nature have planted there, and which no human legislator ever can eradicate. I should have chosen to have mentioned Virginia, as the most ancient state, or indeed any other in the union rather than the one that gave me birth, if I were not afraid of putting suppositions which may give offense, a liberty which my neighbors will pardon. Yet I shall say nothing that is not applicable to all the other twelve.

In this society of Massachusettensians then there is, it is true, a moral and political equality of rights and duties among all the individuals and as yet no appearance of artificial inequalities of conditions, such as hereditary dignities, titles, magistracies, or legal distinctions; and no established marks, as stars, garters, crosses, or ribbons; there are, nevertheless, inequalities of great moment in the consideration of a legislator, because they have a natural and inevitable influence in society. Let us enumerate some of them: 1. There is an inequality of wealth; some individuals, whether by descent from their ancestors or from greater skill, industry, and success in business, have estates both in lands and goods of great value; others have no property at all; and of all the rest of society, much the greater number are possessed of wealth in all the variety of degrees between these extremes; it will easily be conceived that all the rich men will have many of the poor in the various trades, manufactures, and other occupations in life dependent upon them for their daily bread; many of smaller fortunes will be in their debt and in many ways under obligations to them; others, in better circumstances, neither dependent nor in debt, men of letters, men of the learned professions, and others, from acquaintance, conversation, and civilities, will be connected with them and attached to them. Nay, further, it will not be denied that among the wisest people that live there is a degree of admiration, abstracted from all dependence, obligation, expectation, or even acquaintance, which accompanies splendid wealth, insures some respect, and bestows some influence. 2. Birth. Let no man be surprised that this species of inequality is introduced here. Let the page in history be quoted where any nation, ancient or modern, civilized or savage, is mentioned, among whom no difference was made between the citizens on account of their extraction. The truth is that more influence is allowed to this advantage in free republics than in despotic governments, or than would be allowed to it in simple monarchies, if severe laws had not been made from age to age to secure it. The children of illustrious families have generally greater advantages of education and earlier opportunities to be acquainted with public characters and informed of public affairs than those of meaner ones, or even than those in middle life; and what is more than all, an habitual national veneration for their names and the characters of their ancestors, described in history or coming down by tradition, removes them farther from vulgar jealousy and popular envy and secures them in some degree the favor, the affection, and respect of the public. Will any man pretend that the name of Andros and that of Winthrop are heard with the same sensations in any village of New England? Is not gratitude the sentiment that attends the latter and disgust the feeling excited by the former? In the Massachusetts, then, there are persons descended from some of their ancient governors, counsellors, judges, whose fathers, grandfathers, and great-grandfathers are remembered with esteem by many living, and who are mentioned in history with applause as benefactors to the country, while there are others who have no such advantage. May we go a step further—Know thyself is as useful a precept to nations as to men. Go into every village in New England, and you will find that the office of justice of the peace, and even the place of representative, which has ever depended only on the freest election of the people, have generally descended from generation to generation in three or four families at most. The present subject is one of those which all men respect and all men deride. It may be said of this part of our nature, as Pope said of the whole:

> Of human nature, wit her worst may write,
> We all revere it in our own despite.

If, as Harrington says, the ten commandments were voted by the people of Israel and have been enacted as laws by all other nations; and if we should presume to say that nations had a civil right to repeal them, no nation would think proper to repeal the fifth, which enjoins honor to parents. If there is a difference between right and wrong, if anything can be sacred, if there is one idea of moral obligation, the decree of nature must force upon every thinking being and upon every feeling heart the conviction that honor, affection, and gratitude are due from children to those who gave them birth, nurture, and education. The sentiments and affections which naturally arise from reflecting on the love, the cares, and the blessings of parents, abstracted from the consideration of duty, are some of the most forcible and most universal. When religion, law, morals, affection, and even fashion thus conspire to fill every mind with attachment to parents and to stamp deep upon the heart their impressions, is it to be expected that men should reverence their parents while they live and begin to despise or neglect their memories as soon as they are dead? This is in nature impossible. On the contrary, every little unkindness and severity is forgotten, and nothing but endearments remembered with pleasure.

The son of a wise and virtuous father finds the world about him sometimes as much disposed as he himself is to honor the memory of his father, to congratulate him as the successor to his estate, and frequently to compliment him with elections to the offices he held. A sense of duty, his passions, and his interest thus conspiring to prevail upon him to avail himself of this advantage, he finds a few others in similar circumstances with himself; they naturally associate together and aid each other. This is a faint sketch of the source and rise of the family spirit; very often the disposition to favor the family is as strong in the town, county, province, or kingdom as it is in the house itself. The enthusiasm is indeed sometimes wilder and carries away, like a torrent, all before it.

These observations are not peculiar to any age; we have seen the effects of them in San Marino, Biscay, and the Grisons, as well as in Poland and all other countries. Not to mention any notable examples which have lately happened near us, it is not many months since I was witness to a conversation between some citizens of Massachusetts. One was haranguing on the jealousy which a free people ought to entertain of their liberties and was heard by all the company with pleasure. In less than ten minutes the conversation turned upon their governor; and the jealous republican was very angry at the opposition to him. "The present governor," says he, "has done us such services that he ought to rule us, he and his posterity after him, for ever and ever." "Where is your jealousy of liberty?" demanded the other. "Upon my honor," replies the orator, "I had forgot that; you have caught me in an inconsistency; for I cannot know whether a child of five years old will be a son of liberty or a tyrant." His jealousy was the dictate of his understanding. His confidence and enthusiasm the impulse of his heart.

The pompous trumpery of ensigns, armorials, and escutcheons are not, indeed, far advanced in America. Yet there is a more general anxiety to know their originals, in proportion to their numbers, than in any nation of Europe, arising from the easier circumstances and higher spirit of the common people. And there are certain families in every state equally attentive to all the proud frivolities of heraldry. That kind of pride which looks down on commerce and manufactures as degrading may, indeed, in many countries of Europe be a useful and necessary quality in the nobility. It may prevent, in some degree, the whole nation from being entirely delivered up to the spirit of avarice. It may be the cause why honor is preferred by some to money. It may prevent the nobility from becoming too rich and acquiring too large a proportion of the landed property. In America, it would not only be mischievous, but would expose the highest pretensions of the kind to universal ridicule and contempt. Those other hauteurs, of keeping the commons at a distance and disdaining to converse with any but a few of a certain race, may in Europe be a favor to the people by relieving them from a multitude of assiduous attentions and humiliating compliances, which would be troublesome. It may prevent the nobles from caballing with the people and gaining too much influence with them in elections and otherwise. In America it would justly excite universal indignation; the vainest of all must be of the people or be nothing. While every office is equally open to every competitor and the people must decide upon every pretension to a place in the legislature, that of governor and senator as well as representative, no such airs will ever be endured. At the same time it must be acknowledged that some men must take more pains to deserve and acquire an office than others and must behave better in it, or they will not hold it.

We cannot presume that a man is good or bad merely because his father was one or the other; and we should always inform ourselves first whether the virtues and talents are inherited before we yield our confidence. Wise men beget fools, and honest men knaves; but these instances, although they may be frequent, are not general. If there is often a likeness in feature and figure, there is generally more in mind and heart because education contributes to the formation of these as well as nature. The influence of example is very great and almost universal, especially that of parents over their children. In all countries it has been observed that vices as well as virtues very often run down in families from age to age. Any man may go over in his thoughts the circle of his acquaintance, and he will probably recollect instances of a disposition to mischief, malice, and revenge, descending in certain breeds from grandfather to father and son. A young woman was lately convicted at Paris of a trifling theft, barely within the law which decreed a capital punishment. There were circumstances, too, which greatly alleviated her fault, some things in her behavior that seemed innocent and modest; every spectator, as well as the judges, was affected at the scene, and she was advised to petition for a pardon, as there was no doubt it would be granted. "No," says she; "my grandfather, father, and brother were all hanged for stealing; it runs in the blood of our family to steal and be hanged. If I am pardoned now, I shall steal again in a few months more inexcusably; and, therefore, I will be hanged now." An hereditary passion for the halter is a strong instance, to be sure, and cannot be very common; but something like it too often descends in certain breeds from generation to generation.

If vice and infamy are thus rendered less odious by being familiar in a family, by the example of parents and by education, it would be as unhappy as unaccountable if virtue and honor were not recommended and rendered more amiable to children by the same means.

There are, and always have been, in every state, numbers possessed of some degree of family pride, who have been invariably encouraged, if not flattered in it, by the people. These have most acquaintance, esteem, and friendship with each other and mutually aid each other's schemes of interest, convenience, and ambition. Fortune, it is true, has more influence than birth. A rich man of an ordinary family and common decorum of conduct may have greater weight than any family merit commonly confers without it.

It will be readily admitted there are great inequalities of merit, or talents, virtues, services, and what is of more moment, very often of reputation. Some in a long course of service in an army have devoted their time, health, and fortunes, signalized their courage and address, exposed themselves to hardships and dangers, lost their limbs, and shed their blood for the people. Others have displayed their wisdom, learning, and eloquence in council and in various other ways acquired the confidence and affection of their fellow citizens to such a degree that the public have settled into a kind of habit of following their example and taking their advice.

There are a few in whom all these advantages of birth, fortune, and fame are united.

These sources of inequality, which are common to every people and can never be altered by any because they are founded in the constitution of nature—this natural aristocracy among mankind has been dilated on because it is a fact essential to be considered in the institution of a government. It forms a body of men which contains the greatest collection of virtues and abilities in a free government, is the brightest ornament and glory of the nation, and may always be made the greatest blessing of society if it be judiciously managed in the constitution. But if this be not done, it is always the most dangerous; nay, it may be added, it never fails to be the destruction of the commonwealth.

What shall be done to guard against it? Shall they be all massacred? This experiment has been more than once attempted, and once at least executed. Guy Faux attempted it in England; and a king of Denmark,[13] aided by a popular party, effected it once in Sweden; but it answered no good end. The moment they were dead another aristocracy instantly arose, with equal art and influence, with less delicacy and discretion, if not principle, and behaved more intolerably than the former. The country for centuries never recovered from the ruinous consequences of a deed so horrible that one would think it only to be met with in the history of the kingdom of darkness.

There is but one expedient yet discovered to avail the society of all the benefits from this body of men which they are capable of affording, and at the same time to prevent them from undermining or invading the public liberty; and that is to throw them all, or at least the most remarkable of them, into one assembly together, in the legislature; to keep all the executive power entirely out of their hands as a body; to erect a first magistrate over them, invested with the whole executive authority; to make them dependent on that executive magistrate for all public executive employments; to give that first magistrate a negative on the legislature, by which he may defend both himself and the people from all their enterprises in the legislature; and to erect on the

---

[13] This is an allusion to the massacre of Stockholm, committed by Christian II, denominated the Nero of the North.—C. F. A.

other side an impregnable barrier against them in a house of commons, fairly, fully, and adequately representing the people, who shall have the power both of negativing all their attempts at encroachment in the legislature and of withholding from them and from the crown all supplies by which they may be paid for their services in executive offices, or even the public service may be carried on to the detriment of the nation.

We have seen both by reasoning and in experience what kind of equality is to be found or expected in the simplest people in the world. There is not a city nor a village, any more than a kingdom or a commonwealth, in Europe or America; not a horde, clan, or tribe among the Negroes of Africa or the savages of North or South America; nor a private club in the world, in which inequalities are not more or less visible. There is, then, a certain degree of weight, which property, family, and merit will have in the public opinion and deliberations. If M. Turgot had discovered a mode of ascertaining the quantity which they ought to have and had revealed it to mankind, so that it might be known to every citizen, he would have deserved more of gratitude than is due to all the inventions of philosophers. But as long as human nature shall have passions and imaginations, there is too much reason to fear that these advantages in many instances will have more influence than reason and equity can justify.

Let us then reflect, how the single assembly in the Massachusetts, in which our great statesman wishes all authority concentrated, will be composed. There being no senate nor council, all the rich, the honorable, and meritorious will stand candidates for seats in the house of representatives, and nineteen in twenty of them will obtain elections. The house will be found to have all the inequalities in it that prevailed among the people at large. Such an assembly will be naturally divided into three parts. The first is, some great genius—some one masterly spirit who unites in himself all the qualities which constitute the natural foundations of authority, such as benevolence, wisdom, and power, and all the adventitious attractions of respect, such as riches, ancestry, and personal merit. All eyes are turned upon him for president or speaker. The second division comprehends a third, or a quarter, or, if you will, a sixth or an eighth of the whole and consists of those who have the most to boast of resembling their head. In the third class are all the rest, who are nearly on a level in understanding and in all things. Such an assembly has in it, not only all the persons of the nation who are most eminent for parts and virtues, but all those who are most inflamed with ambition and avarice, and who are most vain of their descent. These latter will, of course, constantly endeavor to increase their own influence by exaggerating all the attributes they possess and by augmenting them in every way they can think of, and will have friends whose only chance of rising into public view will be under their protection, who will be even more active and zealous in their service than themselves. Notwithstanding all the equality that can ever be hoped for among men, it is easy to see that the third class will in general be but humble imitators and followers of the second. Every man in the second class will have constantly about him a circle of members of the third, who will be his admirers, perhaps afraid of his influence in the districts they represent, or related to him by blood, or connected with him in trade, or dependent upon him for favors. There will be much envy, too, among individuals of the second class against the speaker, although a sincere veneration is shown him by the majority and great external respect by all. I said there would be envy because there will be among the second class several whose fortunes, families, and merits, in the acknowledged judgment of all, approach near to the first; and from the ordinary illusions of self-love and self-interest they and their friends will be much disposed to claim the first place as their own right. This will introduce controversy and debate as well as emulation; and those who wish for the first place and cannot obtain it will of course endeavor to keep down the speaker as near upon a level with themselves as possible by paring away the dignity and importance of his office, as we saw was the case in Venice, Poland, and, indeed, everywhere else.

A single assembly thus constituted, without any counterpoise, balance, or equilibrium, is to have all authority—legislative, executive, and judicial—concentrated in it. It is to make a constitution and laws by its own will, execute those laws at its own pleasure, and adjudge all controversies that arise concerning the meaning and application of them at its own discretion. What is there to restrain it from making tyrannical laws in order to execute them in a tyrannical manner? Will it be pretended that the jealousy and vigilance of the people and their power to discard them at the next election will restrain them? Even this idea supposes a balance, an equilibrium, which M. Turgot holds in so much contempt; it supposes the people at large to be a check and control over the representative assembly. But this would be found a mere delusion. A jealousy between the electors and the elected neither ought to exist, nor is it possible to exist. It is a contradiction to suppose that a body of electors should have at one moment a warm affection and entire confidence in a man so as to entrust him with authority, limited or unlimited, over their lives and fortunes; and the next moment after his election to commence a suspicion of him that shall prompt them to watch all his words, actions, and motions, and dispose them to renounce and punish him. They choose him, indeed, because they think he knows more and is better disposed than the generality and very often even than themselves. Indeed, the best use of a representative assembly arises from the cordial affection and unreserved confidence which subsists between it and the collective body of the people. It is by such kind and candid intercourse alone that the wants and desires of the people can be made known on the one hand, or the necessities of the public communicated or reconciled to them on the other. In what did such a confidence in one assembly end—in Venice, Geneva, Biscay, Poland—but in an aristocracy and an oligarchy? There is no special providence for Americans, and their nature is the same with that of others. . . .

CONCLUSION

By the authorities and examples already recited you will be convinced that three branches of power have an unalterable foundation in nature; that they exist in every society natural and artificial; and that, if all of them are not acknowledged in any constitution of government, it will be found to be imperfect, unstable, and soon enslaved; that the legislative and executive authorities are naturally distinct; and that liberty and the laws depend entirely on a separation of them in the frame of government; that the legislative power is naturally and necessarily sovereign and supreme over the executive; and, therefore, that the latter must be made an essential branch of the former, even with a negative, or it will not be able to defend itself, but will be soon invaded, undermined, attacked, or in some way or other totally ruined and annihilated by the former. This is applicable to every state in America in its individual capacity; but is it equally applicable to the United States in their federal capacity?

The people of America and their delegates in congress were of opinion that a single assembly was every way adequate to the management of all their federal concerns, and with very good reason, because congress is not a legislative assembly, nor a representative assembly, but only a diplomatic assembly.[14] A single council has been found to answer the purposes of confederacies very well. But in all such cases the deputies are responsible to the states, their authority is clearly ascertained, and the states in

---

[14] This sentence drew from Mr. Jefferson a remonstrating comment. In a letter dated Paris, 23 February, 1787, hitherto unpublished, occurs the following passage, which, in view of the subsequent history of both the parties, is worthy of record.

"I have read your book with infinite satisfaction and improvement. It will do great good in America. Its learning and its good sense will, I hope, make it an institute for our politicians, old as well as young. There is one opinion in it, however, which I will ask you to reconsider, because it appears to me not entirely accurate and not likely to do good. 'Congress is not a legislative, but a diplomatic assembly.' Separating into parts the whole sovereignty of our states, some of these parts are yielded to congress. Upon these I should think them both legislative and executive, and that they could have been judiciary also, had not the confederation required them for certain purposes to appoint a judiciary. It has accordingly been the decision of our courts that the confederation is a part of the law of the land, and superior in authority to the ordinary laws, because it cannot be altered by the legislature of any one state. I doubt whether they are at all a diplomatic assembly."

ite capacities are the checks. These are able to form
ial balance and at all times to control their delegates. The
against the dangers of this kind of government will
a. id upon the accuracy and decision with which the governments of the separate states have their own orders arranged and
balanced.

The necessity we are under of submitting to a federal government is an additional and a very powerful argument for three
branches and a balance by an equal negative in all the separate
governments. Congress will always be composed of members
from the natural and artificial aristocratical body in every state,
even in the northern, as well as in the middle and southern states.
Their natural dispositions, then, in general will be (whether they
shall be sensible of it or not, and whatever integrity or abilities
they may be possessed of) to diminish the prerogatives of the
governors and the privileges of the people and to augment the
influence of the aristocratical parties. There have been causes
enough to prevent the appearance of this inclination hitherto;
but a calm course of prosperity would very soon bring it forth, if
effectual provision against it be not made in season. It will be
found absolutely necessary, therefore, to give negatives to the
governors to defend the executive against the influence of this
body, as well as the senate and representatives in their several
states. The necessity of a negative in the house of representatives
will be called in question by nobody. . . .

In the present state of society and manners in America, with
a people living chiefly by agriculture, in small numbers, sprinkled
over large tracts of land, they are not subject to those panics and
transports, those contagions of madness and folly, which are seen
in countries where large numbers live in small places in daily
fear of perishing for want. We know, therefore, that the people
can live and increase under almost any kind of government, or
without any government at all. But it is of great importance to
begin well; misarrangements now made will have great, extensive, and distant consequences; and we are now employed, how
little soever we may think of it, in making establishments which
will affect the happiness of a hundred millions of inhabitants at

a time in a period not very distant. All nations, under all governments, must have parties; the great secret is to control them.
There are but two ways, either by a monarchy and standing army
or by a balance in the constitution. Where the people have a voice
and there is no balance, there will be everlasting fluctuations,
revolutions, and horrors, until a standing army with a general at
its head commands the peace, or the necessity of an equilibrium
is made appear to all and is adopted by all.

MARCHAMONT NEDHAM

THE RIGHT CONSTITUTION OF A COMMONWEALTH EXAMINED

Volume II of the *Defence* is an examination in detail of some
"Italian Republics of the Middle Ages," and it consists for the
most part of translations from Italian writers of whom the
better known are Machiavelli and Guicciardini. Volume III
is a criticism of Marchamont Nedham's *The Excellency of a
Free State,* published for the first time in 1656 and republished
in 1767 by Thomas Hollis. Nedham had attempted to defend
simple democracy in a way in which Turgot did at a later
date. Adams' criticism is incisive and pungent, and in some
respects this is the most interesting of the three volumes.

. . . Marchamont Nedham lays it down as a fundamental principle and an undeniable rule, "that the people, that is, such as
shall be successively chosen to represent the people, are the best
keepers of their own liberties, and that for many reasons. First,
because they never think of usurping over other men's rights,
but mind which way to preserve their own."
Our first attention should be turned to the proposition itself—
"The people are the best keepers of their own liberties."
But who are the people?
"Such as shall be successively chosen to represent them."
Here is a confusion both of words and ideas, which, though it
may pass with the generality of readers in a fugitive pamphlet or
with a majority of auditors in a popular harangue, ought, for that

very reason, to be as carefully avoided in politics as it is in philosophy or mathematics. If by "the people" is meant the whole body of a great nation, it should never be forgotten that they can never act, consult, or reason together because they cannot march five hundred miles, nor spare the time, nor find a space to meet; and, therefore, the proposition that they are the best keepers of their own liberties is not true. They are the worst conceivable; they are no keepers at all. They can neither act, judge, think, or will, as a body politic or corporation. If by "the people" is meant all the inhabitants of a single city, they are not in a general assembly at all times the best keepers of their own liberties, nor perhaps at any time, unless you separate from them the executive and judicial power and temper their authority in legislation with the maturer counsels of the one and the few. If it is meant by "the people," as our author explains himself, a representative assembly, "such as shall be successively chosen to represent the people," still they are not the best keepers of the people's liberties or their own if you give them all the power— legislative, executive, and judicial. They would invade the liberties of the people, at least the majority of them would invade the liberties of the minority, sooner and oftener than an absolute monarchy such as that of France, Spain, or Russia, or than a well-checked aristocracy like Venice, Bern, or Holland.

An excellent writer has said, somewhat incautiously, that "a people will never oppress themselves or invade their own rights." This compliment, if applied to human nature, or to mankind, or to any nation or people in being or in memory, is more than has been merited. If it should be admitted that a people will not unanimously agree to oppress themselves, it is as much as is ever, and more than is always, true. All kinds of experience show that great numbers of individuals do oppress great numbers of other individuals; that parties often, if not always, oppress other parties; and majorities almost universally minorities. All that this observation can mean then, consistently with any color of fact, is that the people will never unanimously agree to oppress themselves. But if one party agrees to oppress another, or the majority the minority, the people still oppress themselves, for one part of them oppress another.

"The people never think of usurping over other men's rights."
What can this mean? Does it mean that the people never *unanimously* think of usurping over other men's rights? This would be trifling; for there would by the supposition be no other men's rights to usurp. But if the people never, jointly nor severally, think of usurping the rights of others, what occasion can there be for any government at all? Are there no robberies, burglaries, murders, adulteries, thefts, nor cheats? Is not every crime a usurpation over other men's rights? Is not a great part, I will not say the greatest part, of men detected every day in some disposition or other, stronger or weaker, more or less, to usurp over other men's rights? There are some few, indeed, whose whole lives and conversations show that, in every thought, word, and action, they conscientiously respect the rights of others. There is a larger body still, who in the general tenor of their thoughts and actions discover similar principles and feelings yet frequently err. If we should extend our candor so far as to own that the majority of men are generally under the dominion of benevolence and good intentions, yet it must be confessed that a vast majority frequently transgress; and, what is more directly to the point, not only a majority but almost all confine their benevolence to their families, relations, personal friends, parish, village, city, county, province, and that very few indeed extend it impartially to the whole community. Now grant but this truth and the question is decided. If a majority are capable of preferring their own private interest or that of their families, counties, and party to that of the nation collectively, some provision must be made in the constitution in favor of justice to compel all to respect the common right, the public good, the universal law, in preference to all private and partial considerations.

The proposition of our author, then, should be reversed, and it should have been said that they mind so much their own that they never think enough of others. Suppose a nation, rich and poor, high and low, ten millions in number, all assembled together; not more than one or two millions will have lands, houses, or any personal property; if we take into the account the women and children, or even if we leave them out of the question, a great majority of every nation is wholly destitute of property

except a small quantity of clothes and a few trifles of other mov-
ables. Would Mr. Nedham be responsible that, if all were to be
decided by a vote of the majority, the eight or nine millions who
have no property would not think of usurping over the rights
of the one or two millions who have? Property is surely a right
of mankind as really as liberty. Perhaps, at first, prejudice, habit,
shame or fear, principle or religion would restrain the poor from
attacking the rich, and the idle from usurping on the industrious;
but the time would not be long before courage and enterprise
would come and pretexts be invented by degrees to countenance
the majority in dividing all the property among them, or at least
in sharing it equally with its present possessors. Debts would be
abolished first; taxes laid heavy on the rich, and not at all on the
others; and at last a downright equal division of everything be
demanded, and voted. What would be the consequence of this?
The idle, the vicious, the intemperate would rush into the utmost
extravagance of debauchery, sell and spend all their share, and
then demand a new division of those who purchased from them.
The moment the idea is admitted into society that property is not
as sacred as the laws of God, and that there is not a force of law
and public justice to protect it, anarchy and tyranny commence.
If "Thou shalt not covet" and "Thou shalt not steal" were not
commandments of Heaven, they must be made inviolable pre-
cepts in every society before it can be civilized or made free.

If the first part of the proposition, namely, that "the people
never think of usurping over other men's rights," cannot be
admitted, is the second, namely, "they mind which way to preserve their own," better founded?

There is in every nation and people under heaven a large
proportion of persons who take no rational and prudent precautions to preserve what they have, much less to acquire more.
Indolence is the natural character of man to such a degree that
nothing but the necessities of hunger, thirst, and other wants
equally pressing can stimulate him to action, until education is
introduced in civilized societies and the strongest motives of
ambition to excel in arts, trades, and professions are established
in the minds of all men. Until this emulation is introduced, the

lazy savage holds property in too little estimation to give himself trouble for the preservation or acquisition of it. In societies the most cultivated and polished, vanity, fashion, and folly prevail over every thought of ways to preserve their own. They seem rather to study what means of luxury, dissipation, and extravagance they can invent to get rid of it.

"The case is far otherwise among kings and grandees," says our author, "as all nations in the world have felt to some purpose."

That is, in other words, kings and grandees think of usurping over other men's rights, but do not mind which way to preserve their own. It is very easy to flatter the democratical portion of society by making such distinctions between them and the monarchical and aristocratical; but flattery is as base an artifice and as pernicious a vice, when offered to the people, as when given to the others. There is no reason to believe the one much honester or wiser than the other; they are all of the same clay; their minds and bodies are alike. The two latter have more knowledge and sagacity, derived from education, and more advantages for acquiring wisdom and virtue. As to usurping others' rights, they are all three equally guilty when unlimited in power. No wise man will trust either with an opportunity; and every judicious legislator will set all three to watch and control each other. We may appeal to every page of history we have hitherto turned over, for proofs irrefragable, that the people, when they have been unchecked, have been as unjust, tyrannical, brutal, barbarous, and cruel as any king or senate possessed of uncontrollable power. The majority has eternally and without one exception usurped over the rights of the minority. . . .

If "the life of liberty and the only remedy against self-interest lies in succession of powers and persons," the United States of America have taken the most effectual measures to secure that life and that remedy in establishing annual elections of their governors, senators, and representatives. This will probably be allowed to be as perfect an establishment of a succession of powers and persons as human laws can make; but in what manner annual elections of governors and senators will operate remains to be ascertained. It should always be remembered that this is not the first experiment that was ever made in the world of elections to great offices of state; how they have hitherto operated in every great nation and what has been their end is very well known. Mankind have universally discovered that chance was preferable to a corrupt choice and have trusted Providence rather than themselves. First magistrates and senators had better be made hereditary at once than that the people should be universally debauched and bribed, go to loggerheads, and fly to arms regularly every year. Thank Heaven! Americans understand calling conventions; and if the time should come, as it is very possible it may, when hereditary descent shall become a less evil than annual fraud and violence, such a convention may still prevent the first magistrate from becoming absolute as well as hereditary. But if this argument of our author is considered, as he intended it, as a proof that a succession of powers and persons in one assembly is the most perfect commonwealth, it is totally fallacious.

Though we allow benevolence and generous affections to exist in the human breast, yet every moral theorist will admit the selfish passions in the generality of men to be the strongest. There are few who love the public better than themselves, though all may have some affection for the public. We are not, indeed, commanded to love our neighbor better than ourselves. Self-interest, private avidity, ambition, and avarice will exist in every state of society and under every form of government. A succession of powers and persons by frequent elections will not lessen these passions in any case, in a governor, senator, or representative, nor will the apprehension of an approaching election restrain them from indulgence if they have the power. The only remedy is to take away the power by controlling the selfish avidity of the governor by the senate and house, of the senate by the governor and house, and of the house by the governor and senate. Of all possible forms of government, a sovereignty in one assembly, successively chosen by the people, is perhaps the best calculated to facilitate the gratification of self-love and the pursuit of the private interest of a few individuals; a few eminent conspicuous characters will be continued in their seats in the sovereign assembly from one election to another, whatever changes are made in the seats around them; by superior art, address, and opulence, by more splendid birth, reputations, and connections they will be able to intrigue with the people and their leaders, out of doors, until they worm out most of their opposers and introduce their friends; to this end, they will bestow all offices, contracts, privileges in commerce, and other emoluments on the latter and their connections, and throw every vexation and disappointment in the way of the former, until they establish such a system of hopes and fears throughout the state as shall enable them to carry a majority in every fresh election of the house. The judges will be appointed by them and their party and, of consequence, will be obsequious enough to their inclinations. The whole judicial authority, as well as the executive, will be employed, perverted and prostituted to the purposes of electioneering. No justice will be attainable, nor will innocence or virtue be safe, in the judicial courts but for the friends of the prevailing leaders; legal prosecutions will be instituted and carried on against opposers, to their vexation and ruin; and as they have the public purse at command, as well as the executive and judicial power, the public money will be expended in the same way. No favors will be attainable but by those who will court the ruling demagogues in the house by voting for their friends and instruments; and pensions and pecuniary rewards and gratifications, as well as honors and offices of every kind, will be voted to friends and partisans. The leading minds and most influential characters among the clergy will be courted, and the views of the youth in this department will be turned upon those men, and the road to promotion and employment in the church will be obstructed against such as will not worship the general idol. Capital characters among the physicians will not be forgotten, and the means of acquiring reputation and practice in the healing art will be to get the state trumpeters on the side of youth. The bar, too, will be made so subservient that a young gentleman will have no chance to obtain a character or clients but by falling in with the views of the judges and their creators. Even the theatres, and actors and actresses, must become politicians and convert the public pleasures into engines of popularity for the governing members of the house. The press, that great barrier and bulwark of the rights of mankind, when it is protected in its freedom by law, can now no longer be free; if the authors, writers, and printers will not accept of the hire that will be offered them, they must submit to the ruin that will be denounced against them. The presses, with much secrecy and concealment, will be made the vehicles of calumny against the minority, and of panegyric and empirical applauses of the leaders of the majority, and no remedy can possibly be obtained. In one word, the whole system of affairs and every conceivable motive of hope and fear will be employed to promote the private interests of a few and their obsequious majority; and there is no remedy but in arms. Accordingly, we find in all the Italian republics the minority always were driven to arms in despair. . . .

Thus far is very well; but when our author goes on to say, "which might all have been prevented, could they have settled the state free, indeed, by placing an orderly succession of supreme authority in the hands of the people," he can be followed by no one who knows what is in man and in society, because that supreme authority falls out of the whole body into a majority at the first vote. To expect self-denial from men, when they have a majority in their favor and consequently power to gratify themselves, is to disbelieve all history and universal experience; it is to disbelieve Revelation and the Word of God, which informs us the heart is deceitful above all things and desperately wicked. There have been examples of self-denial and will be again; but such exalted virtue never yet existed in any large body of men and lasted long; and our author's argument requires it to be proved, not only that individuals but that nations and majorities of nations are capable, not only of a single act, or a few acts, of disinterested justice and exalted self-denial, but of a course of such heroic virtue for ages and generations; and not only that they are capable of this, but that it is probable they will practise it. There is no man so blind as not to see that to talk of founding a government upon a supposition that nations and great bodies of men, left to themselves, will practise a course of self-denial is either to babble like a new-born infant or to deceive like an unprincipled impostor.

Nedham has himself acknowledged in several parts of this work the depravity of men in very strong terms. In this fifth reason he avers "temptations of honor and profit" to be "sails too big for any human bulk." Why then does he build a system on a foundation which he owns to be so unstable? If his mind had been at liberty to follow his own ideas and principles, he must have seen that a succession of supreme authority in the hands of the people by their house of representatives is at first an aristocracy as despotical as a Roman senate and becomes an oligarchy even sooner than that assembly fell into the decemvirate. There is this infallible disadvantage in such a government, even in comparison with an hereditary aristocracy, that it lets in vice, profligacy, and corruption, like a torrent, with tyranny; whereas the latter often guards the morals of the people with the utmost severity. Even the despotism of aristocracy preserves the morals of the people.

It is pretended by some that a sovereignty in a single assembly, annually elected, is the only one in which there is any responsibility for the exercise of power. In the mixed government we contend for, the ministers, at least of the executive power, are responsible for every instance of the exercise of it; and if they dispose of a single commission by corruption, they are responsible to a house of representatives, who may by impeachment make them responsible before a senate, where they may be accused, tried, condemned, and punished by independent judges. But in a single sovereign assembly, each member at the end of his year is only responsible to his constituents; and the majority of members who have been of one party and carried all before them are to be responsible only to their constituents, not to the constituents of the minority who have been overborne, injured, and plundered. And who are these constituents to whom the majority are accountable? Those very persons to gratify whom they have prostituted the honors, rewards, wealth, and justice of the state. These, instead of punishing, will applaud; instead of discarding, will reëlect, with still greater eclat and a more numerous majority, for the losing cause will be deserted by numbers. And this will be done in hopes of having still more injustice done, still more honors and profits divided among themselves, to the exclusion and mortification of the minority. It is then astonishing that such a simple government should be preferred to a mixed one, by any rational creature, on the score of responsibility.

There is, in short, no possible way of defending the minority in such a government from the tyranny of the majority but by giving the former a negative on the latter—the most absurd institution that ever took place among men. As the major may bear all possible relations of proportion to the minor part, it may be fifty-one against forty-nine in an assembly of a hundred, or it may be ninety-nine against one only. It becomes therefore necessary to give the negative to the minority in all cases, though it be ever so small. Every member must possess it, or he can never be secure that himself and his constituents shall not be sacrificed by all the rest. This is the true ground and original of the *liberum veto* in Poland; but the consequence has been ruin to that noble but ill-constituted republic. One fool, or one knave, one member of the diet, which is a single sovereign assembly, bribed by an intriguing ambassador of some foreign power, has prevented measures the most essential to the defense, safety, and existence of the nation. Hence humiliations and partitions! This also is the reason on which is founded the law of the United Netherlands, that all the seven provinces must be unanimous in the assembly of the states-general, and all the cities and other voting bodies in the assemblies of the separate states. Having no sufficient checks in their uncouth constitution nor any mediating power possessed of the whole executive, they have been driven to demand unanimity instead of a balance. And this must be done in every government of a single assembly, or the majority will instantly oppress the minority. But what kind of government would that be in the United States of America, or any one of them, that should require unanimity or allow of the *liberum veto*? It is sufficient to ask the question, for every man will answer it alike.

No controversy will be maintained with our author that "a free state is more excellent than simple monarchy or simple aristocracy." But the question is, What is a free state? It is plain our author means a single assembly of representatives of the people periodically elected and vested with the supreme power. This is denied to be a free state. It is at first a government of grandees and will soon degenerate into a government of a junto or oligarchy of a few of the most eminent of them, or into an absolute monarchy of one of them. The government of these grandees, while they are numerous as well as when they become few, will be so oppressive to the people that the people from hatred or fear of the gentlemen will set up one of them to rule the rest and make him absolute.

Will it be asked how this can be proved? It is proved, as has been often already said, by the constitution of human nature, by the experience of the world, and the concurrent testimony of all history. The passions and desires of the majority of the representatives in an assembly, being in their nature insatiable and unlimited by anything within their own breasts and having nothing to control them without, will crave more and more indulgence and, as they have the power, they will have the gratification; and Nedham's government will have no security for continuing free but the presumption of self-denial and self-government in the members of the assembly, virtues and qualities that never existed in great bodies of men, by the acknowledgment of all the greatest judges of human nature as well as by his own, when he says that "temptations of honor and profit are sails too big for any human bulk." It would be as reasonable to say that all government is altogether unnecessary because it is the duty of all men to deny themselves and obey the laws of nature and the laws of God. However clear the duty, we know it will not be performed; and, therefore, it is our duty to enter into associations and compel one another to do some of it.

It is agreed that the people are the best keepers of their own liberties and the only keepers who can be always trusted; and, therefore, the people's fair, full, and honest consent to every law, by their representatives, must be made an essential part of the constitution; but it is denied that they are the best keepers, or any keepers at all, of their own liberties when they hold, collectively or by representation, the executive and judicial power, or the whole and uncontrolled legislative; on the contrary, the experience of all ages has proved that they instantly give away their liberties into the hand of grandees or kings, idols of their own creation. The management of the executive and judicial powers together always corrupts them and throws the whole power into the hands of the most profligate and abandoned among themselves. The honest men are generally nearly equally divided in sentiment, and, therefore, the vicious and unprincipled, by joining one party, carry the majority; and the vicious and unprincipled always follow the most profligate leader, him who bribes the highest and sets all decency and shame at defiance. It becomes more profitable, and reputable too, except with a very few, to be a party man than a public-spirited one.

It is agreed that "the end of all government is the good and ease of the people in a secure enjoyment of their rights without oppression"; but it must be remembered that the rich are *people* as well as the poor; that they have rights as well as others; that they have as clear and as *sacred* a right to their large property as others have to theirs which is smaller; that oppression to them is as possible and as wicked as to others; that stealing, robbing, cheating are the same crimes and sins, whether committed against them or others. The rich, therefore, ought to have an effectual barrier in the constitution against being robbed, plundered, and murdered, as well as the poor; and this can never be without an independent senate. The poor should have a bulwark against the same dangers and oppressions; and this can never be without a house of representatives of the people. But neither the rich nor the poor can be defended by their respective guardians in the constitution without an executive power, vested with a negative equal to either, to hold the balance even between them and decide when they cannot agree. If it is asked, When will this negative be used? it may be answered, Perhaps never. The known existence of it will prevent all occasion to exercise it; but if it has not a being, the want of it will be felt every day. If it has not been used in England for a long time past, it by no means follows that there have not been occasions when it might have been employed with propriety. But one thing is very certain, that there have been many occasions since the Revolution when the constitution would have been overturned if the negative had not been an indubitable prerogative of the crown.

It is agreed that the people are "most sensible of their own burdens, and being once put into a capacity and freedom of acting are the most likely to provide remedies for their own relief." For this reason they are an essential branch of the legislature and have a negative on all laws, an absolute control over every grant of money, and an unlimited right to accuse their enemies before an impartial tribunal. Thus far they are most sensible of their burdens and are most likely to provide remedies. But it is affirmed that they are not only incapable of managing the executive power but would be instantly corrupted by it in such numbers as would destroy the integrity of all elections. It is denied that the legislative power can be wholly entrusted in their hands with a moment's safety. The poor and the vicious would instantly rob the rich and virtuous, spend their plunder in debauchery or confer it upon some idol, who would become the despot; or, to speak more intelligibly if not more accurately, some of the rich, by debauching the vicious to their corrupt interest, would plunder the virtuous and become more rich until they acquired all the property, or a balance of property and of power, in their own hands and domineered as despots in an oligarchy.

It is agreed that the "people know where the shoe wrings, what grievances are most heavy," and, therefore, they should always hold an independent and essential part in the legislature and be always able to prevent the shoe from wringing more and the grievances from being made more heavy; they should have a full hearing of all their arguments, and a full share of all consultations, for easing the foot where it is in pain and for lessening the weight of grievances or annihilating them. But it is denied that they have right or that they should have power to take from one man his property to make another easy, and that they *only* know "what fences they stand in need of to shelter them from

the injurious assaults of those powers that are above them"—
meaning by the "powers above them" senators and magistrates,
though, properly speaking, there are no powers above them but
the law, which is above all men, governors and senators, kings
and nobles, as well as commons. . . .

Our author is not explicit. If he meant that a fundamental law
should be made, that no man should be chosen more than one
year, he has nowhere said so. He knew the nation would not
have borne it. Cromwell and his creatures would all have detested it; nor would the members of the Long Parliament or their
constituents have approved it. The idea would have been universally unpopular. No people in the world will bear to be
deprived at the end of one year of the service of their best men
and be obliged to confer their suffrages from year to year on the
next best until the rotation brings them to the worst. The men
of greatest interest and influence, moreover, will govern; and if
they cannot be chosen themselves, they will generally influence
the choice of others so decidedly that they may be said to have
the appointment. If it is true that "the strongest obligation that
can be laid upon a man in public matters is to see that he engage
in nothing but what must either offensively or beneficially reflect
upon himself," it is equally true at least in a mixed government
as in a simple democracy. It is, indeed, more clearly and universally true, because in the first the representatives of the people,
being the special guardians of equality, equity, and liberty for the
people, will not consent to unequal laws; but in the second,
where the great and rich will have the greatest influence in the
public councils, they will continually make unequal laws in their
own favor unless the poorer majority unite, which they rarely
do, set up an opposition to them, and run them down by making
unequal laws against them. In every society where property exists,
there will ever be a struggle between rich and poor. Mixed in
one assembly, equal laws can never be expected. They will either
be made by numbers, to plunder the few who are rich, or by
influence, to fleece the many who are poor. Both rich and poor,
then, must be made independent, that equal justice may be done
and equal liberty enjoyed by all. To expect that in a single

sovereign assembly no load shall be laid upon any but what is common to all, nor to gratify the passions of any but only to supply the necessities of their country, is altogether chimerical. Such an assembly, under an awkward, unwieldy form, becomes at once a simple monarchy in effect. Some one overgrown genius, fortune, or reputation becomes a despot, who rules the state at his pleasure while the deluded nation, or rather a deluded majority, thinks itself free; and in every resolve, law, and act of government you see the interest, fame, and power of that single individual attended to more than the general good. . . .

If Socrates and Plato, Cicero and Seneca, Hutcheson and Butler are to be credited, reason is rightfully supreme in man, and, therefore, it would be most suitable to the reason of mankind to have no civil or political government at all. The moral government of God, and his viceregent, Conscience, ought to be sufficient to restrain men to obedience, to justice, and benevolence at all times and in all places; we must therefore descend from the dignity of our nature when we think of civil government at all. But the nature of mankind is one thing, and the reason of mankind another; and the first has the same relation to the last as the whole to a part. The passions and appetites are parts of human nature as well as reason and the moral sense. In the institution of government it must be remembered that, although reason ought always to govern individuals, it certainly never did since the Fall, and never will till the Millennium; and human nature must be taken as it is, as it has been, and will be. If, as Cicero says, "man is a noble creature, born with affections to rule rather than obey, there being in every man a natural desire of principality," it is yet certain that every man ought to obey as well as to rule, ἄρχειν καὶ ἄρχεσθαι, and that every man cannot rule alone. Each man must be content with his share of empire; and if the nature and reason of mankind, the nobleness of his qualities and affections, and his natural desires prove his right to a share in the government, they cannot surely prove more than the constitutions of the United States have allowed—an annual election of the whole legislative and executive, the governor, senate, and house. If we admit them to prove more, they would prove that every man has every year a right to be governor, senator, and representative, which, being impossible, is absurd. . . .

CONCLUSION

It should have been before observed that the Western Empire fell in the fifth century, and the Eastern in the fifteenth.

Augustulus was compelled by Odoacer, King of the Heruli, in 475, to abdicate the Western Empire, and was the last Roman who possessed the imperial dignity at Rome. The dominion of Italy fell soon afterwards into the hands of Theodoric the Goth. The Eastern Empire lasted many centuries afterwards till it was annihilated by Mahomet the Great, and Constantinople was taken in the year 1453. The *interval* between the fall of these two empires, making a period of about a thousand years, is called the Middle Age.[15] During this term, republics without number arose in Italy, whirled upon their axles or single centers, foamed, raged, and burst, like so many waterspouts upon the ocean. They were all alike ill constituted; all alike miserable; and all ended in similar disgrace and despotism. It would be curious to pursue our subject through all of them whose records have survived the ravages of Goths, Saracens, and bigoted Christians; through those other republics of Castile, Arragon, Catalonia, Galicia, and all the others in Spain; through those in Portugal; through the several provinces that now compose the kingdom of France; through those in Germany, Sweden, Denmark, Holland, England, Scotland, Ireland, etc. But if such a work should be sufficiently encouraged by the public (which is not probable, for mankind, in general, dare not as yet read or think upon *constitutions*), it is too extensive for my forces and ought not to be done in so much haste. The preceding has been produced upon the spur of a particular occasion, which made it necessary to write and publish with precipitation, or it might have been useless to have published at all. The whole has been done in the midst of

[15] Barbeyrac's Preface to his *History of Ancient Treaties. Corps Dipl.* Vol. XXII. Harris' *Philological Inquiries,* Part III, Chap. 1.

other occupations, in so much hurry that scarce a moment could be spared to correct the style, adjust the method, pare off excrescences, or even obliterate repetitions, in all which respects it stands in need of an apology. The investigation may be pursued to any length.

All nations from the beginning have been agitated by the same passions. The principles developed here will go a great way in explaining every phenomenon that occurs in the history of government. The vegetable and animal kingdoms, and those heavenly bodies whose existence and movements we are as yet only permitted faintly to perceive, do not appear to be governed by laws more uniform or certain than those which regulate the moral and political world. Nations move by unalterable rules; and education, discipline, and laws make the greatest difference in their accomplishments, happiness, and perfection. It is the master artist alone who finishes his building, his picture, or his clock. The present actors on the stage have been too little prepared by their early views, and too much occupied with turbulent scenes, to do more than they have done. Impartial justice will confess that it is astonishing they have been able to do so much. It is for the young to make themselves masters of what their predecessors have been able to comprehend and accomplish but imperfectly.

A prospect into futurity in America is like contemplating the heavens through the telescopes of Herschell.[d] Objects stupendous in their magnitudes and motions strike us from all quarters and fill us with amazement! When we recollect that the wisdom or the folly, the virtue or the vice, the liberty or servitude, of those millions now beheld by us, only as Columbus saw these times in vision,[16] are certainly to be influenced, perhaps decided, by the manners, examples, principles, and political institutions of the present generation, that mind must be hardened into stone that is not melted into reverence and awe. With such affecting scenes before his eyes, is there, can there be, a young American indolent and incurious, surrendered up to dissipation and frivolity, vain of imitating the loosest manners of countries which can never be made much better or much worse? A profligate Amer-

[16] Barlow's *Vision of Columbus*.

ican youth must be profligate indeed and richly merits the scorn of all mankind.

The world has been too long abused with notions that climate and soil decide the characters and political institutions of nations. The laws of Solon and the despotism of Mahomet have at different times prevailed at Athens; consuls, emperors, and pontiffs have ruled at Rome. Can there be desired a stronger proof that policy and education are able to triumph over every disadvantage of climate? Mankind have been still more injured by insinuations that a certain celestial virtue, more than human, has been necessary to preserve liberty. Happiness, whether in despotism or democracy, whether in slavery or liberty, can never be found without virtue. The best republics will be virtuous, and have been so; but we may hazard a conjecture that the virtues have been the effect of the well ordered constitution rather than the cause. And, perhaps, it would be impossible to prove that a republic cannot exist even among highwaymen by setting one rogue to watch another; and the knaves themselves may in time be made honest men by the struggle.

It is now in our power to bring this work to a conclusion with unexpected dignity. In the course of the last summer two authorities have appeared, greater than any that have been before quoted, in which the principles we have attempted to defend have been acknowledged.

The first is an *Ordinance* of Congress, of the thirteenth of July, 1787, for the Government of the Territory of the United States, Northwest of the River Ohio.

The second is the *Report* of the Convention at Philadelphia, of the seventeenth of September, 1787.

The former confederation of the United States was formed upon the model and example of all the confederacies, ancient and modern, in which the federal council was only a diplomatic body. Even the Lycian, which is thought to have been the best, was no more. The magnitude of territory, the population, the wealth and commerce, and especially the rapid growth of the United States have shown such a government to be inadequate to their wants; and the new system, which seems admirably calculated to unite their interests and affections and bring them to an uniformity of principles and sentiments, is equally well combined to unite their wills and forces as a single nation. A result of accommodation cannot be supposed to reach the ideas of perfection of anyone; but the conception of such an idea and the deliberate union of so great and various a people in such a plan is, without all partiality or prejudice, if not the greatest exertion of human understanding, the greatest single effort of national deliberation that the world has ever seen. That it may be improved is not to be doubted, and provision is made for that purpose in the report itself. A people who could conceive and can adopt it, we need not fear will be able to amend it, when by experience its inconveniences and imperfections shall be seen and felt.[17]

---

[17] Dr. Price, whose publication gave rise to this work, seems to have been convinced by it. In a letter addressed to the author, he says—

"I cannot be sorry that I have given occasion for your book by the publication of M. Turgot's *Letter*. At the time of this publication, I was entirely ignorant that you had delivered any opinion with respect to the sentiment in the passage to which you have objected. I have lately written several letters to America, and in some of them I have taken occasion to mention your publication and to say that you have convinced me of the main point which it is intended to prove; and that I wish I had inserted a note to signify the difference of opinion between M. Turgot and me on that point. The subject of civil government, next to religion, is of the highest importance to mankind. It is now, I believe, better understood than ever it was. Your book will furnish a help towards further improvement, and your country will, I hope, give such an example of this improvement as will be useful to the world."—C. F. A.

II. THREE LETTERS TO ROGER SHERMAN ON THE CONSTITUTION OF THE UNITED STATES [1]

In these three letters to Roger Sherman written in the summer of 1789, John Adams cogently sets forth some of his major objections to the Constitution of the United States. He found the same difficulties in the Constitution of Massachusetts of 1780; namely, that in both systems the executive power had been dangerously weakened. The essence of free republican government, he reasoned, consists in a proper balance of powers in the legislature. Which is to say, there should be a strong independent executive, a powerful senate, and a broadly representative lower house. In the Constitution of the United States he believed that the limited veto power of the President, plus the necessity for Senate concurrence in appointments, so weakened the chief executive as to upset the delicate tripartite balance. His comments on the Constitution read in the light of his own administration are strangely prophetic, for it is true that during his Presidency some of his own cabinet officers rendered their allegiance not to him but to Hamilton, apparent leader of the Federalist Party. Although many of Adams' fears about the system established by this Constitution were not realized, he did perceive with clarity and understanding those areas in the framework that have led to friction and difficulty.

1

RICHMOND HILL (New York), 17 July, 1789.

Dear Sir: I read over with pleasure your observations on the new federal constitution and am glad to find an opportunity to communicate to you my opinion of some parts of them. It is by a free and amicable intercourse of sentiments that the friends of our country may hope for such a unanimity of opinion and such a concert of exertions as may sooner or later produce the blessings of good government.

[1] [*Works*, VI, 427–436.]

You say, "it is by some objected that the executive is blended with the legislature, and that those powers ought to be entirely distinct and unconnected." But is not that a gross error in politics? The united wisdom and various interests of a nation should be combined in framing the laws by which all are to be governed and protected, though it should not be convenient to have them executed by the whole legislature. The supreme executive in Great Britain is one branch of the legislature and has a negative on all the laws; perhaps that is an extreme not to be imitated by a republic, but the negative vested in the president by the new constitution on the acts of congress and the consequent revision may be very useful to prevent laws being passed without mature deliberation and to preserve stability in the administration of government; and the concurrence of the senate in the appointment to office will strengthen the hands of the executive, and secure the confidence of the people much better than a select council, and will be less expensive.

Is it, then, "an extreme not to be imitated by a republic," to make the supreme executive a branch of the legislature and give it a negative on all the laws? If you please, we will examine this position and see whether it is well founded. In the first place, what is your definition of a republic? Mine is this: *A government whose sovereignty is vested in more than one person.* Governments are divided into *despotisms, monarchies,* and *republics.* A despotism is a government in which the three divisions of power, the legislative, executive and judicial, are all vested in one man. A monarchy is a government where the legislative and executive are vested in one man, but the judicial in other men. In all governments the sovereignty is vested in that man or body of men who have the legislative power. In despotisms and monarchies, therefore, the legislative authority being in one man, the sovereignty is in one man. In republics, as the sovereignty, that is, the legislative, is always vested in more than one, it may be vested in as many more as you please. In the United States it might be vested in two persons, or in three millions, or in any other intermediate number, and in every such supposable case the government would be a republic. In conformity to these ideas, republics have been divided into three species—monarchical, aristocratical, and democratical republics. England is a republic, a monarchical republic it is true, but a republic still, because the sovereignty, which is the legislative power, is vested in more than one man; it is equally divided, indeed, between the one, the few, and the many, or in other words, between the natural division of mankind in society—the monarchical, the aristocratical, and democratical. It is essential to a monarchical republic that the supreme executive should be a branch of the legislature and have a negative on all the laws. I say essential, because, if monarchy were not an essential part of the sovereignty, the government would not be a monarchical republic. Your position is therefore clearly and certainly an error because the practice of Great Britain in making the supreme executive a branch of the legislature and giving it a negative on all the laws must be imitated by every monarchical republic.

I will pause here, if you please; but if you will give me leave, I will write another letter or two upon this subject. Meantime I am, with unalterable friendships, yours.

2

Dear Sir: In my letter of yesterday I think it was demonstrated that the English government is a republic, and that the regal negative upon the laws is essential to that republic. Because without it that government would not be what it is, a monarchical republic, and, consequently, could not preserve the balance of power between the executive and legislative powers, nor that other balance which is in the legislature—between the one, the few, and the many in which two balances the excellence of that form of government must consist.

Let us now inquire whether the new constitution of the United States is or is not a monarchical republic like that of Great Britain. The monarchical and the aristocratical power in our constitution, it is true, are not hereditary; but this makes no difference in the nature of the power, in the nature of the balance, or in the name of the species of government. It would make no difference in the power of a judge or justice, or general or admiral, whether his commission were for life or years. His authority during the time it lasted would be the same whether it were for one year or twenty, or for life, or descendible to his eldest son. The people, the nation, in whom all power resides originally, may delegate their power for one year or for ten years, for years or for life; or may delegate it in fee simple or fee tail, if I may so express myself; or during good behavior, or at will, or till further orders.

A nation might unanimously create a dictator or a despot for one year or more, or for life, or for perpetuity with hereditary descent. In such a case, the dictator for one year would as really be a dictator for the time his power lasted as the other would be whose power was perpetual and descendible. A nation in the same manner might create a simple monarchy for years, life, or perpetuity, and in either case the creature would be equally a simple monarch during the continuance of his power. So the people of England might create king, lords, and commons for a year, or for several years, or for life, and in any of these cases their government would be a monarchical republic, or, if you will, a limited monarchy during its continuance, as much as it is now when the king and nobles are hereditary. They might make their house of commons hereditary too. What the consequence of this would be it is easy to foresee; but it would not in the first moment make any change in the legal power, nor in the name of the government.

Let us now consider what our constitution is and see whether any other name can with propriety be given it, than that of a monarchical republic or, if you will, a limited monarchy. The duration of our president is neither perpetual nor for life; it is only for four years; but his power during those four years is much greater than that of an avoyer, a consul, a podestà, a doge, a stadtholder; nay, than a king of Poland; nay, than a king of Sparta. I know of no first magistrate in any republican government, excepting England and Neuchâtel, who possesses a constitutional dignity, authority, and power comparable to his. The power of sending and receiving ambassadors, of raising and commanding armies and navies, of nominating and appointing and commissioning all officers, of managing the treasures, the internal and external affairs of the nation; nay, the whole executive power, coextensive with the legislative power, is vested in him, and he has the right, and his is the duty, to take care that the laws be faithfully executed. These rights and duties, these prerogatives and dignities are so transcendent that they must naturally and necessarily excite in the nation all the jealousy, envy, fears, apprehensions, and opposition that are so constantly observed in England against the crown.[2]

That these powers are necessary I readily admit. That the laws cannot be executed without them; that the lives, liberties, properties and characters of the citizens cannot be secure without their protection, is most clear. But it is equally certain, I think, that they ought to have been still greater, or much less. The limitations upon them in the cases of war, treaties, and appointments to office, and especially the limitation on the president's independence as a branch of the legislative, will be the destruction of this constitution and involve us in anarchy, if not amended. I shall pass over all particulars for the present, except the last, because that is now the point in dispute between you and me. Longitude and the philosopher's stone have not been sought with more earnestness by philosophers than a guardian of the laws has been studied by legislators from Plato to Montesquieu; but every project has been found to be no better than committing the lamb to the custody of the wolf, except that one which is called a *balance of power.* A simple sovereignty in one, a few, or many has no balance and therefore no laws. A divided sovereignty without a balance, or, in other words, where the division is unequal, is always at war and consequently has no laws. In our constitution the sovereignty—that is, the legislative power—is divided into three branches. The house and senate are equal, but

[2] M. de Tocqueville has taken a similar view of the President's powers:
"Le président des États-Unis possède des prérogatives presque royales, dont il n'a pas l'occasion de se servir; et les droits dont jusqu'à présent il peut user sont très circonscrits; *les lois lui permettent d'être fort, les circonstances le maintiennent foible.*" De la Démocratie en Amérique, Vol. I, Chap. 8.

the third branch, though essential, is not equal. The president must pass judgment upon every law, but in some cases his judgment may be overruled. These cases will be such as attack his constitutional power; it is, therefore, certain he has not equal power to defend himself, or the constitution, or the judicial power, as the senate and house have.

Power naturally grows. Why? Because human passions are insatiable. But that power alone can grow which already is too great, that which is unchecked, that which has no equal power to control it. The legislative power in our constitution is greater than the executive; it will, therefore, encroach because both aristocratical and democratical passions are insatiable. The legislative power will increase, the executive will diminish. In the legislature the monarchical power is not equal either to the aristocratical or democratical; it will, therefore, decrease while the other will increase. Indeed, I think the aristocratical power is greater than either the monarchical or democratical. That will, therefore, swallow up the other two.

In my letter of yesterday, I think it was proved that a republic might make the supreme executive an integral part of the legislature. In this, it is equally demonstrated, as I think, that our constitution ought to be amended by a decisive adoption of that expedient. If you do not forbid me, I shall write to you again.

3

Dear Sir: There is a sense and degree in which the executive, in our constitution, is blended with the legislature. The president has the power of suspending a law—of giving the two houses an opportunity to pause, to think, to collect themselves, to reconsider a rash step of a majority. He has a right to urge all his reasons against it, by speech or message, which, becoming public, is an appeal to the nation. But the rational objection here is, not that the executive is blended with the legislature, but that it is not enough blended; that it is not incorporated with it and made an essential part of it. If it were an integral part of it, it might negative a law without much noise, speculation, or confusion among the people. But as it now stands, I beg you to consider it is almost impossible that a president should ever have the courage to make use of his partial negative. What a situation would a president be in to maintain a controversy against a majority of both houses before a tribunal of the public? To put a stop to a law that more than half the senate and house and, consequently, we may suppose, more than half the nation have set their hearts upon?[3] It is, moreover, possible that more than two thirds of the nation, the senate and house, may in times of calamity, distress, misfortune, and ill success of the measures of government, from the momentary passion and enthusiasm, demand a law which will wholly subvert the constitution. The constitution of Athens was overturned in such a manner by Aristides himself. The constitution should guard against a possibility of its subversion; but we may take stronger ground and assert that it is probable such cases will happen, and that the constitution will, in fact, be subverted in this way. Nay, I go further and say that from the constitution of human nature and the constant course of human affairs it is certain that our constitution will be subverted, if not amended, and that in a very short time, merely for want of a decisive negative in the executive.

There is another sense and another degree in which the executive is blended with the legislature which is liable to great and just objection, which excites alarms, jealousies, and apprehensions in a very great degree. I mean, first, the negative of the senate upon appointments to office; secondly, the negative of the senate upon treaties; and thirdly, the negative of the two houses upon war. I shall confine myself at present to the first. The negative of the senate upon appointments is liable to the following objections:

1. It takes away, or at least it lessens the responsibility of the executive. Our constitution obliges me to say that it lessens the responsibility of the president. The blame of an injudicious, weak, or wicked appointment is shared so much between him and the senate that his part of it will be too small. Who can

---

[3] Thus far, this has not been found so difficult as was here predicted. But it must be admitted that the occasions in which the negative has been exercised were not of a kind in which the popular passions are greatly excited. C. F. A.

censure him without censuring the senate and the legislatures who appoint them? All their friends will be interested to vindicate the president in order to screen them from censure. Besides, if an impeachment against an officer is brought before them, are they not interested to acquit him, lest some part of the odium of his guilt should fall upon them who advised to his appointment?

2. It turns the minds and attention of the people to the senate, a branch of the legislature, in executive matters. It interests another branch of the legislature in the management of the executive. It divides the people between the executive and the senate; whereas all the people ought to be united to watch the executive, to oppose its encroachments, and resist its ambition. Senators and representatives and their constituents, in short the aristocratical and democratical divisions of society, ought to be united on all occasions to oppose the executive or the monarchical branch when it attempts to overleap its limits. But how can this union be effected when the aristocratical branch has pledged its reputation to the executive by consenting to an appointment?

3. It has a natural tendency to excite ambition in the senate. An active, ardent spirit who is rich and able and has a great reputation and influence will be solicited by candidates for office. Not to introduce the idea of bribery, because, though it certainly would force itself in, in other countries and will probably here when we grow populous and rich, it is not yet to be dreaded, I hope, ambition must come in already. A senator of great influence will be naturally ambitious and desirous of increasing his influence. Will he not be under a temptation to use his influence with the president as well as his brother senators to appoint persons to office in the several states, who will exert themselves in elections to get out his enemies or opposers both in senate and house of representatives, and to get in his friends, perhaps his instruments? Suppose a senator to aim at the treasury office for himself, his brother, father, or son. Suppose him to aim at the president's chair or vice-president's at the next election or at the office of war, foreign, or domestic affairs. Will he not naturally be tempted to make use of his whole patronage, his whole influence in advising to appointments, both with president and sen-

ators, to get such persons nominated as will exert themselves in elections of president, vice-president, senators, and house of representatives to increase his interest and promote his views? In this point of view I am very apprehensive that this defect in our constitution will have an unhappy tendency to introduce corruption of the grossest kinds, both of ambition and avarice, into all our elections, and this will be the worst of poisons to our constitution. It will not only destroy the present form of government, but render it almost impossible to substitute in its place any free government, even a better limited-monarchy, or any other than a despotism or a simple monarchy.

4. To avoid the evil under the last head it will be in danger of dividing the continent into two or three nations, a case that presents no prospect but of perpetual war.

5. This negative on appointments is in danger of involving the senate in reproach, censure, obloquy, and suspicion without doing any good. Will the senate use their negative or not? If not, why should they have it? Many will censure them for not using it; many will ridicule them and call them servile, etc. If they do use it, the very first instance of it will expose the senators to the resentment of not only the disappointed candidate and all his friends, but of the president and all his friends, and these will be most of the officers of government, through the nation.

6. We shall very soon have parties formed, a court and country party, and these parties will have names given them. One party in the house of representatives will support the president and his measures and ministers; the other will oppose them. A similar party will be in the senate; these parties will study with all their arts, perhaps with intrigue, perhaps with corruption, at every election to increase their own friends and diminish their opposers. Suppose such parties formed in the senate, and then consider what factious divisions we shall have there upon every nomination.

7. The senate have not time. The convention and Indian treaties.[4]

----

[4] This seems to be an imperfect sentence. The sense is explained at the close of the letter. C. F. A.

You are of opinion "that the concurrence of the senate in the appointments to office will strengthen the hands of the executive and secure the confidence of the people much better than a select council, and will be less expensive."

But in every one of these ideas I have the misfortune to differ from you.

It will weaken the hands of the executive by lessening the obligation, gratitude, and attachment of the candidate to the president by dividing his attachment between the executive and legislative, which are natural enemies. Officers of government, instead of having a single eye and undivided attachment to the executive branch, as they ought to have, consistent with law and the constitution, will be constantly tempted to be factious with their factious patrons in the senate. The president's own officers, in a thousand instances, will oppose his just and constitutional exertions and screen themselves under the wings of their patrons and party in the legislature.[5] Nor will it secure the confidence of the people. The people will have more confidence in the executive, in executive matters, than in the senate. The people will be constantly jealous of factious schemes in the senators to unduly influence the executive, to serve each other's private views. The people will also be jealous that the influence of the senate will be employed to conceal, connive at, and defend guilt in executive officers, instead of being a guard and watch upon them, and a terror to them. A council, selected by the president himself, at his pleasure, from among the senators, representatives, and nation at large would be purely responsible. In that case, the senate would be a terror to privy counsellors; its honor would never be pledged to support any measure or instrument of the executive beyond justice, law, and the constitution. Nor would a privy council be more expensive. The whole senate must now deliberate on every appointment, and if they ever find time for it, you will find that a great deal of time will be required and consumed in this service. Then, the president might have a constant executive council; now, he has none.

[5] A singular prediction of what actually happened, afterwards, to himself. C. F. A.

I said, under the seventh head, that the senate would not have time. You will find that the whole business of this government will be infinitely delayed by this negative of the senate on treaties and appointments. Indian treaties and consular conventions have been already waiting for months, and the senate have not been able to find a moment of time to attend to them; and this evil must constantly increase. So that the senate must be constantly sitting and must be paid as long as they sit. . . .

But I have tired your patience. Is there any truth in these broken hints and crude surmises, or not? To me they appear well founded and very important.

I am, with usual affection, yours,

JOHN ADAMS.

III. DISCOURSES ON DAVILA [1]

In the first year of his Vice Presidency John Adams published a series of letters in the *Gazette of the United States* entitled *Discourses on Davila,* which he thought of as "the fourth volume of the *Defence of the Constitutions of the United States."* Some of the letters, particularly the thirty-second, the last one of the papers, aroused the ire of the Jeffersonian Republicans and led to unwarranted charges that Adams favored monarchy and even that he was "anti-republican." According to his own statement, ". . . the rage and fury of the Jacobinical journals against these discourses, increased as they proceeded, intimidated the printer, John Fenno, and convinced me, that to proceed would do more hurt than good. I therefore broke off abruptly." [2] The bulk of the *Discourses* consists of translations from Enrico Caterino Davila's *History of the Civil Wars of France,* which covers part of the intrigues, rivalries, machinations, and battles in France raging during a part of the sixteenth century. However, at the end of the first essay Adams wrote: "Before we proceed in our discourses on Davila, it will assist us, in comprehending this narration, as well as in making many useful reflections in morals and policy, to turn our thoughts for a few moments to the constitution of the human mind." [3] He then proceeded in a most stimulating and lively fashion to reflect on human nature. At first one is delighted and amazed at such original speculations until in the ninth paper, Charles Francis Adams, the editor of John Adams' *Works,* cites Adam Smith as the source of one of the extended quotations. We then discover that practically the whole of these "useful reflections" is based on Adam Smith's chapter on "The Origin of Ambition, and of the Distinction of Ranks," found in his *Theory of Moral Sentiments.* In these letters Adams elaborated on that phase of human nature wherein pride or the "passion for distinction" is said to be the motivating force. He also appealed to the poets, quoting from Edward Young's *Love of Fame, The Universal Passion,* Alexander Pope's *Essay on Man,* Dr. Samuel Johnson's *The Vanity of*

[1] [*Works* VI, 232–281, passim.]
[2] [VI, 272 (note).]
[3] [VI, 232.]

Human Wishes, and from several of Shakespeare's plays. After these diverting speculations on human nature, Adams returned to Davila in the fourteenth paper and continued in this vein to the end of the series. Despite the extended borrowing the *Discourses* are well worth reading. The selections below from the *Discourses on Davila* are devoted to Adams' provocative comments on "The constitution of the human mind."

1 [4]

C'est là le propre de l'esprit humain, que les exemples ne corrigent personne; les sottises des pères sont perdues pour leurs enfans; il faut que chaque génération fasse les siennes.

[FONTENELLE]

Men in their primitive conditions, however savage, were undoubtedly gregarious; and they continue to be social, not only in every stage of civilization, but in every possible situation in which they can be placed. As nature intended them for society, she has furnished them with passions, appetites, and propensities, as well as a variety of faculties calculated both for their individual enjoyment and to render them useful to each other in their social connections. There is none among them more essential or remarkable than the *passion for distinction*. A desire to be observed, considered, esteemed, praised, beloved, and admired by his fellows is one of the earliest as well as keenest dispositions discovered in the heart of man. If anyone should doubt the existence of this propensity, let him go and attentively observe the journeymen and apprentices in the first workshop or the oarsmen in a cockboat, a family or a neighborhood, the inhabitants of a house or the crew of a ship, a school or a college, a city or a village, a savage or civilized people, a hospital or a church, the bar or the exchange, a camp or a court. Wherever men, women, or children are to be found, whether they be old or young, rich or poor, high or low, wise or foolish, ignorant or learned, every individual is seen to be strongly actuated by a desire to be seen, heard, talked of, approved and respected by the people about him and within his knowledge.

[4] [*Works* VI, 232 (Chapter II).]

Moral writers have by immemorial usage a right to make a free use of the poets.

> The love of praise, howe'er conceal'd by art,
> Reigns, more or less, and glows, in every heart;
> The proud, to gain it, toils on toils endure,
> The modest shun it, but to make it sure.
> O'er globes and sceptres, now on thrones it swells,
> Now, trims the midnight lamp in college cells.
> 'T is tory, whig—it plots, prays, preaches, pleads,
> Harangues in Senates, squeaks in masquerades.
> It aids the dancer's heel, the writer's head,
> And heaps the plain with mountains of the dead;
> Nor ends with life; but nods in sable plumes,
> Adorns our hearse, and flatters on our tombs.[5]

A regard to the sentiments of mankind concerning him and to their dispositions towards him, every man feels within himself; and if he has reflected and tried experiments, he has found that no exertion of his reason, no effort of his will can wholly divest him of it. In proportion to our affection for the notice of others is our aversion to their neglect; the stronger the desire of the esteem of the public, the more powerful the aversion to their disapprobation; the more exalted the wish for admiration, the more invincible the abhorrence of contempt. Every man not only desires the consideration of others, but he frequently compares himself with others, his friends or his enemies; and in proportion as he exults when he perceives that he has more of it than they, he feels a keener affliction when he sees that one or more of them are more respected than himself.

This passion, while it is simply a desire to excel another, by fair industry in the search of truth and the practice of virtue is properly called *Emulation*. When it aims at power as a means of distinction, it is *Ambition*. When it is in a situation to suggest the sentiments of fear and apprehension that another who is now inferior will become superior, it is denominated *Jealousy*. When it is in a state of mortification at the superiority of another and desires to bring him down to our level or to depress him

[5] [Quoted from *Love of Fame, The Universal Passion*, Satire I, lines 51–58, 61–64, by Edward Young.]

below us, it is properly called *Envy*. When it deceives a man into a belief of false professions of esteem or admiration or into a false opinion of his importance in the judgment of the world, it is *Vanity*. These observations alone would be sufficient to show that this propensity in all its branches is a principal source of the virtues and vices, the happiness and misery of human life, and that the history of mankind is little more than a simple narration of its operation and effects.

There is in human nature, it is true, simple *Benevolence* or an affection for the good of others; but alone it is not a balance for the selfish affections. Nature then has kindly added to benevolence the desire of reputation in order to make us good members of society. *Spectemur agendo* [a] expresses the great principle of activity for the good of others. Nature has sanctioned the law of self-preservation by rewards and punishments. The rewards of selfish activity are life and health; the punishments of negligence and indolence are want, disease, and death. Each individual, it is true, should consider that nature has enjoined the same law on his neighbor, and therefore a respect for the authority of nature would oblige him to respect the rights of others as much as his own. But reasoning as abstruse, though as simple, as this would not occur to all men. The same nature therefore has imposed another law, that of promoting the good, as well as respecting the rights of mankind, and has sanctioned it by other rewards and punishments. The rewards in this case, in this life, are *esteem* and *admiration* of others; the punishments are *neglect* and *contempt;* nor may anyone imagine that these are not as real as the others. The desire of the esteem of others is as real a want of nature as hunger; and the neglect and contempt of the world as severe a pain as the gout or stone. It sooner and oftener produces despair and a detestation of existence of equal importance to individuals, to families, and to nations. It is a principal end of government to regulate this passion, which in its turn becomes a principal means of government. It is the only adequate instrument of order and subordination in society and alone commands effectual obedience to laws, since without it neither human reason nor standing armies would ever produce that great effect. Every personal quality and every blessing of fortune is cherished in proportion to its capacity of gratifying this universal affection for the esteem, the sympathy, admiration and congratulations of the public. Beauty in the face, elegance of figure, grace of attitude and motion, riches, honors, everything is weighed in the scale and desired, not so much for the pleasure they afford as the attention they command. As this is a point of great importance, it may be pardonable to expatiate a little upon these particulars.

Why are the personal accomplishments of beauty, elegance, and grace held in such high estimation by mankind? Is it merely for the pleasure which is received from the sight of these attributes? By no means. The taste for such delicacies is not universal; in those who feel the most lively sense of them, it is but a slight sensation and of shortest continuance; but those attractions command the notice and attention of the public; they draw the eyes of spectators. This is the charm that makes them irresistible. Is it for such fading perfections that a husband or a wife is chosen? Alas, it is well known that a very short familiarity totally destroys all sense and attention to such properties; and, on the contrary, a very little time and habit destroy all the aversion to ugliness and deformity, when unattended with disease or ill temper. Yet beauty and address are courted and admired, very often more than discretion, wit, sense, and many other accomplishments and virtues, of infinitely more importance to the happiness of private life as well as to the utility and ornament of society. Is it for the momentous purpose of dancing and drawing, painting and music, riding or fencing, that men or women are destined in this life or any other? Yet those who have the best means of education bestow more attention and expense on those than on more solid acquisitions. Why? Because they attract more forcibly the attention of the world and procure a better advancement in life. Notwithstanding all this, as soon as an establishment in life is made they are found to have answered their end, are neglected and laid aside.

Is there anything in birth, however illustrious or splendid, which should make a difference between one man and another?

If from a common ancestor the whole human race is descended, they are all of the same family. How then can they distinguish families into the more or the less ancient? What advantage is there in an illustration of an hundred or a thousand years? Of what avail are all these histories, pedigrees, traditions? What foundation has the whole science of genealogy and heraldry? Are there differences in the breeds of men as there are in those of horses? If there are not, these sciences have no foundation in reason; in prejudice they have a very solid one. All that philosophy can say is that there is a general presumption, that a man has had some advantages of education if he is of a family of note. But this advantage must be derived from his father and mother chiefly, if not wholly; of what importance is it then, in this view, whether the family is twenty generations upon record or only two?

The mighty secret lies in this: An illustrious descent attracts the notice of mankind. A single drop of royal blood, however illegitimately scattered, will make any man or woman proud or vain. Why? Because, although it excites the indignation of many and the envy of more, it still attracts the *attention* of the world. Noble blood, whether the nobility be hereditary or elective, and indeed more in republican governments than in monarchies, least of all in despotisms, is held in estimation for the same reason. It is a name and a race that a nation has been interested in and is in the habit of respecting. Benevolence, sympathy, congratulation have been so long associated to those names in the minds of the people that they are become national habits. National gratitude descends from the father to the son, and is often stronger to the latter than the former. It is often excited by remorse upon reflection on the ingratitude and injustice with which the former has been treated. When the names of a certain family are read in all the gazettes, chronicles, records, and histories of a country for five hundred years, they become known, respected, and delighted in by everybody. A youth, a child of this extraction and bearing this name, attracts the eyes and ears of all companies long before it is known or inquired whether he be a wise man or a fool. His name is often a greater distinction than a title, a star, or a garter. This it is which makes so many men proud, and so many others envious of illustrious descent. The pride is as irrational and contemptible as the pride of riches, and no more. A wise man will lament that any other distinction than that of merit should be made. A good man will neither be proud nor vain of his birth but will earnestly improve every advantage he has for the public good. A cunning man will carefully conceal his pride but will indulge it in secret the more effectually and improve his advantage to greater profit. But was any man ever known so wise, or so good, as really to despise birth or wealth? Did you ever read of a man rising to public notice from obscure beginnings who was not reflected on? Although with every liberal mind it is an honor and a proof of merit, yet it is a disgrace with mankind in general. What a load of sordid obloquy and envy has every such man to carry! The contempt that is thrown upon obscurity of ancestry augments the eagerness for the stupid adoration that is paid to its illustration.

This desire of the consideration of our fellow men and their congratulations in our joys is not less invincible than the desire of their sympathy in our sorrows. It is a determination of our nature that lies at the foundation of our whole moral system in this world and may be connected essentially with our destination in a future state.

2 [6]

O fureur de se distinguer, que ne pouvez vous point! VOLTAIRE.

Why do men pursue riches? What is the end of avarice?

The labor and anxiety, the enterprises and adventures, that are voluntarily undertaken in pursuit of gain are out of all proportion to the utility, convenience, or pleasure of riches. A competence to satisfy the wants of nature, food and clothes, a shelter from the seasons, and the comforts of a family may be had for very little. The daily toil of the million, and of millions of millions, is adequate to a complete supply of these necessities and conveniences. With such accommodations, thus obtained, the

[6] [VI, 237–240.]

appetite is keener, the digestion more easy and perfect, and repose is more refreshing than among the most abundant superfluities and the rarest luxuries. For what reason, then, are any mortals averse to the situation of the farmer, mechanic or laborer? Why do we tempt the seas and encompass the globe? Why do any men affront heaven and earth to accumulate wealth which will forever be useless to them? Why do we make an ostentatious display of riches? Why should any man be proud of his purse, houses, lands, or gardens; or, in better words, why should the rich man glory in his riches? What connection can there be between wealth and pride?

The answer to all these questions is, *because riches attract the attention, consideration, and congratulations of mankind;* it is not because the rich have really more of ease or pleasure than the poor. Riches force the opinion on a man that he is the object of the congratulations of others, and he feels that they attract the complaisance of the public. His senses all inform him that his neighbors have a natural disposition to harmonize with all those pleasing emotions and agreeable sensations which the elegant accommodations around him are supposed to excite.

His imagination expands and his heart dilates at these charming illusions. His attachment to his possessions increases as fast as his desire to accumulate more, not for the purposes of beneficence or utility, but from the desire of illustration.

Why, on the other hand, should any man be ashamed to make known his poverty? Why should those who have been rich or educated in the houses of the rich entertain such an aversion, or be agitated with such terror, at the prospect of losing their property or of being reduced to live at a humbler table, in a meaner house, to walk instead of riding, or to ride without their accustomed equipage or retinue? Why do we hear of madness, melancholy, and suicides upon bankruptcy, loss of ships, or any other sudden fall from opulence to indigence or mediocrity? Ask your reason what disgrace there can be in poverty? What moral sentiment of approbation, praise, or honor can there be in a palace? What dishonor in a cottage? What glory in a coach? What shame in a wagon? Is not the sense of propriety and sense of merit as much connected with an empty purse as a full one? May not a man be as estimable, amiable, and respectable, attended by his faithful dog, as if preceded and followed by a train of horses and servants? All these questions may be very wise, and the stoical philosophy has her answers ready. But if you ask the same questions of nature, experience, and mankind, the answers will be directly opposite to those of Epictetus, namely, that there is more respectability in the eyes of the greater part of mankind in the gaudy trappings of wealth than there is in genius or learning, wisdom or virtue.

The poor man's conscience is clear; yet he is ashamed. His character is irreproachable; yet he is neglected and despised. He feels himself out of the sight of others, groping in the dark. Mankind take no notice of him. He rambles and wanders un-heeded. In the midst of a crowd, at church, in the market, at a play, at an execution or coronation, he is in as much obscurity as he would be in a garret or a cellar. He is not disapproved, censured, or reproached; *he is only not seen.* This total inatten-tion is to him mortifying, painful, and cruel. He suffers a misery from this consideration, which is sharpened by the consciousness that others have no fellow-feeling with him in this distress. If you follow these persons, however, into their scenes of life, you will find that there is a kind of figure which the meanest of them all endeavors to make, a kind of little grandeur and respect which the most insignificant study and labor to procure in the small circle of their acquaintances. Not only the poorest mechanic, but the man who lives upon common charity, nay, the common beg-gars in the streets; and not only those who may be all innocent, but even those who have abandoned themselves to common infamy, as pirates, highwaymen, and common thieves, court a set of admirers and plume themselves upon that superiority which they have or fancy they have over some others. There must be one, indeed, who is the last and lowest of the human species. But there is no risk in asserting that there is no one who believes and will acknowledge himself to be the man. To be wholly over-looked and to know it are intolerable. Instances of this are not uncommon. When a wretch could no longer attract the notice of a man, woman, or child, he must be respectable in the eyes of his dog. "Who will love me then?" was the pathetic reply of one who starved himself to feed his mastiff, to a charitable passenger who advised him to kill or sell the animal. In this "who will love me then?" there is a key to the human heart, to the history of human life and manners, and to the rise and fall of empires. To feel ourselves unheeded chills the most pleasing hope, damps the most fond desire, checks the most agreeable wish, disappoints the most ardent expectations of human nature.

Is there in science and letters a reward for the labor they require? Scholars learn the dead languages of antiquity as well as the living tongues of modern nations; those of the east as well as the west. They puzzle themselves and others with metaphysics and mathematics. They renounce their pleasures, neglect their exercises, and destroy their health—for what? Is curiosity so strong? Is the pleasure that accompanies the pursuit and acquisition of knowledge so exquisite? If Crusoe on his island had the library of Alexandria and a certainty that he should never again see the face of man, would he ever open a volume? Perhaps he might; but it is very probable he would read but little. A sense of duty, a love of truth, a desire to alleviate the anxieties of ignorance may, no doubt, have an influence on some minds. But the universal object and idol of men of letters is *reputation*. It is the *notoriety*, the *celebration*, which constitutes the charm that is to compensate the loss of appetite and sleep and sometimes of riches and honors.

The same ardent desire of the *congratulations* of others in our joys is the great incentive to the pursuit of honors. This might be exemplified in the career of civil and political life. That we may not be too tedious, let us instance in military glory.

Is it to be supposed that the regular standing armies of Europe engage in the service for pure motives of patriotism? Are their officers men of contemplation and devotion who expect their reward in a future life? Is it from a sense of moral or religious duty that they risk their lives and reconcile themselves to wounds? Instances of all these kinds may be found. But if anyone supposes that all or the greater part of these heroes are actuated by such principles, he will only prove that he is unacquainted with them. Can their pay be considered as an adequate encouragement? This, which is no more than a very simple and moderate subsistence, would never be a temptation to renounce the chances of fortune in other pursuits, together with the pleasures of domestic life, and submit to this most difficult and dangerous employment. No, it is the consideration and the chances of laurels which they acquire by the service.

The soldier compares himself with his fellows and contends for promotion to be a corporal. The corporals vie with each other to be sergeants. The sergeants will mount breaches to be ensigns. And thus every man in an army is constantly aspiring to be something higher, as every citizen in the commonwealth is constantly struggling for a better rank, that he may draw the observation of more eyes.

3 [7]

. . . There is a voice within us which seems to intimate that real merit should govern the world, and that men ought to be respected only in proportion to their talents, virtues, and services. But the question always has been, how can this arrangement be accomplished? How shall the men of merit be discovered? How shall the proportions of merit be ascertained and graduated? Who shall be the judge? When the government of a great nation is in question, shall the whole nation choose? Will such a choice be better than chance? Shall the whole nation vote for senators? Thirty millions of votes, for example, for each senator in France! It is obvious that this would be a lottery of millions of blanks to one prize, and that the chance of having wisdom and integrity in a senator by hereditary descent would be far better. There is no individual personally known to an hundredth part of the nation. The voters, then, must be exposed to deception from intrigues and maneuvers without number, that is to say, from all the chicanery, impostures, and falsehoods imaginable, with scarce a possibility of preferring real merit. Will you divide the

[7] [VI, 249–252.]

nation into districts and let each district choose a senator? This is giving up the idea of national merit and annexing the honor and the trust to an accident, that of living on a particular spot. A hundred or a thousand men of the first merit in a nation may live in one city, and none at all of this description in several whole provinces. Real merit is so remote from the knowledge of whole nations that, were magistrates to be chosen by that criterion alone and by a universal suffrage, dissensions and venality would be endless. The difficulties arising from this source are so obvious and universal that nations have tried all sorts of experiments to avoid them.

As no appetite in human nature is more universal than that for honor, and real merit is confined to a very few, the numbers who thirst for respect are out of all proportion to those who seek it only by merit. The great majority trouble themselves little about merit but apply themselves to seek for honor by means which they see will more easily and certainly obtain it by displaying their taste and address, their wealth and magnificence, their ancient parchments, pictures, and statues, and the virtues of their ancestors; and if these fail, as they seldom have done, they have recourse to artifice, dissimulation, hypocrisy, flattery, imposture, empiricism, quackery, and bribery. What chance has humble, modest, obscure, and poor merit in such a scramble? Nations, perceiving that the still small voice of merit was drowned in the insolent roar of such dupes of impudence and knavery in national elections without a possibility of a remedy, have sought for something more permanent than the popular voice to designate honor. Many nations have attempted to annex it to land, presuming that a good estate would at least furnish means of a good education, and have resolved that those who should possess certain territories should have certain legislative, executive, and judicial powers over the people. Other nations have endeavored to connect honor with offices; and the names and ideas at least of certain moral virtues and intellectual qualities have been by law annexed to certain offices, as veneration, grace, excellence, honor, serenity, majesty. Other nations have attempted to annex honor to families without regard to lands or offices. The Romans allowed none but those who had possessed curule offices to have statues or portraits. He who had images or pictures of his ancestors was called noble. He who had no statue or pictures but his own was called a new man. Those who had none at all were ignoble. Other nations have united all those institutions—connected lands, offices, and families, made them all descend together, and honor, public attention, consideration, and congratulation along with them.

This has been the policy of Europe; and it is to this institution she owes her superiority in war and peace, in legislation and commerce, in agriculture, navigation, arts, sciences, and manufactures, to Asia and Africa.[8] These families, thus distinguished by property, honors, and privileges, by defending themselves have been obliged to defend the people against the encroachments of despotism. They have been a civil and political militia, constantly watching the designs of the standing armies and courts; and by defending their own rights, liberties, properties, and privileges, they have been obliged in some degree to defend those of the people by making a common cause with them. But there were several essential defects in this policy; one was that the people took no rational measures to defend themselves, either against these great families or the courts. They had no adequate representation of themselves in the sovereignty. Another was that it never was determined where the sovereignty resided. Generally it was claimed by kings, but not admitted by the nobles. Sometimes every baron pretended to be sovereign in his own territory; at other times the sovereignty was claimed by an assembly of nobles, under the name of States or Cortes. Sometimes the united authority of the king and states was called the sovereignty. The common people had no adequate and independent share in the legislatures and found themselves harassed to discover who was the sovereign and whom they ought to obey, as much as they ever had been or could be to determine who had the most merit.

[8] This is a truth, but by no means a justification of the system of nobility in France, nor in other parts of Europe. Not even in England without a more equitable representation of the Commons in the legislature. J. A. 1812.

A thousand years of barons' wars, causing universal darkness, ignorance, and barbarity, ended at last in simple monarchy, not by express stipulation but by tacit acquiescence, in almost all Europe—the people preferring a certain sovereignty in a single person to endless disputes about merit and sovereignty, which never did and never will produce anything but aristocratical anarchy; and the nobles contenting themselves with a security of their property and privileges by a government of fixed laws, registered and interpreted by a judicial power, which they called sovereign tribunals, though the legislation and execution were in a single person.

In this system to control the nobles, the church joined the kings and common people. The progress of reason, letters, and science has weakened the church and strengthened the common people, who, if they are honestly and prudently conducted by those who have their confidence, will most infallibly obtain a share in every legislature. But if the common people are advised to aim at collecting the whole sovereignty in single national assemblies, as they are by the Duke de la Rochefoucauld and the Marquis of Condorcet, or at the abolition of the regal executive authority, or at a division of the executive power, as they are by a posthumous publication of the Abbé de Mably [9]—they will fail of their desired liberty as certainly as emulation and rivalry are founded in human nature and inseparable from civil affairs. It is not to flatter the passions of the people, to be sure, nor is it the way to obtain a present enthusiastic popularity, to tell them that in a single assembly they will act as arbitrarily and tyrannically as any despot, but it is a sacred truth, and as demonstrable as any proposition whatever, that a sovereignty in a single assembly must necessarily and will certainly be exercised by a majority as tyrannically as any sovereignty was ever exercised by kings or nobles. And if a balance of passions and interests is not scientifically concerted, the present struggle in Europe will be little beneficial to mankind [10] and produce nothing but another thousand years of feudal fanaticism under new and strange names.

[9] Witness the quintuple directory and the triumvirate consulate. J. A.
[10] Witness France and Europe in 1813. J. A.

4 [11]

> First follow nature; and your judgment frame
> By her just standard, which is still the same.   POPE.

The world grows more enlightened. Knowledge is more equally diffused. Newspapers, magazines, and circulating libraries have made mankind wiser. Titles and distinctions, ranks and orders, parade and ceremony are all going out of fashion. This is roundly asserted in the streets and sometimes on theatres of higher *rank*.[12] Some truth there is in it; and if the opportunity were temperately improved, to the reformation of abuses, the rectification of errors, and the dissipation of pernicious prejudices, a great advantage it might be. But, on the other hand, false inferences may be drawn from it, which may make mankind wish for the age of dragons, giants, and fairies. If all decorum, discipline, and subordination are to be destroyed and universal Pyrrhonism, anarchy, and insecurity of property are to be introduced, nations will soon wish their books in ashes, seek for darkness and ignorance, superstition and fanaticism as blessings, and follow the standard of the first mad despot who, with the enthusiasm of another Mahomet,[13] will endeavor to obtain them.

Are riches, honors, and beauty going out of fashion? Is not the rage for them, on the contrary, increased faster than improvement in knowledge? As long as either of these are in vogue, will there not be emulations and rivalries? Does not the increase of knowledge in any man increase his emulation, and the diffusion of knowledge among men multiply rivalries? Has the progress of science, arts, and letters yet discovered that there are no passions in human nature—no ambition, avarice, or desire of fame? Are these passions cooled, diminished, or extinguished? Is the rage for admiration less ardent in men or women? Have these propensities less a tendency to divisions, controversies, seditions, mutinies, and civil wars than formerly? On the contrary, the more

[11] [VI, 274–281, passim.]
[12] Read the history of the world, from 1790 to 1813, as a comment.
[13] Napoleon is not all this. J. A. 1813.

knowledge is diffused, the more the passions are extended, and the more furious they grow. Had Cicero less vanity, or Caesar less ambition, for their vast erudition? Had the King of Prussia [14] less of one than the other? There is no connection in the mind between science and passion by which the former can extinguish or diminish the latter. It, on the contrary, sometimes increases them by giving them exercise. Were the passions of the Romans less vivid in the age of Pompey than in the time of Mummius? Are those of the Britons more moderate at this hour than in the reigns of the Tudors? Are the passions of monks the weaker for all their learning? Are not jealousy, envy, hatred, malice, and revenge, as well as emulation and ambition, as rancorous in the cells of Carmelites [b] as in the courts of princes? Go to the Royal Society of London. [c] Is there less emulation for the chair of Sir Isaac Newton than there was, and commonly will be, for all elective presidencies? Is there less animosity and rancor arising from mutual emulations in that region of science than there is among the most ignorant of mankind? Go to Paris—How do you find the men of letters? United, friendly, harmonious, meek, humble, modest, charitable? Prompt to mutual forbearance? Unassuming? Ready to acknowledge superior merit? Zealous to encourage the first symptoms of genius? Ask Voltaire and Rousseau, Marmontel and De Mably.

The increase and dissemination of knowledge, instead of rendering unnecessary the checks of emulation and the balances of rivalry in the orders of society and constitution of government, augment the necessity of both. It becomes the more indispensable that every man should know his place and be made to keep it. Bad men increase in knowledge as fast as good men; and science, arts, taste, sense, and letters are employed for the purposes of injustice and tyranny as well as those of law and liberty, for corruption as well as for virtue.

FRENCHMEN! Act and think like yourselves! confessing human nature, be magnanimous and wise. Acknowledging and boasting yourselves to be men, avow the feelings of men. The affectation of being exempted from passions is inhuman. The grave preten-

[14] [Reference is to Frederick the Great.]

sion to such singularity is solemn hypocrisy. Both are unworthy of your frank and generous natures. Consider that government is intended to set bounds to passions which nature has not limited; and to assist reason, conscience, justice, and truth in controlling interest which without it would be as unjust as uncontrollable.[15]

AMERICANS! Rejoice, that from experience you have learned wisdom; and instead of whimsical and fantastical projects, you have adopted a promising essay towards a well-ordered government. Instead of following any foreign example, to return to *the legislation of confusion,* contemplate the means of restoring decency, honesty, and order in society by preserving and completing, if anything should be found necessary to complete, the balance of your government. In a well-balanced government, reason, conscience, truth, and virtue must be respected by all parties, and exerted for the public good.[16] Advert to the principles on which you commenced that glorious self-defense, which, if you behave with steadiness and consistency, may ultimately loosen the chains of all mankind. If you will take the trouble to read over the memorable proceedings of the town of Boston, on the twenty-eighth day of October, 1772, when the Committee of Correspondence of twenty-one persons [d] was appointed to state the rights of the colonists as men, as Christians, and as subjects, and to publish them to the world, with the infringements and violations of them,[17] you will find the great principles of civil and religious liberty for which you have contended so successfully, and which the world is contending for after your example. I could transcribe with pleasure the whole of this immortal pamphlet, which is a real picture of the sun of liberty rising on the human race, but shall select only a few words more directly to the present purpose. . . .

[15] Frenchmen neither saw, heard, nor felt or understood this. J. A. 1813.

[16] Americans paid no attention or regard to this. And a blind, mad rivalry between the north and the south is destroying all morality and sound policy. God grant that division, civil war, murders, assassination, and massacres may not soon grow out of these rivalries of states, families, and individuals.

[17] This Boston pamphlet was drawn by the great James Otis. J. A. 1813.

This is all enchanting. But amidst our enthusiasm there is great reason to pause and preserve our sobriety. It is true that the first empire of the world is breaking the fetters of human reason and exerting the energies of redeemed liberty. In the glowing ardor of her zeal, she condescends, Americans, to pay the most scrupulous attention to your maxims, principles, and example. There is reason to fear she has copied from you errors which have cost you very dear. Assist her, by your example, to rectify them before they involve her in calamities as much greater than yours, as her population is more unwieldly and her situation more exposed to the baleful influence of rival neighbors. Amidst all their exultations Americans and Frenchmen should remember that the perfectibility of man is only human and terrestrial perfectibility. Cold will still freeze, and fire will never cease to burn; disease and vice will continue to disorder, and death to terrify mankind. Emulation next to self-preservation will forever be the great spring of human actions, and the balance of a well-ordered government will alone be able to prevent that emulation from degenerating into dangerous ambition, irregular rivalries, destructive factions, wasting seditions, and bloody, civil wars.[18]

The great question will forever remain, *who shall work?* Our species cannot all be idle. Leisure for study must ever be the portion of a few. The number employed in government must forever be very small. Food, raiment, and habitations, the indispensable wants of all, are not to be obtained without the continual toil of ninety-nine in a hundred of mankind. As rest is rapture to the weary man, those who labor little will always be envied by those who labor much, though the latter in reality be probably the most enviable. With all the encouragements, public and private, which can ever be given to general education, and it is scarcely possible they should be too many or too great, the laboring part of the people can never be learned. The controversy between the rich and the poor, the laborious and the idle, the learned and the ignorant, distinctions as old as the creation

[18] View France, Europe, and America, in 1813, and compare the state of them all with this paragraph written twenty-three years ago! J. A.

and as extensive as the globe, distinctions which no art or policy, no degree of virtue or philosophy can ever wholly destroy, will continue, and rivalries will spring out of them. These parties will be represented in the legislature, and must be balanced, or one will oppress the other. There will never probably be found any other mode of establishing such an equilibrium than by constituting the representation of each an independent branch of the legislature, and an independent executive authority, such as that in our government, to be a third branch and a mediator or an arbitrator between them. Property must be secured, or liberty cannot exist. But if unlimited or unbalanced power of disposing property be put into the hands of those who have no property, France will find, as we have found, the lamb committed to the custody of the wolf. In such a case, all the pathetic exhortations and addresses of the national assembly to the people to respect property will be regarded no more than the warbles of the songsters of the forest. The great art of lawgiving consists in balancing the poor against the rich in the legislature and in constituting the legislative a perfect balance against the executive power at the same time that no individual or party can become its rival. The essence of a free government consists in an effectual control of rivalries. The executive and the legislative powers are natural rivals; and if each has not an effectual control over the other, the weaker will ever be the lamb in the paws of the wolf. The nation which will not adopt an equilibrium of power must adopt a despotism. There is no other alternative. Rivalries must be controlled, or they will throw all things into confusion; and there is nothing but despotism or a balance of power which can control them. Even in the simple monarchies the nobility and the judicatures constitute a balance, though a very imperfect one, against the royalties.

Let us conclude with one reflection more which shall barely be hinted at, as delicacy, if not prudence, may require in this place some degree of reserve. Is there a possibility that the government of nations may fall into the hands of men who teach the most disconsolate of all creeds, that men are but fireflies and that this *all* is without a father? Is this the way to make man, as

man, an object of respect? Or is it to make murder itself as indifferent as shooting a plover, and the extermination of the Rohilla
nation[e] as innocent as the swallowing of mites on a morsel of
cheese? If such a case should happen, would not one of these,
the most credulous of all believers, have reason to pray to his
eternal nature or his almighty chance (the more absurdity there
is in this address the more in character) *give us again the gods of
the Greeks; give us again the more intelligible as well as more
comfortable systems of Athanasius and Calvin; nay, give us again
our popes and hierarchies, Benedictines and Jesuits, with all their
superstition and fanaticism, impostures and tyranny.* A certain
duchess of venerable years and masculine understanding,[19] said
of some of the philosophers of the eighteenth century admirably
well, "On ne croit pas dans le Christianisme, mais on croit toutes
les sottises possibles."

[19] The Duchess d'Enville, the mother of the Duc de la Rochefoucauld.
The author heard those words from that lady's own lips; with many other
striking effusions of the strong and large mind of a great and excellent
female character. J. A.

IV. LETTERS TO JOHN TAYLOR, OF CAROLINE, VIRGINIA [1]

In 1814, John Taylor of Caroline, Virginia, published *An Inquiry into the Principles and Policy of the Government of the United States,* which contained a running commentary on John Adams' *Defence.* It was Adams' view that Taylor had misconceived or not properly comprehended the main thesis of the *Defence.* Hence these letters represent Adams' second look at his own *Defence* and are in addition a rejoinder to Taylor's strictures. The writing is lively, not ponderous, at times quite penetrating, and represents well Adams' political views in his old age. The caustic tone of some of the letters may not be interpreted to mean that Adams and Taylor were enemies. Adams always took delight in controversial, even heated, debate on matters of government. In fact, he and John Taylor despite political differences became firm in their friendship in part as a result of this very exchange of views. Two years before Adams' death in 1826, John Taylor expressed his esteem for his old friend by requesting him "to file among your archives some facts [which Taylor had recorded in his letter,] which may meet the eye of a historian, as well as to give some pleasure to a patriot, who I believe has served his country faithfully and has done what man can do to please his God." [2]

1 [3]

QUINCY, 15 April, 1814.

Sir: I have received your *Inquiry* in a large volume neatly bound. Though I have not read it in course, yet, upon an application to it of the *Sortes Virgilianæ,* scarce a page has been found in which my name is not mentioned and some public sentiment or expression of mine examined. Revived as these subjects are, in this manner, in the recollection of the public, after an oblivion of so many years, by a gentleman of your high rank, ample fortune, learned education, and powerful connec-

[1] [*Works* VI, 447–521 passim.]
[2] [X, 412.]   [3] [VI, 447–449.]

195

tions, I flatter myself it will not be thought improper in me to solicit your attention to a few explanations and justifications of a book that has been misunderstood, misrepresented, and abused more than any other, except the Bible, that I have ever read.

In the first words of the first section, you say, "Mr. Adams' political system deduces government from a *natural* fate; the policy of the United States deduces it from *moral* liberty."

This sentence, I must acknowledge, passes all my understanding. I know not what is meant by fate, nor what distinction there is, or may be made or conceived, between a natural and artificial or unnatural fate. Nor do I well know what "moral liberty" signifies. I have read a great deal about the words *fate* and *chance;* but though I close my eyes to abstract my meditations, I never could conceive any idea of either. When an action or event happens or occurs without a cause, some say it happens by chance. This is equivalent to saying that chance is no cause at all; it is nothing. Fate, too, is no cause, no agent, no power; it has neither understanding, will, affections, liberty, nor choice; it has no existence; it is not even a figment of imagination; it is a mere invention of a word without a meaning; it is a nonentity; it is nothing. Mr. Adams most certainly never deduced any system from chance or fate, natural, artificial, or unnatural.

Liberty, according to my metaphysics, is an intellectual quality, an attribute that belongs not to fate nor chance. Neither possesses it, neither is capable of it. There is nothing moral or immoral in the idea of it. The definition of it is a self-determining power in an intellectual agent. It implies thought and choice and power; it can elect between objects, indifferent in point of morality, neither morally good nor morally evil. If the substance in which this quality, attribute, adjective—call it what you will—exists, has a moral sense, a conscience, a moral faculty; if it can distinguish between moral good and moral evil, and has power to choose the former and refuse the latter, it can, if it will, choose the evil and reject the good, as we see in experience it very often does.

"Mr. Adams' system" and "the policy of the United States" are drawn from the same sources, deduced from the same principles, wrought into the same frame; indeed, they are the same and ought never to have been divided or separated; much less set in opposition to each other, as they have been.

That we may more clearly see how these hints apply, certain technical terms must be defined.

1. Despotism. A sovereignty unlimited, that is, the *suprema lex*, the *summa potestatis* in one.[a] This has rarely, if ever, existed but in theory.

2. Monarchy. Sovereignty in one, variously limited.

3. Aristocracy. Sovereignty in a few.

4. Democracy. Sovereignty in the many, that is, in the whole nation, the whole body, assemblage, congregation, or if you are an Episcopalian,[b] you may call it, if you please, *church*, of the whole people. This sovereignty must, in all cases, be exerted or exercised by the whole people assembled together. This form of government has seldom, if ever, existed but in theory—as rarely, at least, as an unlimited despotism in one individual.

5. The infinite variety of mixed governments are all so many different combinations, modifications, and intermixtures of the second, third, and fourth species or divisions.

Now, every one of these sovereigns possesses intellectual liberty to act for the public good or not. Being men, they have all what Dr. Rush calls a *moral faculty*; Dr. Hutcheson, a *moral sense*; and the Bible and the generality of the world, *a conscience*. They are all, therefore, under moral obligations to do to others as they would have others *do to them*—to consider themselves born, authorized, empowered for the good of society as well as their own good. Despots, monarchs, aristocrats, democrats, holding such high trusts, are under the most solemn and the most sacred moral obligations to consider their trusts and their power to be instituted for the benefit and happiness of their nations, not their nations as servants to them or their friends or parties. In other words, to exert all their intellectual liberty to employ all their faculties, talents, and power for the public, general, universal good of their nations, not for their own separate good or the interest of any party.

In this point of view, there is no difference in forms of government. All of them, and all men concerned in them—all are under equal moral obligations. The intellectual liberty of aristocracies and democracies can be exerted only by votes and ascertained only by ayes and noes. The sovereign judgment and will can be determined, known, and declared only by majorities. This will, this decision, is sometimes determined by a single vote, often by two or three, very rarely by a large majority, scarcely ever by a unanimous suffrage. And from the impossibility of keeping together at all times the same number of voters, the majorities are apt to waver from day to day and swing like a pendulum from side to side.

Nevertheless, the minorities have, in all cases, the same intellectual liberty and are under the same moral obligations as the majorities.

In what manner these theoretical, intellectual liberties have been exercised, and these moral obligations fulfilled, by despots, monarchs, aristocrats, and democrats, is obvious enough in history and in experience. They have all in general conducted themselves alike.

But this investigation is not at present before us.

2 *

. . . There is no necessity of "confronting Mr. Adams' opinion, that aristocracy is natural and therefore unavoidable, with the other, that it is artificial or factitious and therefore avoidable," because the opinions are both true and perfectly consistent with each other.

By *natural aristocracy,* in general, may be understood those superiorities of influence in society which grow out of the constitution of human nature. By *artificial aristocracy,* those inequalities of weight and superiorities of influence which are created and established by civil laws. Terms must be defined before we can reason. By aristocracy, I understand all those men who can command, influence, or procure more than an average of votes; by an aristocrat, every man who can and will influence one man

* [VI, 451–452.]

to vote besides himself. Few men will deny that there is a
natural aristocracy of virtues and talents in every nation and in
every party, in every city and village. Inequalities are a part of
the natural history of man.

3 ⁵

3 ⁵

I believe that none but Helvetius will affirm that all children
are born with equal genius.

None will pretend that all are born of dispositions exactly
alike—of equal weight, equal strength, equal length, equal
delicacy of nerves, equal elasticity of muscles, equal complexions,
equal figure, grace, or beauty.

I have seen, in the Hospital of Foundlings, the "*Enfans
Trouvés,*" at Paris, fifty babes in one room—all under four days
old, all in cradles alike, all nursed and attended alike, all dressed
alike, all equally neat. I went from one end to the other of the
whole row and attentively observed all their countenances. And
I never saw a greater variety or more striking inequalities in the
streets of Paris or London. Some had every sign of grief, sorrow,
and despair; others had joy and gayety in their faces. Some were
sinking in the arms of death; others looked as if they might live
to fourscore. Some were as ugly and others as beautiful, as
children or adults ever are; these were stupid; those sensible.
These were all born to equal rights, but to very different fortunes,
to very different success and influence in life.

The world would not contain the books if one should produce
all the examples that reading and experience would furnish.
One or two permit me to hint.

Will any man say, would Helvetius say, that all men are born
equal in strength? Was Hercules no stronger than his neighbors?
How many nations, for how many ages, have been governed by
his strength and by the reputation and renown of it by his posterity? If you have lately read Hume, Robertson, or the Scottish
Chiefs, let me ask you if Sir William Wallace was no more than
equal in strength to the average of Scotchmen, and whether

⁵ [VI, 452–454.]

Wallace could have done what he did without that extraordinary strength?

Will Helvetius or Rousseau say that all men and women are born equal in beauty? Will any philosopher say that beauty has no influence in human society? If he does, let him read the histories of Eve, Judith, Helen, the fair Gabrielle, Diana of Poitiers, Pompadour, du Barry, Susanna, Abigail, Lady Hamilton, Mrs. Clark, and a million others. Are not despots, monarchs, aristocrats, and democrats equally liable to be seduced by beauty to confer favors and influence suffrages?

Socrates calls beauty a short-lived tyranny; Plato, the privilege of nature; Theophrastus, a mute eloquence; Diogenes, the best letter of recommendation; Carneades, a queen without soldiers; Theocritus, a serpent covered with flowers; Bion, a good that does not belong to the possessor, because it is impossible to give ourselves beauty or to preserve it. Madame du Barry expressed the philosophy of Carneades in more laconic language when she said, "La véritable royauté, c'est la beauté"—the genuine royalty is beauty. And she might have said with equal truth that it is genuine aristocracy; for it has as much influence in one form of government as in any other and produces aristocracy in the deepest democracy that ever was known or imagined, as infallibly as in any other form of government. What shall we say to all these philosophers, male and female? Is not beauty a privilege granted by nature, according to Plato and to truth, often more influential in society, and even upon laws and government, than stars, garters, crosses, eagles, golden fleeces, or any hereditary titles or other distinctions? The grave elders were not proof against the charms of Susanna. The Grecian sages wondered not at the Trojan war when they saw Helen. Holofernes' guards, when they saw Judith, said, "One such woman let go would deceive the whole earth."

Can you believe, Mr. Taylor, that the brother of such a sister, the father of such a daughter, the husband of such a wife, or even the gallant of such a mistress, would have but one vote in your moral republic? Ingenious—but not historical, philosophical, or political—learned, classical, poetical Barlow! I mourn over thy life and thy death. Had truth, instead of popularity and party, been thy object, your pamphlet on privileged orders would have been a very different thing!

That all men are born to equal rights is true. Every being has a right to his own, as clear, as moral, as sacred as any other being has. This is as indubitable as a moral government in the universe. But to teach that all men are born with equal powers and faculties, to equal influence in society, to equal property and advantages through life, is as gross a fraud, as glaring an imposition on the credulity of the people as ever was practised by monks, by Druids,c by Brahmins, by priests of the immortal Lama, or by the self-styled philosophers of the French revolution. For honor's sake, Mr. Taylor, for truth and virtue's sake, let American philosophers and politicians despise it.

Mr. Adams leaves to Homer and Virgil, to Tacitus and Quintilian, to Mahomet and Calvin, to Edwards and Priestley, or, if you will, to Milton's angels reasoning high in pandemonium, all their acute speculations about fate, destiny, foreknowledge absolute, necessity, and predestination. He thinks it problematical whether there is, or ever will be, more than one Being capable of understanding this vast subject. In his principles of legislation he has nothing to do with these interminable controversies. He considers men as free, moral, and accountable agents; and he takes men as God has made them. And will Mr. Taylor deny that God has made some men deaf and some blind, or will he affirm that these will infallibly have as much influence in society and be able to procure as many votes as any who can see and hear?

Honor the day,6 and believe me no enemy. . . .

4 7

When your new democratical republic meets, you will find half a dozen men of independent fortunes; half a dozen, of more eloquence; half a dozen, with more learning; half a dozen, with eloquence, learning, and fortune.

Let me see. We have now twenty-four; to these we may

6 19 April. The anniversary of the action at Lexington.
7 [VI, 456–458.]

add six more, who will have more art, cunning, and intrigue than learning, eloquence, or fortune. These will infallibly soon unite with the twenty-four. Thus we make thirty. The remaining seventy are composed of farmers, shopkeepers, merchants, tradesmen, and laborers. Now, if each of these thirty can, by any means, influence one vote besides his own, the whole thirty can carry sixty votes—a decided and uncontrolled majority of the hundred. These thirty I mean by aristocrats, and they will instantly convert your democracy of ONE HUNDRED into an aristocracy of THIRTY.

Take at random, or select with your utmost prudence, one hundred of your most faithful and capable domestics from your own numerous plantations and make them a democratical republic. You will immediately perceive the same inequalities and the same democratical republic, in a very few of the first sessions, transformed into an aristocratical republic, as complete and perfect an aristocracy as the senate of Rome, and much more so. Some will be beloved and followed, others hated and avoided by their fellows.

It would be easy to quote Greek and Latin to produce a hundred authorities to show the original signification of the word *aristocracy* and its infinite variations and application in the history of ages. But this would be all waste water. Once for all I give you notice that whenever I use the word *aristocrat* I mean a citizen who can command or govern two votes or more in society, whether by his virtues, his talents, his learning, his loquacity, his taciturnity, his frankness, his reserve, his face, figure, eloquence, grace, air, attitude, movements, wealth, birth, art, address, intrigue, good fellowship, drunkenness, debauchery, fraud, perjury, violence, treachery, pyrrhonism, deism, or atheism; for by every one of these instruments have votes been obtained and will be obtained. You seem to think aristocracy consists altogether in artificial titles, tinsel decorations of stars, garters, ribbons, golden eagles and golden fleeces, crosses and roses and lilies, exclusive privileges, hereditary descents, established by kings or by positive laws of society. No such thing! Aristocracy was from the beginning, now is, and ever will be, world without end, independent of all these artificial regulations as really and as efficaciously as with them!

Let me say a word more. Your democratical republic picked in the streets and your democratical African republic, or your domestic republic, call it which you will, in its first session will become an aristocratical republic. In the second session it will become an oligarchical republic, because the seventy-four democrats and the twenty-six aristocrats will, by this time, discover that thirteen of the aristocrats can command four votes each; these thirteen will now command the majority and, consequently, will be sovereign. The thirteen will then be an oligarchy. In the third session, it will be found that among these thirteen oligarchs there are seven, each of whom can command eight votes, equal in all to fifty-six, a decided majority. In the fourth session, it will be found that there are among these seven oligarchs four who can command thirteen votes apiece. The republic then becomes an oligarchy whose sovereignty is in four individuals. In the fifth session, it will be discovered that two of the four can command twenty-six votes each. Then two will have the command of the sovereign oligarchy. In the sixth session, there will be a sharp contention between the two which shall have the command of the fifty-two votes. Here will commence the squabble of Danton and Robespierre, of Julius and Pompey, of Anthony and Augustus, of the white rose and the red rose,[d] of Jefferson and Adams, of Burr and Jefferson, of Clinton and Madison, or, if you will, of Napoleon and Alexander.

This, my dear sir, is the history of mankind, past, present, and to come.

5 [8]

When superior genius gives greater influence in society than is possessed by inferior genius, or a mediocrity of genius, that is, than by the ordinary level of men, this superior influence I call natural aristocracy. This cause, you say, is "fluctuating." What then? It is aristocracy still, while it exists. And is not democracy

[8] [VI. 493–496.]

"fluctuating" too? Are the waves of the sea, or the winds of the air, or the gossamer that idles in the wanton summer air more fluctuating than democracy? While I admit the existence of democracy, notwithstanding its instability, you must acknowledge the existence of natural aristocracy, notwithstanding its fluctuations.

I find it difficult to understand you when you say that "knowledge and ignorance are fluctuating." Knowledge is unchangeable; and ignorance cannot change, because it is nothing. It is a nonentity. Truth is one, uniform and eternal; knowledge of it cannot fluctuate any more than itself. Ignorance of truth, being a nonentity, cannot surely become entity and fluctuate and change like Proteus, or wind, or water. You sport away so merrily upon this topic that I will have the pleasure of transcribing you. You say, "The aristocracy of superior abilities will be regulated by the extent of the space between knowledge and ignorance; as the space contracts or widens, it will be diminished or increased; and if aristocracy may be thus diminished, it follows that it may be thus destroyed."

What is the amount of this argument? Ignorance may be destroyed and knowledge increased *ad infinitum*. And do you expect that all men are to become omniscient, like the almighty and omniscient Hindu, perfect Brahmins? Are your hopes founded upon an expectation that knowledge will one day be equally divided? Will women have as much knowledge as men? Will children have as much as their parents? If the time will never come when all men will have equal knowledge, it *seems* to follow that some will know more than others; and that those who know most will have more influence than those who know least, or than those who know half way between the two extremes, and consequently will be aristocrats. "Superior abilities" comprehend abilities acquired by education and study as well as genius and natural parts; and what a source of inequality and aristocracy is here! Suffer me to dilate a little in this place. Massachusetts has probably educated as many sons to letters, in proportion to her numbers, as any State in the Union, perhaps as any nation, ancient or modern. What proportion do the scholars bear to the

whole number of people? I wish I had a catalogue of our Harvard University that I might state exact numbers. Say that, in
almost two hundred years, there have been three or four thousand educated, from perhaps two or three millions of people. Are
not these aristocrats or, in other words, have they not had more
influence than any equal number of uneducated men? In fact,
these men governed the province from its first settlement; these
men have governed and still govern the state. These men, in
schools, academies, colleges, and universities; these men, in the
shape of ministers, lawyers, and physicians; these men, in
academies of arts and sciences, in agricultural societies, in historical societies, in medical societies and in antiquarian societies,
in banking institutions and in Washington benevolent societies
govern the state, at this twenty-sixth of December, 1814. The
more you educate, without a balance in the government, the more
aristocratical will the people and the government be. There never
can be, in any nation, more than one fifth—no, not one tenth—
of the men regularly educated to science and letters. I hope, then,
you will acknowledge that "abilities" form a *distinction* and
confer a privilege, in fact, though they give no peculiar rights
in society.

2. You appear, sir, to have overlooked or forgotten one great
source of natural aristocracy, mentioned by me in my Apology
and dilated on in subsequent pages—I mean *birth*. I should be
obliged to you for your candid sentiments upon this important
subject. Exceptions have been taken to the phrase *well born;* but
I can see no more impropriety in it than in the epithets *well
bred, well educated, well brought up, well taught, well informed,
well read, well to live, well dressed, well fed, well clothed, well
armed, well accoutered, well furnished, well made, well fought,
well aimed, well meant, well mounted, well fortified, well tempered, well fatted, well spoken, well argued, well reasoned, well
decked, well ducked, well trimmed, well wrought,* or any other
well in common parlance.

And here, sir, permit me, by way of digression, to remark
another discouragement to honest political literature and the
progress of real political science. If a *well-meant* publication

appears, it is instantly searched for an unpopular word or one that can be made so by misconstruction, misrepresentation, or by any credible and imposing deception. Some ambitious, popular demagogue gives the alarm—"heresy?" Holy, democratical church has decreed that word to be "heresy!" Down with him! And if there was no check to their passions and no balance to their government, they would say, *à la lanterne! à la guillotine! roast him! bake him! boil him! fry him!* The Inquisition in Spain would not celebrate more joyfully an *auto-da-fé*.[e]

Some years ago, more than forty, a writer unfortunately made use of the term *better sort*. Instantly, a popular clamor was raised and an odium excited, which remains to this day to such a degree that no man dares to employ that expression at the bar, in conversation, in a newspaper, or pamphlet, no, nor in the pulpit; though the "baser sort" are sufficiently marked and distinguished in the New Testament to prove that there is no wrong in believing a "better sort." And if there is any difference between virtue and vice, there is a "better sort" and a worse sort in every human society.

With sincere reverence let me here quote one of the most profound philosophical, moral, and religious sentiments that ever was expressed: *"We know not what spirit we are of."*

6 [9]

That the first want of man is his dinner, and the second his girl, were truths well known to every democrat and aristocrat long before the great philosopher Malthus arose to think he enlightened the world by the discovery.

It has been equally well known that the second want is frequently so impetuous as to make men and women forget the first and rush into rash marriages, leaving both the first and second wants, their own as well as those of their children and grandchildren, to the chapter of accidents. The most religious very often leave the consideration of these wants to Him who supplies the young ravens when they cry.

The natural, necessary, and unavoidable consequence of all this

[9] [VI, 516.]

is that the multiplication of the population so far transcends the
multiplication of the means of subsistence that the constant labor
of nine tenths of our species will forever be necessary to prevent
all of them from starving with hunger, cold, and pestilence. Make
all men Newtons, or, if you will, Jeffersons, or Taylors, or Ran-
dolphs, and they would all perish in a heap! . . .

7 [10]

A few words more concerning the characters of literary men.
What sort of men have had the conduct of the presses in the
United States for the last thirty years? In Germany, in England,
in France, in Holland, the presses, even the newspapers, have
been under the direction of learned men. How has it been in
America? How many presses, how many newspapers have been
directed by vagabonds, fugitives from a bailiff, a pillory, or a
halter in Europe?

You know it is one of the sublimest and profoundest discoveries
of the eighteenth century that knowledge is corruption; that arts,
sciences, and taste have deformed the beauty and destroyed the
felicity of human nature, which appears only in perfection in the
savage state—the children of nature. One writer gravely tells us
that the first man who fenced a tobacco yard and said, "this is
mine," ought instantly to have been put to death; another as
solemnly says, the first man who pronounced the word "dieu"
ought to have been dispatched on the spot; yet these are advocates of toleration and enemies of the Inquisition.[11]

I never had enough of the ethereal spirit to rise to these heights.
My humble opinion is that knowledge, upon the whole, pro-
motes virtue and happiness. I therefore hope that you and all
other gentlemen of property, education, and reputation will exert
your utmost influence in establishing schools, colleges, academies,
and universities, and employ every means and opportunity to
spread information, even to the lowest dregs of the people, if any
such there are, even among your own domestics and John Randolph's serfs.[f] I fear not the propagation and dissemination of

[10] [VI, 518–521.]
[11] *Vide* Rousseau and Diderot *passim.*

knowledge. The conditions of humanity will be improved and ameliorated by its expansion and diffusion in every direction. May every human being—man, woman, and child—be as well informed as possible! But, after all, did you ever see a rose without a briar, a convenience without an inconvenience, a good without an evil, in this mingled world? Knowledge is applied to bad purposes as well as to good ones. Knaves and hypocrites can acquire it, as well as honest, candid, and sincere men. It is employed as an engine and a vehicle to propagate error and falsehood, treason and vice, as well as truth, honor, virtue, and patriotism. It composes and pronounces, both panegyrics and philippics, with exquisite art, to confound all distinctions in society between right and wrong. And if I admit, as I do, that truth generally prevails and virtue is or will be triumphant in the end, you must allow that honesty has a hard struggle and must prevail by many a well-fought and fortunate battle, and, after all, must often look to another world for justice, if not for pardon.

There is no necessary connection between knowledge and virtue. Simple intelligence has no association with morality. What connection is there between the mechanism of a clock or watch and the feeling of moral good and evil, right or wrong? A faculty or a quality of distinguishing between moral good and evil, as well as physical happiness and misery, that is, pleasure and pain, or, in other words, a *conscience*—an old word almost out of fashion—is essential to morality.

Now, how far does simple, theoretical knowledge quicken or sharpen conscience? La Harpe, in some part of his great work, his *Course of Literature,* has given us an account of a tribe of learned men and elegant writers who kept a kind of office in Paris for selling at all prices, down to three livres, essays or paragraphs upon any subject, good or evil, for or against any party, any cause, or any person. One of the most conspicuous and popular booksellers in England, both with the courtiers and the citizens, who employed many printers and supported many writers, has said to me, "The men of learning in this country are stark mad. There are in this city a hundred men, gentlemen of liberal education, men of science, classical scholars, fine writers, whom I can hire at any time at a guinea a day to write for me for or against any man, any party, or any cause." Can we wonder, then, at anything we read in British journals, magazines, newspapers, or reviews?

Where are, and where have been, the greatest masses of science, of literature, or of taste? Shall we look for them in the church or the state, in the universities or the academies, among Greek or Roman philosophers, Hindus, Brahmins, Chinese mandarins, Chaldean magi, British druids, Indian prophets, or Christian monks? Has it not been the invariable maxim of them all to deceive the people by any lies, however gross? "Bonus populus vult decipi; ergo decipiatur." [8]

And after all that can be done to disseminate knowledge, you never can equalize it. The number of laborers must and will forever be so much more multitudinous than that of the students that there will always be giants as well as pygmies, the former of which will have more influence than the latter, man for man and head for head; and, therefore, the former will be aristocrats and the latter democrats, if not Jacobins or *sans culottes*.

These morsels and a million others analogous to them, which will easily occur to you if you will be pleased to give them a careful mastication and rumination, must, I think, convince you that no practicable or possible advancement of learning can ever equalize knowledge among men to such a degree that some will not have more influence in society than others; and, consequently, that some will always be aristocrats and others democrats. You may read the history of all the universities, academies, monasteries of the world and see whether learning extinguishes human passions or corrects human vices. You will find in them as many parties and factions, as much jealousy and envy, hatred and malice, revenge and intrigue, as you will in any legislative assembly or executive council, the most ignorant city or village. Are not the men of letters—philosophers, divines, physicians, lawyers, orators, and poets—all over the world, at perpetual strife with one another? Knowledge, therefore, as well as genius, strength, activity, industry, beauty, and twenty other things, will forever be a natural cause of aristocracy.

NOTES

INTRODUCTION

(a) FEDERALIST PARTY: A political party which was organized in 1787 for the purpose of furthering the adoption of the Constitution of the U. S. Conservative in its philosophy, it stood for a strong federal government. Hamilton, who is believed to be its founder, was its leader until his death in 1804.

(b) REPUBLICAN PARTY: A political party, also known as the Democratic-Republican Party, which was founded by Thomas Jefferson, in opposition to the Federalist Party, for the defense of the states' rights. Its major support came from the farmers, small business men, and small townspeople in general.

(c) JACOBIN: A name given pro-French democratic clubs organized in the United States in 1793. The name was derived from the famous political clubs of the French Revolution.

(d) QUID: In United States politics a Democratic Republican who supported John Randolph in opposition to the Jefferson administration.

(e) THE AMERICAN TORIES were the political party that remained loyal to the Crown and opposed the independence of the Colonies, whereas the Whigs desired greater independence from England. Although the names were borrowed from the two major political parties of England, the political division which they signified in America differed from that in England. The Tory party in England was the successor to the Court party and upheld the prerogative of the Crown over Parliament, while the Whigs defended the sovereignty of Parliament. The English Tories were mostly titled landowners and, as to their religious affiliation, Episcopalians. The Whigs drew their strength from the urban elements, especially the merchants, and from the small landowners. They were Puritans, either Presbyterians or Independents.

(f) THE MAGNA CHARTA was signed by John I on June 15, 1215. Although it guaranteed freedom and a voice in the affairs of state solely to the barons of the realm, it is generally considered the basic document in the progress of the British people toward political liberty. The terms of the Magna Charta were often violated by subsequent rulers, and the time from 1215 to 1688 is marked by an almost uninterrupted struggle of the people not only to enforce the basic principles of the Magna Charta, but also to broaden their application by extending the guarantees to the commons and by assigning the major voice in the affairs of state to Parliament. The Revolution of 1688 decided this contest in favor of Parliament.

(g) BILL OF RIGHTS: Act of Parliament passed in 1689, to protect individual liberties. This Bill of Rights became the model for the Bill of Rights adopted by Virginia and later for the first ten Amendments of the Constitution of the United States.

(h) STAMP ACT: An act of the British Parliament (1765) imposing a tax on all papers used in the colonies and declaring invalid all transactions not properly stamped. Repealed in 1766 as the result of the colonial opposition in the Stamp Act Congress. This act had aroused the American colonists more than any other act of oppression by Britain, as it was the first major British attempt to impose taxes in the colonies without the consent of the people.

(i) CONTINENTAL CONGRESS: Governing body of the united colonies during the Revolution and of the states until 1789.

(j) SOCIAL COMPACT: The political theory that legitimate government originates in a contract (compact) between people. Used in the seventeenth and eighteenth centuries as an argument to throw off oppressive governments. Best known expositions of these theories are found in Locke's *Second Treatise of Government* and Rousseaus' *Social Contract*.

(k) BOSTON MASSACRE (March 5, 1770): Incident in which a small squad of British soldiers upon provocation fired upon a group of rioters, killing three and wounding eight.

A DISSERTATION ON THE CANON AND FEUDAL LAW

(a) SOLIDARITAS CLUB: Informal Boston Club of which John Adams was a member.

(b) PURITANS: Religious dissenters who wished to reform the Church of England, and being unable to do so formed their own churches, the Presbyterian and the Congregational Churches. A number of Puritans left England after 1627 and established the Massachusetts Bay Colony, which became first a theocracy under the domination of the Congregational Church.

(c) DIOCESAN EPISCOPACY: Church organization used by the Church of England in which the diocese is an administrative unit of organization headed by a bishop.

(d) PRESBYTERIAN ORDINATION: Arrangement under which applicants are admitted into the Christian ministry by the authority of a Presbytery, itself a church governing body organized on a district basis, made up of ministers and church elders. The terms Episcopalian, Presbyterian, and Congregational refer to church organizational arrangements in which the Episcopalian is the most highly centralized, employing bishops and dioceses, the Presbyterian less highly organized, and the Congregational largely decentralized with each separate church a practically self-governing unit. (Cf. preceding notes on *Puritans,* and *Diocesan Episcopacy.*

(e) JACOBITE: A partisan of or adherent to James II after his abdication of the English throne in 1688.

NOVANGLUS AND MASSACHUSETTENSIS

(a) CONTINENTAL CONGRESS: See page 212, note (i).

(b) BATTLE OF LEXINGTON: April 19, 1775, opening skirmish in the American War of Independence.

(c) WHIGS: See page 211, note (e).

(d) GRENVILLIAN ADMINISTRATION: George Grenville's ministry in Great Britain, which lasted from 1763 to 1765.

(e) HANOVER: The House of Hanover, King George I and descendants.

(f) HORACE: "He annoys, he soothes, he fills with useless fears, like a sorcerer."

(g) SENATUS CONSULTA: Decrees of the Senate (ancient Rome) from 100 to 300 A. D. *Senatus consulta* were *leges* (laws) enacted without consultation of the tribunes.

(h) QUOD PRINCIPI PLACUIT LEGIS HABET VIGOREM: "What pleases the prince is law" was a legal principle in Roman law which established absolute authority of the Roman emperors.

Derived from Ulpian (170?–228 A. D.), it was included in the Corpus Juris Civilis (Dig. i.4.1.) and became, during the Middle Ages, the major basis for the claims of princes to absolute authority.

(i) DELENDA EST CARTHAGO: "Carthage must be destroyed." Phrase used by Cato the Elder.

(j) MASSACHUSETTS BAY COMPANY: A royal chartered company authorized to colonize and trade in New England. The company settled in Massachusetts in 1629, thereby establishing that colony. (Cf. preceding note on the *Puritans*, p. 213.)

(k) CASUS OMISSUS: A case omitted or not provided for, as by a statute (and therefore governed by the common law).

(l) NE EXEAT REGNO: "Let him not go out of the Kingdom." In England a high prerogative writ used in matters of state to restrain a person from leaving the country; later, a writ issued out of chancery or equity to restrain a person from leaving the jurisdiction of the court pending an action.

(m) HIC LABOR HOC OPUS EST: "This is labor, this work" (This is the task, this is the thing to be done).

(n) PROCUL A JOVE A FULMINE PROCUL: "Far away from Jove, far away from this thunderbolt."

THOUGHTS ON GOVERNMENT

(a) VIRGINIA PLAN: Strong central government plan submitted by the Virginia delegates in the Federal Constitutional Convention of 1787.

(b) LONG PARLIAMENT: English Parliament which sat without renewal from 1640 to 1660.

(c) THE PRINCIPLE OF ROTATION of officers Adams in all likelihood borrowed from James Harrington's *The Commonwealth of Oceana*, first published in England in 1656. Though Harrington first formulated the idea in modern times, he undoubtedly was influenced in this respect by his thorough knowledge of the political affairs of the ancient Greeks and Romans.

CONSTITUTION OF MASSACHUSETTS

(a) GENERAL COURT OF MASSACHUSETTS: Massachusetts legislature.

(b) PROVINCIAL CONGRESS: Congress of the colony.

(c) VIRGINIA BILL OF RIGHTS: Declaration of rights of the State of Virginia established as part of its constitution during the American Revolution. (Cf. note on the *Bill of Rights,* p. 212.)

(d) UNIVERSITY AT CAMBRIDGE: Reference is to the Harvard College, later Harvard University, Cambridge, Massachusetts.

DEFENCE OF THE CONSTITUTIONS OF GOVERN-MENT OF THE UNITED STATES OF AMERICA

(a) FEDERAL CONSTITUTIONAL CONVENTION: Convention called by the States in 1787 which drew up the Constitution of the United States.

(b) SHAYS'S REBELLION: Popular uprising in western and central Massachusetts in 1786 as a result of economic discontent. The "rebellion" was short-lived and indirectly influenced the calling of the Federal Constitutional Convention in 1787.

(c) CENTRALIZING SCHEMES OF DR. FRANKLIN AND TOM PAINE: Plans for a strong central government.

(d) CICERO: "This indeed hold fast which I said initially: unless there be this even counterweighting in the state between law and the public office and public duty and that there be a sufficiency of authority in the wise counsel of the leaders and a sufficient degree of freedom for the people, this constitution of the state cannot be preserved unchanged."

DISCOURSES ON DAVILA

(a) SPECTEMUR AGENDO: "Let us be watched in the doing."

(b) CARMELITES: One of the Roman Catholic monastic orders which came to Louisiana in the early days of French settlement.

(c) ROYAL SOCIETY OF LONDON: A society incorporated in England in 1662 to give governmental support to scientific investigation.

(d) COMMITTEE OF CORRESPONDENCE: Extra-constitutional committees organized by the American colonists to carry on propaganda against Great Britain and to co-ordinate efforts of the patriots.

LETTERS TO JOHN TAYLOR

(a) SUPREMA LEX: "Supreme law"; SUMMA POTESTATIS: "Highest power, supreme power."

(b) EPISCOPALIAN: Name of Anglican Church in America.

(c) DRUIDS: Members of an ancient pagan religious order in Britain, France and Ireland.

(d) WHITE ROSE AND RED ROSE: The symbol of the House of York and the House of Lancaster respectively in England. These two houses contended intermittently for the throne in England in the fifteenth century.

(e) AUTO-DA-FE: The medieval burning of a heretic; act of faith.

BIOGRAPHICAL INDEX

ADAMS, SAMUEL (1722–1803). Cousin of John Adams; revolutionary leader and political writer.

ADDISON, JOSEPH (1672–1719). English essayist and poet.

ANDROS, SIR EDMUND (1637–1714). Soldier and colonial governor who served in Massachusetts Bay from 1686 until his return to England because of the Revolution of 1688.

ATHANASIUS, Saint (293?–373). Greek father of the Church. Strong opponent of Arianism.

BARLOW, JOEL (1754–1812). Liberal American poet and statesman.

BECCARIA CESARE (1735–1794). Philosophical writer; best known for his *Treatise on Crimes and Punishments*. His opposition to capital punishment led to establishment of more just principles of penal law.

BECCARIA, GIOVANNI (1716–1781). Italian philosopher.

BELKNAP, JEREMY (1744–1798). New England Congregational clergyman and writer, defender of the American Revolution.

BERNARD, SIR FRANCIS (1712–1779). Colonial governor both in New Jersey and Massachusetts.

BLACKSTONE, WILLIAM (1723–1780). Famous English jurist. His *Commentaries on the Laws of England* (1765–1769) exerted a strong influence on British and American jurisprudence.

BOLINGBROKE (1678–1751). English statesman and writer. Author of *Dissertation on Parties* and *Letters on the Study of History*.

BOYLSTON, ZABDIEL (1679–1766). He was an American physician, the first to introduce the practice of inoculation against smallpox into America.

BROOKES, HENRY (1703–1783). Irish author. He wrote a philosophical poem in six books entitled "Universal Beauty."

BUFFON, GEORGE LOUIS (1707–1788). French naturalist and member of the French Academy.

BURKE, EDMUND (1729–1797). British Statesman and political writer. He eloquently espoused the cause of the American colonies for more self-government. Author a.o. of *On The Sublime and Beautiful*, and *Reflection on the French Revolution* (1790). Best remembered for his speeches: "American Taxation" (1744) and "Conciliation with America" (1775).

BERNET, WILLIAM (1688–1729). Able colonial governor of New York and New Jersey from 1720-1727, and of Massachusetts in 1728.

BURR, AARON (1756–1836). Revolutionary soldier, lawyer, United States senator and Vice-President of the United States during the term of Thomas Jefferson's first administration of 1801–1804.

CALHOUN, JOHN C. (1782–1850). From South Carolina. Was Secretary of War, Vice-President of the United States under John Quincy Adams, senator from South Carolina, Secretary of State, and one of America's outstanding political philosophers, ably defending the states' rights position. Author of *A Disquisition on Government* and *A Discourse on the Constitution and Government of the United States.*

CALVIN, JOHN (1509–1564). French divine and reformer. He systematized the Protestant doctrine. His major work is the *Institutes of the Christian Religion.* His teachings had a great influence on the reform movement in England and the established church in the Colony of Massachusetts Bay. (Cf. Note on Puritans, p. 212.)

CHATHAM, EARL OF, William Pitt (1708–1778). He entered the House of Commons in 1735 and became its greatest leader from 1754 to 1763.

CLINTON, GEORGE (1739–1812). Revolutionary soldier, statesman, served seven times as governor of the state of New York. He was Vice-President of the United States in Jefferson's second administration and James Madison's first administration.

CONDORCET, MARIE JEAN (1743–1794). French mathematician, philosopher, and revolutionary. Member of the National Convention 1793.

COPLEY, JOHN SINGLETON (1738–1815). American portrait painter, native of Boston.

DANTON, GEORGE JACQUES (1759–1794). French revolutionary leader.

DELOLME, JEAN LOUIS (1740–1806). Swiss jurist and constitutional writer. While in exile in England until 1775, he wrote the *Constitution de l'Angleterre,* a study of the English constitution.

DIDEROT, DENIS (1713–1784). French man of letters and encyclopedist.

DUDLEY, PAUL (1675–1751). The son of Governor Joseph Dudley of Massachusetts; was Chief Justice in that colony from 1745 to 1751.

DWIGHT, TIMOTHY (1752–1817). A native of Massachusetts, well-known Congregational divine, author and President of Yale College from 1795–1817. For years he was the dominant figure in the established order of Connecticut.

EDWARDS, JONATHAN (1703–1758). Congregational clergyman, theologian, and philosopher; leader of the "Great Awakening" movement (1734–1735). Author of *Freedom of the Will* and of many influential theological works.

EDWARDS, JONATHAN (1745–1801). Theologian and second son of Jonathan Edwards.

Affairs for the United States under the Articles of Confederation and then became first Chief Justice. Co-author with Alexander Hamilton and James Madison of *The Federalist*.

JEFFERSON, THOMAS (1743–1826). Statesman, diplomat, author, apostle of freedom and enlightenment. He wished to be remembered as the author of the Declaration of Independence, of the Virginia Statute for Religious Freedom and founder of the University of Virginia. He was Secretary of State under George Washington, Vice-President of the United States under John Adams, and President of the United States from 1801 to 1809.

JENINGS, EDMUND. Friend and correspondent of John Adams.

JOHNSON, DR. SAMUEL (1709–1784). Famous English writer and author of a dictionary. He was probably the leading literary figure in the eighteenth century in England.

JUNIUS. The pseudonym of a writer who contributed a series of letters to the *London Public Advertiser* from January 21, 1769 to January 2, 1772. The "Letters of Junius" were written to discredit the ministry of the Duke of Grafton.

KAMES, LORD (1696–1782). Scottish lawyer, judge, and philosopher.

KING, WILLIAM (1650–1729). British divine, archbishop of Dublin. King was a supporter of the Revolution of 1688.

LEONARD, DANIEL (1740–1829). Able Massachusetts lawyer and staunch loyalist. Leonard is well known for his defense of the Tory view under the pen name "Massachusettensis." This view John Adams opposed under the name of "Novanglus."

LOCKE, JOHN (1632–1704). English philosopher. His major political work, the *Two Treatises of Government* (1689) strongly influenced both English and American political thought.

ABBE DE MABLY (1709–1785). French author, moral and political philosopher.

MACHIAVELLI, NICCOLO (1469–1527). Italian statesman and writer. His best known work is *The Prince*.

MADISON, JAMES (1750–1836). Statesman, writer, member of Congress, and fourth President of the United States. He was one of the most influential members of the Constitutional Convention of 1787, which drew up the Constitution of the United States. He later served in Congress as a leader of the party of Jefferson, was Secretary of State under Jefferson, and succeeded Jefferson to the Presidency. Co-author with Alexander Hamilton and John Jay of *The Federalist*.

MARSHALL, JOHN (1755–1835). Born in Virginia. Revolutionary soldier, a leader of the Federalist party in Virginia, and judicial statesman. He was appointed Chief Justice of the United States by President

John Adams, and served from 1801 to 1835. In this capacity he established his reputation as being one of America's greatest constitutional statesmen. The decision of the Supreme Court under his leadership had a major influence in formulating a legal interpretation of the Constitution designed to strengthen the union of the states.

MARMONTEL, JEAN F. (1723–1799). French author, dramatist and contributor to the *Encyclopédie*.

MONTESQUIEU, CHARLES DE SECONDAT. French philosophical historian. Best known for his exposition, in his *The Spirit of the Laws*, of the doctrine of separation of powers.

MONTGOMERY, RICHARD (1738–1775). American soldier and brigadier-general in the Continental Army.

MUMMIUS, LUCIUS (second century B. C.). Roman statesman and general.

NEDHAM, MARCHAMONT. Seventeenth-century English political writer, whose *Excellency of a Free State* provides the basis for the third part of John Adams' *Defence*.

NILES, HEZEKIAH (1777-1839). Editor, native of Pennsylvania. From 1811 to 1836, he edited and published *Niles "Weekly Register"* which consistently advocated strong union, internal improvements, and protection to industry.

OTIS, JAMES (1725–1783). Massachusetts lawyer, politician and publicist. He is probably best known for his opposition to the "Writs of Assistance," which allowed customs collectors wide discretion to search for and seize contraband goods. Otis insisted that the writs were void and that the courts should hold the act of Parliament establishing them as unconstitutional and hence illegal.

PAINE, THOMAS (1737–1809). A native of England; American revolutionary political pamphleteer, agitator and author. Paine's political tract, *Common Sense*, which advocated in ringing terms separation of the colonies from England, was widely read and influential. His other well-known political work is *Rights of Man* (Part I, 1791; Part II, 1792).

PARKER, THEODORE (1810–1860). Theologian, Unitarian clergyman, publicist of Massachusetts.

PENN, JOHN (1740–1788). Signer of the Declaration of Independence and member of the Continental Congress representing North Carolina.

PENN, WILLIAM (1644–1718). Founder and Proprietor of Pennsylvania colony. A member of the Society of Friends, he preached and practiced religious toleration and granted the colony a liberal constitution.

KING PHILIP (died 1676). Sachem of the Wampanoag Indians and leader of the most severe Indian war in New England history, 1675–1676, which was called King Philip's War.

Hutchinson, a rift arose between him and Adams.

SIDNEY, ALGERNON (1622–1683). English politician and political philosopher.

SHERMAN, ROGER (1721–1793). American political leader, signer of the Declaration of Independence, and active member of the Federal Constitutional Convention of 1787.

SMITH, ADAM (1723–1790). British economist and moral philosopher. Best known for his work entitled *Inquiry into the Nature and Causes of the Wealth of Nations.*

SPENCER, HERBERT (1820–1903). English moral and political philosopher.

SWIFT, JONATHAN (1677–1745). Dean of St. Patrick's, Dublin; British satirist, author, and moral philosopher.

TAYLOR, JOHN (1753–1824). Best known as John Taylor of Caroline (Virginia). Political writer and agriculturist. United States senator three different times.

TILLOTSON, DR. JOHN (1630–1694). English archbishop and writer on theology.

TOCQUEVILLE DE, ALEXIS (1805–1859). French author and political philosopher. His *Democracy in America* is still considered an outstanding work on American politics and society.

TURGOT, ANNE ROBERT JACQUES (1727–1781). French statesman, economist, and political writer, known principally for his efforts to further free trade.

TRUMBULL, BENJAMIN (1735–1820). Congregational clergyman, historian. He wrote a history of Connecticut.

TRUMBULL, JOHN (1750–1831). Poet and jurist. Friend of John Adams.

VANE, SIR HENRY (1613–1662). English statesman and author; defender of popular government; executed in 1662 for high treason against the king.

VOLTAIRE (1694–1778). Famous French author, dramatist, poet and moral philosopher.

WALLACE, WILLIAM (about 1270–1305). Popular national hero and military leader of Scotland. He was executed in London as a traitor to the English king.

WARREN, JAMES (1726–1808). Massachusetts political leader and a close friend of John and Samuel Adams.

WARREN, JOSEPH (1741–1775). Physician, revolutionary patriot. A close friend of John Adams.

WEST, BENJAMIN (1738–1820). English historical and portrait painter.

WINTHROP, JOHN (1588–1649). Puritan leader and first governor of Massachusetts Bay Colony. This colony's early success was due to his wisdom and skill.

WYTHE, GEORGE (1726–1806). Signer of the Declaration of Independence, statesman, professor of law and chancellor of the University of Virginia. He established the first chair of law in an American college.

YOUNG, EDWARD (1683–1765). English poet and author.